Gerard Manley Hopkins

PADDY KITCHEN

Gerard Manley Hopkins

HAMISH HAMILTON
LONDON

B

1

Unlike writers in many countries, British writers are not paid for the borrowing of their books from public libraries, even though our public library system is the largest in the western world. Whether you are yourself a borrower or a buyer of books, if you want literature to go on being written in Great Britain, please tell your MP and your local authority that you support Public Lending Right, under which writers will be paid, from central funds, a small fee for each borrowing of their work.

821·8
KIT

First published in Great Britain 1978
by Hamish Hamilton Limited
90 Great Russell Street London WC1B 3PT

Copyright © 1978 by Paddy Kitchen

British Library Cataloguing in Publication Data

Kitchen, Paddy
 Gerard Manley Hopkins.
  1. Hopkins, Gerard Manley—Biography
  2. Poets, English—19th century—Biography
  821'.8   PR4803.H44Z/
 ISBN 0-241-89938-9

Printed and bound in Great Britain at
The Camelot Press Ltd, Southampton

To Lewis Mumford
whose letters are treasured

Any writer knows you can only march to the beat of your personal drummer.'

TOM STOPPARD

Contents

Illustrations

Preface

This is not an official or definitive biography of Gerard Manley Hopkins. Many of his writings are still in copyright, and the copyright belongs to the Society of Jesus. The writings are virtually all published, apart from some confessional passages in his diaries. The latter have not so far been considered suitable for publication. I have read them and decided to comment on their content for this book. This is a breach of courtesy to the copyright holders, but not, I think, harmful to Hopkins.

For extensive quotations from the poems I have used the 1918 Robert Bridges edition which—apart from Bridges's own editorial contributions—is out of copyright. In order to help readers who may wish to refer to the poems, I have included, after the first mention of each title, the number of the poem in the Oxford University Press paperback fourth edition of *The Poems of Gerard Manley Hopkins*, edited by W. H. Gardner and N. H. MacKenzie (1970), and also its number in the Bridges edition if included there (the number being prefaced by 'RB').

Since this is a personal rather than an academic study, I have not given detailed references to sources. There is a selected bibliography, and much of the information is taken from Hopkins's published writings. I should emphasise that my task would have been impossible but for the earlier, painstaking work of others—particularly Claude Colleer Abbott, W. H. Gardner, Humphry House, N. H. MacKenzie, Graham Storey and Alfred Thomas.

My reason for writing the book is simple: Hopkins is my favourite poet, and I was curious to explore the creative chemistry behind the words that affect me, an agnostic, so strongly.

I should like to thank the Phoenix Trust for financial help. I hope my friends and family realise how much I have appreciated their moral and practical support.

Preface

This is not an official or definitive biography of Gerard Manley Hopkins. Many of his writings are still in copyright, and the copyright belongs to the Society of Jesus. The writings are virtually all published, apart from some confessional passages in his diaries. The latter have not so far been considered suitable for publication. I have read them and decided to comment on their content for this book. This is a breach of courtesy to the copyright holders, but not, I think, harmful to Hopkins.

For extensive quotations from the poems I have used the 1918 Robert Bridges edition which—apart from Bridges's own editorial contributions—is out of copyright. In order to help readers who may wish to refer to the poems, I have included, after the first mention of each title, the number of the poem in the Oxford University Press paperback fourth edition of *The Poems of Gerard Manley Hopkins*, edited by W. H. Gardner and N. H. MacKenzie (1970), and also its number in the Bridges edition if included there (the number being prefaced by 'RB').

Since this is a personal rather than an academic study, I have not given detailed references to sources. There is a selected bibliography, and much of the information is taken from Hopkins's published writings. I should emphasise that my task would have been impossible but for the earlier, painstaking work of others— particularly Claude Colleer Abbott, W. H. Gardner, Humphry House, N. H. MacKenzie, Graham Storey and Alfred Thomas.

My reason for writing the book is simple: Hopkins is my favourite poet, and I was curious to explore the creative chemistry behind the words that affect me, an agnostic, so strongly.

I should like to thank the Phoenix Trust for financial help. I hope my friends and family realise how much I have appreciated their moral and practical support.

Prologue

WHEN GERARD Manley Hopkins, as an Oxford undergraduate, decided to become a Roman Catholic, he approached John Henry Newman for counsel, and it was Newman who two months later received him into that Church.

This was more than thirty years after the Oxford Movement had first tried to infuse the Anglican Church with increased authority and sanctity, and twenty years after the wet night when Newman knelt at the feet of an affable, shabby Italian monk and begged to be admitted into the bosom of the Roman Catholic Church. However, the reverberations from these events still coloured the religious—and much of the emotional—climate of Hopkins's Oxford, and it is for this reason that they are summarily presented here.

That Oxford in the 1830's should have provided a centre for an Anglo-Catholic movement is entirely unsurprising. The powerful new secular forces of utilitarianism, industrial economics, and political reform were disquieting to many members of the University, two-thirds of whose undergraduates were due to go into Holy orders, and the gathering tide of rationalism which those forces perpetrated could not be ignored (indeed, some of its most challenging elements sprang from within the University itself). To many there seemed an urgent need for a strengthening of spiritual values and for a clear redefinition of the position of the Church in relation to the State.

In that pre-Victorian era only members of the Church of England were allowed to enter the University, while its Fellows were obliged to take orders and to remain celibate. Yet despite this, the young men who went up to Oxford at the same time as Newman were not altogether unlike those who go there today. They carried the psychological marks of their mothers and fathers; some were snobbish and arrogant; they experienced love and intellectual excitement; many were overtaken by silliness, laziness and despair;

and some of them burned, as they still do, with an urgent need to sweep away lethargy and worldliness and to redirect people's energies towards a spiritual goal.

The three founders of the Oxford Movement provide an intriguing example of effects caused by the interaction of differing personal chemistries. Had they not met, John Henry Newman would probably not have become England's most famous Roman Catholic convert. John Keble would still have been a county clergyman in the old Tory High Church tradition, but would not have had an Oxford college founded in his memory. And Richard Hurrell Froude, who acted as the trio's catalyst, would be quite forgotten. Indeed to many people today he is unknown, while to many others the recital of these Oxford Movement names causes an uneasy disquiet. Their lingering odour of aspiring sanctity distresses the psychologically-knowing, who mutter about repression and shudder at asceticism. They were, however, very much men of their time, just as were the social and political reformers. Their temperaments led them to seek the salvation of souls—particularly their own—while the reformers were drawn to improve conditions on this earth.

Newman in particular came to regard this world as a shadowy and unpleasant rehearsal for the next. As a small boy it had occurred to him that he might himself be an angel, and that the world was a deception in which his fellow-angels were hiding from him; but by the time he was fifteen he had begun to question his traditional, though not strict, Christian upbringing, and was reading authors such as Hume and Paine. However, 'the heavy hand of God', as he described it, halted his slide (or ascent) to rationalism, and 'turned me right round when I was more like a devil than a wicked boy . . .' Three things contributed to this turn-around: his father's bank failed; as a result he was forced to stay at school during the summer holidays and became ill; and at the same time, when he was at his most vulnerable, he fell under the influence of a young Evangelical clergyman schoolteacher. The strong emphasis of the Evangelicals on a supernatural order appealed to Newman's latent childhood instincts, while his father's misfortune had given a severe demonstration as to what happened when one relied too much on the things of this world. It was his first, and most fundamental, conversion. By the autumn, so Newman recalled years later in *Apologia pro Vita Sua* (1864):

another deep imagination . . . took possession of me,—there can be no mistake about the fact; viz. that it would be the will of God that I should lead a single life. This anticipation . . . also strengthened my feeling of separation from the visible world . . .

He was still only fifteen. He went up to Oxford the following year, and verses which he wrote to commemorate his eighteenth birthday contain lines about his 'feeble spirit' aspiring to heaven 'As some long-prisoned dove towards her nest'.

The riotous drunkenness which he encountered at Oxford disgusted him deeply, particularly the feast which took place on Trinity Sunday which meant that the celebration of Holy Communion was almost immediately followed by a bacchanal; indeed he amazed one contemporary by comparing drunkenness to murder. However, his undergraduate years were by no means devoid of earthly pleasures, and in the company of his handsome friend John Bowden—Newman described them as 'inseparables'— he walked and talked and boated, as well as diligently studied.

When he was twenty-three he was elected a Fellow of Oriel College and wrote to Bowden about how he went to receive the congratulations of the other Fellows and 'bore it till Keble took my hand, and then felt so abashed and unworthy of the honour done to me, that I seemed desirous of quite sinking into the ground'. (Throughout his life Newman combined a steely intellectual authority with an innate submissiveness—the latter sometimes manifesting itself in ways closely resembling that eighteenth-century phenomenon, the vapours.)

Oriel's powerful Provost, Richard Whately, undertook to knock the new Fellow into shape (he used to boast that he treated his friends as anvils for his ideas), and assailed Newman with well-grounded liberal views, delivered in a bluff, challenging manner that appealed to the young man's submissive side. For a time Newman hero-worshipped Whately, and began 'to prefer intellectual excellence to moral'; but other influences were to prevent him from doing more than tentatively peer down the path of rational liberal thought. Indeed a decade later he had such 'fierce thoughts against the liberals' he could not bring himself even to look at a tricolour flag fluttering on a French boat.

One of these influences was Edward Bouverie Pusey, who in later years was to support the remnants of the Oxford Movement after

Froude had died and Newman departed. But when he became a Fellow of Oriel, Pusey was some way from being the grave pillar of Anglican orthodoxy known to many generations of Oxford undergraduates. Newman liked his appearance the first time he saw him, remarking that 'his light curly hair was damp with the cold water which his headaches made necessary for his comfort'. The two men became friends, and discussed religious matters with deep seriousness—especially the idea of missionary work. Newman recorded in his diary, 'That Pusey is Thine, O Lord, how can I doubt?' Pusey was not, however, predisposed towards the predominantly middle-class Evangelical movement, being himself used to the traditions of the English gentry, and his influence combined with a seed already implanted by Whately in Newman's mind: namely that the Church was an historic institution whose members perhaps had no private right of entry into heaven. (The Evangelicals believed that as long as a man adhered to the Bible and was in direct personal communion with God, he would be saved without the intervention of an established corporate ritual.)

Emotionally, at that time, Pusey was in a state of turmoil—hence the headaches. From the age of seventeen he had been in love with a charming, impetuous girl whom his father deemed unsuitable, and the fact that this passion obsessed him even more, on occasion, than his love of God, distressed him deeply. He probably confided in Newman, but their friendship could not for the time being develop, as Pusey went abroad to study.

During his first year at Oriel, Newman was offered a curacy and ordained deacon. An hour after the ordination ceremony, he wrote in his diary:

> It is over. I am Thine, O Lord; I seem quite dizzy and cannot altogether believe and understand it. At first, after the hands were laid on me, my heart shuddered within me; the words 'for ever' are so terrible. It was hardly a godly feeling which made me feel melancholy at the idea of giving up all for God. At times indeed my heart burnt within me, particularly during the singing of the Veni Creator. Yet, Lord, I ask not for comfort in comparison of sanctification. I feel as a man thrown suddenly in deep water.

On the following day he noted: 'I have the responsibility of souls on me to the day of my death.' However, a year later, when he was ordained priest, he was much calmer: 'What a divine service is that of Ordination!' he wrote. 'The whole has a fragrance in it; and to think of it is soothing and delightful.' By that time he had become even more convinced of the importance of tradition within the Church, of the idea of passing on an objective body of teaching from one generation to the next.

He was invited to become a tutor at Oriel. It was a post which he wanted very much, for he deplored the slack teaching habits of many college tutors and wanted to demonstrate the importance of assuming responsibility for undergraduates' moral well-being as well as their intellectual development. His appointment coincided with the election of Hurrell Froude to a Fellowship. Newman never quite lost his childhood feeling that a certain élite band of mortals might be angels-on-earth, and, of all his friends, Froude was to be revealed as the one most worthy of such an accolade. Certainly, after his death, Newman decided that Froude was the 'one who had the most angelic mind of any person I ever fell in with . . .'

Hurrell Froude was aristocratic, quick-witted, had a sharp and logical disdain of humbug, and by the time Newman met him was deeply religious. He was also extremely good-looking, with the then familiar bright eyes, boniness, and waxing and waning vitality of a consumptive. It is possible, however, that he might never have qualified for saintly epitaphs if it had not been for his mother, and her early death while he was still an undergraduate. His father, an Archdeacon of High Tory persuasion and no-nonsense attitude, merely elicited the confession from him that 'A want of proper notions respecting my relations to my Father' was the 'great root' of all his 'complicated misdeeds'. But of his mother he could thank God 'That it has pleased thee to bring me into the world under the shadow of my holy Mother' and write in his journal, 'I hope, by degrees, I may get to consider her relics in the light of a friend . . .' Mothers still have an appalling knack of making their sons feel guilty, but at least we need not now approve their behaviour. Froude never stood a chance, given the prevailing attitude to motherhood, and his own, allegedly very beautiful, mother. When advising him to keep a confessional journal, she wrote: 'Try to make every account better than the last . . . and keep clear of passion and then all that we hear of you will make hip hip hurra at home.' Everything about Froude leads one to suppose that quick passion was an endemic part of his nature, and his mother's request rather akin to asking St Francis to keep clear of the animals.

When Froude had been an undergraduate at Oriel, John Keble was his tutor, and when Keble resigned his tutorship in order to become his father's curate he invited Froude to spend the summer vacation with him in Gloucestershire. Together with another two undergraduates—Robert Wilberforce and Isaac Williams—they formed a reading party: the customary form of study during a vacation. Isaac Williams later recorded how he felt quite overcome by the way Keble made 'religion a reality', and found him a 'man wholly made up of love, with charms of conversation, thought and kindness, beyond what one had experienced among boyish companions'. (Remembering his boyish companions at Harrow, Williams once recalled: "The very warm and strong attachments I formed with boys not in every case of the best principles.") Williams and Wilberforce were lodged at a farmhouse four miles from Keble's home, and so Keble was able to write to the Dean of Oriel that he was getting on 'very comfortably here with no wife but Froude'. It was not long after the death of Froude's mother, and he particularly valued the deepening, but not disturbing, friendship with his tutor. Three years later, having referred in the previously-quoted prayer to 'the shadow of my holy Mother', he mentioned Keble, and thanked God

> that I should fall into the way of one whose good instructions have ... convinced me of the error of my ways ... with whose good high friendship I have most unworthily been honoured, and in whose presence I taste the cup of happiness.

During these years he was to compare Keble's spirituality to that of his mother on several occasions.

Keble does frequently sound too good to be true. He is described as a modest, gentle man of ineffable sweetness, whose style of preaching caused one listener to say: 'You seemed to be amidst the rustling of angels' wings.' His one fault was a sort of mindless obstinacy, springing from naivety, so that when he encountered views which opposed his own, however intelligently, he would simply lose his temper and say: 'I cannot think how people can be so stupid.' He was entirely immured in the patriarchal atmosphere of old English country life as created by his father, and regarded all relaxation of tradition (whether social, political or ecclesiastical) as tending towards sin and sensuality. He managed to reorientate Froude's passionate attachment to his mother in a religious direction by substituting his own strong belief in spiritual realities, and by encouraging him to strive for what he called 'moral taste'. Froude later wrote to Keble, but did not post the letter:

> I have been trying almost all the Long to discover a sort of common sense romance, I am convinced there must be such a thing, and that nature did not give us such a high capacity for pleasure without making some other qualification of it beside delusion . . . Perhaps you may think it very odd, but this summer has been the first time I have had resolution to ask for the papers which they found of my mother's after her death.

It was after reading these papers, which included her confessional journal, that he embarked on his own journal of self-examination:

> I thank God some of her writings have been kept; that may be my salvation; but I have spent the evening just as idly as if I had not seen it. I don't know how it is, but it seems to me, that the consciousness of having capacities for happiness, with no objects to gratify them, seems to grow upon me in a dreary way.

Much later, his feelings about his relationship with Keble crystallised into the kind of imagery still possible in those days; he wrote to Newman: Keble 'is my fire, but (craving pardon for the plurality) I may be his poker'.

As Newman and Froude gradually grew to know one another, Froude was able to cement the rather tenuous relationship between Keble and Newman. And under the influence of these two men—especially Froude—Newman came to assimilate the romantic loyalties of High Church Toryism. After riding with Froude (a brilliant horseman), he wrote to Bowden: '. . . King Charles and his Bishops seemed to rise before us along the old road which leads from Oxford to Cuddesdon.' To this allegiance with the past, however, he added his own contemporary apprehensions. He feared that by trying to make Christianity a religion of universal benevolence, the misguided liberals and utilitarians were hiding away the dark and unavoidable mysteries of evil and suffering that pervade this world. Against the 'flimsy, self-invented notions which satisfy the reason of the mere man of letters or prosperous and self-indulgent philosopher' he set 'the overwhelming total of the world's guilt and suffering . . .'. His sermons were full of foreboding, and his Evangelical awareness of the parallel evolution of God's kingdom and the Devil's kingdom was never eroded by his assumption of the historical claims of the Anglican tradition. In 1828, at the age of twenty-seven, he became Vicar of St Mary's, the University church, and for fifteen years this provided him with an extremely influential pulpit from which to promulgate his developing beliefs.

A more specific way in which Froude had influence on Newman was to convince him of his own 'high severe idea of the intrinsic excellence of Virginity'—as Newman later described it. Having failed to resolve his unnamed appetites by some form of 'common sense romance', Froude had privately embarked on a strict routine of fasting and self-denial. He would sleep on the floor instead of in the bed, and force himself to eat as little as possible. As well as giving up material things, he endeavoured to avoid the 'flash' company which he rather enjoyed, and after agreeing to coach a pupil he confided to his diary that he must 'above all watch and pray against being led out of the way by the fascination of his society'. His highest ambition, he claimed, 'was to be a humdrum'. His mother and Keble had succeeded in building a spiritual enclosure around his passions, and the man who paced up and down inside, mettlesome yet safe, was entirely attractive to Newman.

The idea of uniting with a woman appalled Froude: he hated weddings and loved romantic monastic ruins. After drawing a statue of Diana, he wrote to his father:

> I think accustoming the eye to forms so infinitely superior to anything we see in nature must have a tendency to give people a very philosophical indifference to their own looks and those of their acquaintances and make them look on the approximations to beauty, which they occasionally may see, as things rather to be speculated upon than admired, and as for any emotions of another kind to put them completely out of question.

One wonders if Archdeacon Froude, widower of an alleged beauty and father of eight, noticed the implied criticism.

Newman once remarked that one of the reasons he saw very little of Pusey between 1828 (the year he finally married the girl he had loved for a decade) and 1832, was that 'Hurrell Froude with his high views about marriage led me to think with him'. Sam Wiberforce, brother of Robert who had attended Keble's reading party, married during the same month as Pusey, and when he had become engaged he had complained that Froude was 'so fierce

against him'. When yet another Wilberforce brother, Henry, also became engaged, he dared not break the news to Newman—who too looked 'fierce'—but wrote to a mutual friend: 'It is, I am sure, very *foolish* of Newman on mere principles of calculation, if he gives up all his friends on their marriage . . .' About the Wilberforce brothers in general, Newman wrote: '. . . they are hampered with the world. May *we* be kept from forming alliances with things visible—and bringing on ourselves cares.' When poor Keble married in 1835, aged forty-three, he did so, according to Newman, 'telling no one' (which was not surprising), and Newman wrote to Froude abroad referring to marriage in general and Keble's in particular as 'a very second rate business'.

But the best evidence of Newman's physical aversion to the idea of marriage comes in his novel *Loss and Gain*. The novel gives a blow-by-blow account of one Charles Reding's progress from the Church of England to the Church of Rome against an Oxford background, and at one point Reding pauses in a bookshop while on his way to be received into the Roman Church:

> . . . looking round, [he] saw a familiar face. It was that of a young clergyman, with a very pretty girl on his arm, whom her dress pronounced to be a bride. Love was in their eyes, joy in their voices, and affluence in their gait and bearing. Charles had a faintish feeling come over him, somewhat such as might beset a man on hearing a call for pork-chops when he was sea-sick.

No wonder in his sermons, couched in less corporeal language, Newman made men such as John Campbell Shairp, a Scottish Presbyterian, feel 'more than ever ashamed of coarseness, selfishness [and] worldliness'. Shairp wrote of the sermons:

> the tone of voice in which they were spoken, once you grew accustomed to it, sounded like a fine strain of unearthly music. Through the silence of the high Gothic building the words fell on the ear like the measured drippings of water in some vast dim cave.

But the silvery drippings came from the same source as the pork-chop image.

His intimacy with Froude and Keble, and his intensive study of the early Christian Fathers, led Newman to a position within the Anglican Church where he could record in his diary that he was 'slowly advancing and led by God's hand blindly' and declare to his large congregation: 'We are the English Catholics. There is not a dissenter living but, inasmuch, and so far as he dissents, is in sin.' Froude remarked that he hoped 'Pusey may turn out High Church after all', and indeed Pusey, now Professor of Hebrew and Canon of Christ Church, was well embarked on the massive scholarly programme that led him to the most dogmatic of High Church positions. So intensive were these studies, that Keble announced he was 'a little apprehensive of him reading himself to death'.

God's hand may well have been leading Newman into an advanced Anglo-Catholic position, but it was Froude who acted as sheepdog and saw that he reached the hand which was pointing in that particular direction in the first place. Froude's main point of departure, which led him to wish to regenerate the Anglican Church, was his study of the Reformation. His disgust against the ethos (rather than the doctrines) of the reformers was paralleled by his love of the medieval Church, and while Newman read the early Christian Fathers and admired their spiritual and intellectual qualities, Froude studied the lives of the medieval popes and grew closer in sympathy with the mysteries of Catholicism.

In 1832 there was a cholera outbreak in Oxford, and when Froude went home at the end of July, Newman was acutely conscious of the threat of this infection as well as the continuing threat of Froude's worsening consumption. He later wrote a letter:

It was when the cholera was imminent we parted as if, perhaps, we might not see each other again. With reference to the memory of that parting, when I shook hands with him and looked into his face with great affection I afterwards wrote the stanza:

> And when thine eye surveys
> With fond adoring gaze,
> And yearning heart, thy friend,
> Love to its grave doth tend.

However, neither of them caught the cholera, and when Archdeacon Froude decided to take Hurrell to the Mediterranean for the winter for the sake of his health, an invitation was issued to Newman to join them. This put Newman into a turmoil. The idea excited him; he had never travelled abroad before; but would he be neglecting his duties? He was perturbed by the extent of his excitement and wrote to Hurrell:

It makes me quite sad to think what an evidence it has given me of the little real stability of mind I have attained. I cannot make out why I was so little, or rather not at all, excited by the coming of the cholera, and so much by this silly prospect you have put before me.

Silly or no, Newman decided he could safely leave Isaac Williams—who was by now his curate—in charge of St Mary's, and he and the Froudes sailed from Falmouth early in December. Hurrell's health did not improve, and the winter's journeys combined discomfort, exaltation, homesickness, and joy to a disconcerting degree for Newman. When the party were incarcerated for fifteen days in Malta for quarantine purposes, he wrote a poem on the text 'Thy love for me was wonderful, passing the love of women'. In it he wondered whether David and Jonathan's mutual affection would have lasted had Jonathan not been killed by the Philistines. Probably not, he decided, favouring the constancy of memory over that of life: 'He lives to us who dies, he is but lost who lives.' There were signs that the complex intimacies and longueurs of nineteenth-century travel, plus Hurrell's illness and the Archdeacon's continual robust presence, were directing the emotional thoughts aroused in Newman by his friend towards the circumspect sanctuary of an early grave.

They spent five weeks in Rome in a mood fluctuating between horror and admiration. Newman was overwhelmed by the place, finding it 'the first of cities' in spite of the continuous 'jading stimulus' of 'statues of the Madonna and the saints in the streets'. Much of his time abroad was spent in writing long letters to his mother and sisters at home, and in one of these he revealed that while he still detested the *Roman* Catholic system 'to the Catholic system I am more attracted than ever, and quite love the little monks [seminarists] of Rome; they look so innocent and bright, poor boys!' A talk with Dr Wiseman at the English College convinced Newman and Froude that there could be no hope of reconciliation between the Churches of England and Rome. Froude wrote to a friend: '. . . I own it has altogether changed my notions of the Roman Catholics and made me wish for the total overthrow of their system.' Newman was becoming convinced that the whole western world was on the verge of a crisis: 'the Christian world is gradually becoming barren and effete, as land which has been worked out and has become sand'. He decided to leave the Froudes, and travel back to Sicily on his own. Afterwards he wrote to Keble: 'When I went down to Sicily by myself, I had a strong idea that God was going to effect some purpose by me.' He in fact became very ill with fever, and was convinced that this was God's punishment to him for being self willed. His recovery—he had been near to death—served to resurrect and reinforce a feeling he had first experienced in Rome: namely, that God had some special work for him to do in England, and for this reason had spared his life. Impatiently, he waited for a passage home.

Meanwhile the incident had occurred which was to be to the Oxford Movement what the shooting of the Archduke Ferdinand was to the First World War: the Whig government had suppressed ten Irish Protestant bishoprics. It had realised the futility of continuing to exact exorbitant tithes from impoverished Roman Catholic peasants in order to support a top-heavy, alien, Protestant church, and decided to ease out ten of the twenty-two bishoprics in Ireland. Newman was appalled: bishops traced their spiritual authority and office back in an unbroken line to Christ's Apostles. Governments could not simply remove that authority without threatening the whole foundation of the Church. It did not matter that the Irish peasants did not believe in the Church of England's supremacy—they were wrong, and it was the duty of a British government to impose the Church's law on all its subjects. (After all, by 1848 the Church Missionary Society would claim to have converted 10,000 Negroes in Sierra Leone and the whole Maori population of New Zealand.) Newman later wrote of this period: 'My own bishop was my pope; I knew no other; the successor of the apostles, the vicar of Christ.'

When he arrived back in England, he discovered that Froude had already begun to organise a campaign in support of belief in the Apostolical succession; and, on the Sunday after his return, Keble preached the famous sermon on National Apostasy, of which Newman later remarked: 'I have ever considered and kept the day, as the start of the religious movement of 1833.' During the summer and autumn of that year the course of the Oxford Movement, according to Froude's biographer, Piers Brendon,

> was determined by a triumvirate consisting of Newman, who held the reins, Keble, who provided the motive power, and Froude, who wielded the whip and yelled directions.

Their main method of propaganda was to issue a series of pamphlets called *Tracts for the Times* (which resulted in adherents to the Oxford Movement becoming known as Tractarians), and to distribute them as widely as possible up and down the country. They also became involved in a bitter (and inhumane) attack on the newly-appointed Regius Professor of Divinity at Oxford, Dr Renn Dickson Hampden. It was a post that both Pusey and Newman had been tipped for, but it was a government appointment and the liberal Lord Melbourne chose the sedate, rational Hampden, friend of Dr Arnold of Rugby. The reverberations of this battle, which was lengthy, and involved the complex political machinery of the University hierarchy, cemented the lines of demarcation between the Tractarians and the less dogmatic clergy. Arnold called the former 'the Oxford malignants' and declared that their work was to change sense into silliness and holiness into formality and hypocrisy; and Carlyle dismissed them as having but the brains of rabbits.

Nevertheless, for six years the Movement was very successful in terms of the numbers of followers which it attracted. The almost physical enjoyment which Newman and Froude seemed to get from plotting their strategies may be illustrated by part of a letter Newman wrote to his friend while planning a pamphlet on Church grievances. He said his motivation was merely 'to *irritate* and shall (if so) write it as rhetorically and vehemently as I can ... having established a raw, our game is to keep it from healing'. Froude contributed to the excitable, schoolboy element of the Movement by allotting codenames: the Tractarians themselves were the X's; Evangelicals were known as Peculiars; and the middle-of-the-road establishment churchmen were called Z's. Such characteristics were rather different from those highlighted in the entry on the Oxford Movement included in the *Encyclopedia of Religion and Ethics* published in 1917:

> The first Tractarians re-introduced a type of character which had been sadly lacking in the English clergy and laity for a century. They were marked by reserve, resolute self-discipline, unworldliness, shrinking from preferment, hatred of sham and pretence, and a grave distrust of the feelings.

This reverential summary ignores the note of shrillness that appears in some of Newman's work, and which allowed his fictional character, Charles Reding, to denigrate the worldly heads of Oxford colleges thus when expressing his 'hatred of sham and pretence':

> Here are ministers of Christ with large incomes, living in finely furnished houses, with wives and families, and stately butlers and servants in livery, giving dinners all in the best style, condescending and gracious, waving their hands and mincing their words as if they were the cream of the earth, but without anything to make them clergymen but a black coat and a white tie. And then Bishops or Deans come, with women tucked under their arm; and they can't enter church but a fine powdered man runs first with a cushion for them to sit on, and a warm sheepskin to keep their feet from the stones.

In the autumn of 1833 Newman learned from a doctor in Oxford that Froude could not be expected to recover from consumption, and he and Keble persuaded him to go to Barbados in a final desperate bid for convalescence. Pusey, with initial reluctance, was drawn into the vanguard of the Movement, replacing Froude's vehemence with a gravity and orthodoxy that proved invaluable. 'Pusey's presence,' wrote Isaac Williams,

> always checked Newman's lighter and unrestrained mood: and I was myself silenced by so awful a person. Yet I always found in him something most congenial to myself; a nameless something which was wanting even in Newman, and I might perhaps add even in Keble himself.

Newman, Froude and Keble all had a lot of charm—an equivocal quality in a moral leader; Pusey—apart from an occasional slow, disarming smile—did not, conveying an impression of sternness and stability which added much-needed ballast to the Movement.

Froude came home in 1835, and died in March the following year. After his death, Newman added these somewhat ambiguous lines to his poem 'Separation of Friends', which he had first started after Froude had preceded him back to England at the end of their Mediterranean tour:

> Ah! dearest, with a word he could dispel
> All questioning, and raise
> Our hearts to rapture, whispering all was well,
> And turning prayer to praise.

And other secrets too he could declare,
By patterns all divine,
His earthly creed retouching here and there,
And deepening every line.
Dearest! he longs to speak, as I to know,
And yet we both refrain:
It were not good; a little doubt below,
And all will soon be plain.

As he read through Froude's papers, he became determined to preserve a record of his friend's abbreviated life. He underwent the customary urge of needing to prove the invincible worthiness of the object of his love; and he could do so with impunity now that Froude was dead. When he had been alive, Newman had written to him thus:

It is quite impossible that, some way or other, you are not destined to be the instrument of God's purposes. Though I saw the earth cleave, and you fall in, or Heaven open and a chariot appear, I should say just the same . . . You might be of use in the central elemental fire; you might be of use in the depths of the sea.

Now he was dead, he wrote to Bowden:

What a marvel it is! but I really do think that a fresh instrument of influence is being opened to us in these Papers. They do certainly portray a saint. They bring out, in the most natural way, an ethos as different from what is now set up as perfection as the East from the West.

It was during this period that Newman was at the height of his influence in Oxford. As one visitor recorded: 'When he preaches at St Mary's (on every Sunday afternoon) all the men of talent in the University come to hear him, although at the loss of their dinner.' But the publication of Froude's *Remains* under his editorship marked the beginning of a decline in his reputation. Hurrell's private confessions of his guilt-ridden struggles to conform to the ideal of 'moral taste', and his invective against the Reformation, confirmed the worst suspicions of the enemies of the Oxford Movement. In the House of Commons its leaders were denounced as a set of 'damnable and detestable heretics', and Bishops and professors of divinity combined in their condemnation of Froude's

writings. A year later, Newman began to have his first doubts about
the tenability of the Anglican Church.

He was both the most reasoning and the most unreasonable of
men. As he embarked on the six years' reading, meditating, suffering
and insight which led to his final conversion, he published the
following invective against the Roman Church:

> We see its agents smiling and nodding and ducking to attract
> attention, as gipseys [*sic*] make up to truant boys, holding out
> tales for the nursery, and pretty pictures, and gilt gingerbread,
> and physic concealed in jam, and sugar-plums for good
> children ... We Englishmen like manliness, openness, consis-
> tency, truth.

This almost manic fear of the Roman Catholic Church was not, of
course, confined to Newman; such expression was common. When
Ruskin's mother, for example, felt that her son was becoming
familiar with too many Catholics in Italy, she wrote to her
daughter-in-law:

> My dearest Effie, I wish you would use your influence with mine
> to prevent your Husband keeping company with these idolators
> for they are most insidious.

And converts to Roman Catholicism were frequently nicknamed
'perverts'.

In 1840 Newman published *Tract 90* in which, by employing a
strictly historical method, he tried to prove that the Thirty-Nine
Articles of the Church of England need not bear the anti-Roman
sense popularly attributed to them. This resulted in a great outcry,
and he withdrew from public Oxford life in order to found a quasi-
monastic community at Littlemore, a few miles away. It was never
a very flourishing venture, and one visitor, the ascetic Mark
Pattison, noted that Newman's 'lurking fondness for the miracu-
lous' was coming very much to the fore. Silence was the order for
most of the day, but talk was allowed at the frugal dinner table, and
during Pattison's short stay the following subjects were mentioned
by Newman:

> how St Macarius stood upright in his cell for a week without
> eating anything, but chewed a palm-leaf out of humility; how
> St Goderick stood all night in the river up to his neck, and

frozen; how a blasphemer in a Leicestershire public house uttered the common oath, Strike me blind! and was on the instant taken at his word by a flash of lightning, but became a Cistercian and recovered his sight on first receiving the sacrament.

When finally he resigned the vicarage of St Mary's, Newman took farewell of his ministry by celebrating Holy Communion with Pusey. Parry Liddon, Pusey's intimate friend and supporter, witnessed the event, and wrote, 'Some who were present in the gloom of that early October morning felt that they were assisting at the funeral of a religious effort which had failed.'

On St John the Baptist's day, midsummer eve, the following year, an Italian Passionist monk visited Littlemore. His name was Father Dominic Barberi, and as a young man he 'had received an interior understanding from God that he would have work to do in the conversion of England'. He was short, round-faced, bright-eyed, and wore a 'scratch lot of old black clothes, old patched boots and an ancient hat'. Long after, Newman remarked: 'His very look had about it something holy. When his form came in sight I was moved to the depths of my being in the strangest way.'

A month later, on 28 July 1844, Gerard Manley Hopkins was born at Stratford in Essex.

In September, John Bowden, Newman's close friend from their undergraduate days, died—like Froude, of consumption. His death had been expected, and Newman had hoped it would bring 'light to my mind, as to what I ought to do'. But 'it brought none', and he wrote in his journal: 'I sobbed bitterly over his coffin, to think that he left me still dark as to what the way of truth was . . .' That Newman should have expected some kind of spiritual revelation over whether or not he should proceed into the Church of Rome to have resulted from Bowden's death may seem a little odd bearing in mind that Bowden—though closely associated with the Oxford Movement and a contributor to the Tracts—was a Commissioner of Stamps and Taxes with a wife and several children. However, apart from Froude, he was the friend Newman had loved most; and as Newman had allowed Froude to guide him away from the Evangelicals into one form of traditional Catholicism, so perhaps he needed some kind of influence (albeit supernatural) from another beloved friend to provide the final involuntary impulse to Rome; an impulse that would give the culminating spiritual ingredient to bind together the not-quite-absolute results of his long theological quest.

The dark did not lift for some time. Newman's doctor became alarmed by his shrunken and debilitated appearance; although only forty-four, and in what should have been the prime of life, he already seemed to think of himself as an old man.

Then on 8 October 1845 he heard that Father Dominic was to be passing through Oxford again, and he sent a message asking him to come to Littlemore. Meriol Trevor, Newman's biographer, writes:

> It was very late and pouring with rain, the coach had been delayed by the weather. Father Dominic had had five hours of it on top of the coach and was soaked. [He] took a chaise out to Littlemore, arriving about eleven at night. 'I took up my position by the fire to dry myself,' he wrote later to his superiors. 'The door opened— and what a spectacle it was for me to see at my feet John Henry Newman begging me to hear his confession and admit him into the bosom of the Catholic Church.'

After his ordination as deacon, Newman had written: 'I feel as a man thrown suddenly in deep water.' About his reception into the Roman Catholic Church, he wrote that it was 'like coming into port after a rough sea'.

CHAPTER ONE

Skin

'WHAT MUST it be to be someone else?' As a boy Gerard Manley Hopkins was overwhelmed by this concept, its strangeness, and could imagine no answer. His uniqueness was unassailable and indelible; his sense of self utterly distinctive.

In appearance he was very slightly-built, with heavy-lidded eyes, pale skin, and thin, light brown hair; and from his photographs he seems to have had an intense, rather knowing expression. He was the eldest of nine children; his mother, Kate, the eldest of eight; and his father, Manley, the eldest of five. In the midst of a widely-branching yet united family, uniqueness flourished, feeding on a variety of relationships. And at the centre of these relationships were, for Gerard, the procreators: Kate and Manley.

Manley Hopkins (1818–1897) was allegedly somewhat pompous and autocratic, but also loving and humorous, and conscientiously effective as a man of affairs. His father had been a broker and India merchant, but died in 1836 when his fortunes were low, leaving Manley to take charge of the family at the age of eighteen. When he married seven years later, he continued to provide a home for his mother and sister, as well as temporarily for his brothers. His mother, Ann Hopkins (*née* Manley), came from a family in Devon who had owned and farmed their property since the thirteenth century and were fairly prosperous. The Hopkinses lived in comfortable middle-class style, and at some time had acquired a family crest and motto: 'Esse quam videre'—to be, rather than to seem to be.

Manley worked as an average adjuster, the forerunner of marine insurance, and became a leading expert on the protection and safety of shipping. As well as works related to his profession, he wrote poetry and also made an unsuccessful attempt at a novel. (It was rejected for serial publication by Hurrell Froude's younger brother, James Anthony.)

In 1843 he married Kate Smith (1821–1920), a doctor's daughter, and published his first book, *A Philosopher's Stone and other Poems*.

The book was dedicated to Thomas Hood with whom he was acquainted, and who stimulated his interest in puns and wordplay— an interest later shared with Gerard and his brother Lionel. Hood died in 1845, but his riddles and comic verse were no doubt popular in the Hopkins nursery; verses such as:

> Ben Battle was a soldier bold,
> And used to war's alarms:
> But a cannon-ball took off his legs,
> So he laid down his arms!

Gerard was born on 28 July 1844, a year after his parents' marriage and the year in which his father started up his own firm in the City. Their home was Chestnut House, 87 The Grove, Stratford, Essex, a tall brick semi-detached house on the eastern periphery of London. Grandmamma and Aunt Annie (Ann Eleanor Hopkins) were part of the permanent household, and Uncle Marsland (Manley's youngest brother), who was up at Cambridge, spent his vacations there. (The other brothers, Charles and Edward, were abroad.) During this period Marsland, who was soon to be ordained, and Manley were preparing a joint volume of verse, published anonymously, and called: *Pietas Metric; Or, Nature Suggestive of God and Godliness.* It was dedicated to 'The Church . . . By Two of Her Sons'. The Church in this case was the High Anglican Church, of which the family were devout members. It was a thorough, but not an oppressive, influence. Manley Hopkins considered that Christianity when seen 'in its true colours' was 'winning, persuasive, holy, and altogether lovely'. While successful in commerce, and compliant to Christian morality, his life was infused and heightened by an appreciation of beauty and the practice of art.

His sister Ann was a good amateur musician and painter (her rather sentimental watercolour of Gerard at fifteen hangs in the National Portrait Gallery), and she played an important part in the education of Gerard before he was old enough to go to school. He was twenty months old when his brother Cyril was born; Arthur arrived a year later, and Milicent in 1849. While his mother concentrated on the youngest arrivals, Aunt Annie organised the care and teaching of the older ones. Gerard was always small for his age, and when he was four a note, written on his behalf to his mother who was away, said that Uncle Marsland had told him that if he did not eat more meat he would soon be outgrown by Cyril. (It is apparently the only surviving letter from his childhood; the next in time was written when he was seventeen.)

As in most educated Victorian families, reading, music, drawing and writing were activities available to all the children and each was encouraged to develop his or her talents. Kate shared these artistic interests with Manley and Ann—especially music and reading. To judge from photographs (admittedly not the most reliable of evidence), she and Manley appear to have had other similarities: neither is especially handsome, and they both display a mild, intelligent and above all calm, mien. Manley's conviction that Christianity contained 'dignity, beauty, tenderness and amiability' seems to have been a positive influence on their personalities. But as well as conventional artistic interests, he was fascinated by the contemporary preoccupation with curious psychological problems and miscellaneous pieces of esoteric knowledge; he had a questing, active mind, and helped to stimulate Gerard's many-sided approach to learning.

When Gerard was eight, the whole family moved to a more fashionable area—Oak Hill in Hampstead, and he was sent to a day school nearby. The neighbourhood was still surrounded by woods and fields, and was popular with people connected with the arts. A Scottish student who lodged there some years later mentioned 'the classic arcadian calm of Oak Village, its green umbrageous nooks and its breezy atmosphere redolent of culture and the breath of the marigold . . .' Manley became churchwarden of St John's church for a time, and for many years taught in its Sunday school and managed its funds. It is a Georgian church, built by John Sanderson in 1747, with an airy, elegant interior. Just a few minutes' walk from Oak Hill, it must have provided a frequent visual reminder of Manley Hopkins's belief that Christianity contained dignity and beauty, and was 'altogether lovely'.

Another baby, Felix, had been added to the family, but he died shortly after the move. Then Lionel was born in 1854, to be followed by Kate (1856), Grace (1857), and Everard (1860). In 1856 Grandmamma and Aunt Annie moved away from Oak Hill to a small house in Maida Vale in order to be near Marsland, who had married and was Perpetual Curate at St Saviour's church, Paddington.

When he was ten years old, Gerard was sent as a boarder to Sir Roger Cholmeley's School, Highgate. It was a mile and a half away from Oak Hill, across Hampstead Heath, and he was joined

B

there two years later by Cyril. Highgate School, as it came to be known, was in the process of being built up by its autocratic headmaster, the Reverend John Bradley Dyne, 'late Fellow, Dean and Lecturer in Divinity at Wadham College, Oxford'. It was one of many small grammar schools which expanded and flourished during that period, containing only nineteen pupils on Dyne's arrival and 200 on his retirement. He was a good classics teacher, but a tyrannical headmaster. Marcus Clarke, pupil at the same time as Gerard and Cyril, ruefully recalled 'the heartburnings, the miseries, the vexations, the birchings, the humiliations', and when, a few years after he had left, he heard that a celebration ball was to be held at the school, he wrote to Cyril:

> I could understand a musical soirée at the Deaf and Dumb Asylum, or a gymnastic exhibition at the Orthopaedic Institution—but a ball at Highgate schoolhouse . . . !

From the start, Gerard's academic work went well. His report for his fourth term shows that he was top of his class, and gained the best comment available—'Good'—for conduct, exercises, classics, arithmetic and either French or German (it does not specify which). Writing was the only subject for which he received a 'Moderately Good'—this, of course, being hand-writing, not creative output. It developed into an extremely distinctive script: open, generous, a little ornate, and retaining throughout his life an air of both femininity and exuberance. When accompanied by decorated capitals and other motifs, for which he had a facility, it was done with a good deal of flourish. On hearing that the father of his schoolfriend Charles Luxmoore thought he must have taken a whole day to do one particular drawing, Gerard replied tartly (in the letter referred to on p. 27) that 'it was certainly not more than five minutes'.

Luxmoore was the same age as Hopkins, and fourteen when he first went to Highgate. He arrived with a reputation as a scholar, and was immediately spurred by some of the pupils into a competition with Gerard to see who could complete their evening work—composing elegiacs—the faster. It was a dead heat, each writing twenty-four verses in as many minutes. Gerard's facility did not extend to games, which he disliked, but according to Cyril he was 'a fearless climber of trees, and would go up very high in the lofty elm tree, standing in our garden . . . to the alarm of on-lookers like myself'.

One can imagine that Gerard did not climb the elm merely to
show off and tease his brother. His drawings, poems, and journals
are full of trees; the fragment *A Windy Day in Summer* (78),
written when he was eighteen, describes—with a little adjectival
difficulty—elms, willows, chestnuts and aspens, and trees occur
again and again in his poems until, in *Epithalamion* (159, RB 72)
written the year before his death, they are perhaps the most overwhelming and vital presence of all:

> . . . sweetest, freshest, shadowiest;
> Fairyland; silk-beech, scrolled ash, packed sycamore,
>   wild wychelm, hornbeam fretty overstood
> By. Rafts and rafts of flake-leaves light, dealt so,
>   painted on the air,
> Hang as still as hawk or hawkmoth . . .

The association which Ruskin made between acute physical perception of nature and high moral perception pervades Hopkins's
speculations about art, and is one of the foundation stones of his
thought. One can guess from the subtitle of his father's and uncle's
book, *Nature Suggestive of God and Godliness*, and from Manley's
own drawings, that Ruskin was one of the family's mentors; and,
when astride a branch at the top of the elm, Gerard may have
experienced a totality of feeling that embraced the beauty of nature,
the exhilaration of praise, and the fervent wish to express these
magnificently, yet meticulously, in words or line. The one drawing
manual known to have been in the family library, *The Sketcher* by
John Eagles, expounds the connection between visual and verbal
art, encouraging students to accompany drawings with suitable
quotations or poems. Perhaps after gazing from the elm, across Oak
Hill to the landscape beyond, Gerard remained for a while in high
solitude to read from his favourite Keats, whose religion of beauty
was so intoxicating. Later such romanticism was to come to seem
dangerous, but for the moment the poet's visions of forests and
flowers, gods and lovers, may have given an added magic to the
surrounding woods and fields.

Hopkins liked to visit his maternal grandparents, Maria and John
Simms Smith; the latter a successful doctor who had been a fellow-
student of Keats. They lived at Blunt House in Croydon, and had a
two-acre lawn 'beautifully ornamented with stately Timber Trees',
which included two cedars of Lebanon and a very fine old beech.

Another favourite garden was that of his uncle, Judge George Giberne, who was married to Kate Hopkins's sister Maria and lived in Epsom. Giberne became one of the first expert amateur photographers, and took all the early surviving portraits of Gerard. He was also a good draughtsman and his collection of architectural drawings and photographs helped to stimulate his nephew's interest in medieval churches. His younger sister, Maria Rosina, had been a friend of Newman's since 1826. Meriol Trevor describes her as 'an uninhibitedly emotional creature, but she had a determined will and a good deal of common sense; she could be an embarrassment to her friends, but never a liability'. She was devoted to Newman, followed him into the Roman Catholic Church, and in 1859, when she was fifty-seven, decided she had an interior call from the Blessed Virgin telling her she must be a nun. Newman had been helped by her support and outspokenness in the past, but also embarrassed by her bouts of sentimentality. However, he was fond of her (towards the end of her life, when they were both very old, he gave her postal advice on elastic stockings, trusses, and the dangers of having no teeth) and anxious she should not commit herself to a convent for the wrong reasons and in the wrong spirit. He wrote to her:

> It would be more wicked indeed, but not more inconsistent, for a profligate unbelieving woman, some French novelist or Italian red-republicaness, to go to the Visitation convent, than for you, as you showed your feelings the other day.

She accepted this criticism, apparently amended her attitudes, and left for the convent, according to report, 'in full sail and tearless'. It is possible that Maria Rosina may have stayed at Epsom at the same time as Gerard and talked of Newman to him; certainly she would have been mentioned by the family.

The first surviving evidence of Hopkins's future as a poet is his poem *The Escorial* (1). It won the school poetry prize in 1860, a prize which was in Dyne's gift and was not awarded every year. The subject was prescribed (another time it was the Roman emperor, Julian the Apostate, and Marcus Clarke wrote the winning poem, but Dyne would not award him the prize because he had neglected his other studies). At the time Gerard wrote *The Escorial* the poet Philip Worsley, who had been a pupil at Highgate, was staying with Dr Dyne, and he read the poem and made criticisms. Since his own major work was to translate Homer into Spenserian stanzas (making the form, according to Matthew Arnold, yield 'its treasures of fluidity and sweet ease') he was no doubt particularly interested that this was the verse-form Hopkins had chosen. Worsley suffered much ill-health and died of consumption in 1866; an almost pathologically self-effacing man, his gentleness and devotion to poetry probably communicated favourably to Hopkins.

The Escorial has fifteen stanzas (one of which is missing) and is a very sustained effort for a boy of fifteen—despite the deprecatory quotation from Theocritus, 'and I compete like a frog against the cicadas', with which he prefaced it, and which W. H. Gardner suggests 'may perhaps be taken as a precocious recognition of the fact that important poetry seldom emerges from a competition'. It contains an historical description of the Escorial, which was built thirty miles from Madrid by Philip II in order to celebrate his victory over the French at the Battle of St Quentin on St Laurence's Day, 1557. Hopkins makes much of the fact that the buildings were laid out in the shape of a gridiron—to commemorate the legend that St Laurence is said to have been roasted to death on one. He describes the martyr's agony graphically: his 'crack'd flesh' lies 'hissing on the grate', and his collapsed body is likened to a wreck which is beaten by flames rather than wind. He ironically suggests that Philip must have 'grown fantastic in his piety' in supposing that a permanent emblem of the instrument of the saint's torture was the appropriate thanskgiving. He also underlines the contrast between the sombre, pious 'fortress of faith' and the 'zeal-rampant, fiery' people who rushed from it to try to inflict the Inquisition 'upon the stubborn Fleming' and to establish Roman Catholicism with 'the rod / Of forc'd persuasion'. Hopkins regrets the buildings' lack of 'Gothic grace' or classic harmony, and his involvement with Keats's poetry and Ruskin's aesthetics combine to allow him to indulge in a description of the 'Gothic grace' that might have been. Ruskin is acknowledged in the words 'foliag'd crownals (pointing how the ways / Of art best follow nature)' and Keats in 'flowing tracery engemming rays / Of colour in high casements'.*

*Cf. *The Eve of Saint Agnes*:
A casement high and triple-arch'd there was,
All garlanded with carven imag'ries
Of fruits, and flowers, and bunches of knot-grass,
And diamonded with panes of quaint device,
Innumerable of stains and splendid dyes . . .

As well as the theme of clashing faiths adumbrated in the poem, Hopkins included another which was to have significance in his later life: the effect of storm. He describes an avalanche in the mountains near the Escorial, and just one phrase 'Down-splinter'd rocks crush'd cottages' has the authentic, compressed Hopkins diction. It also raises the speculation, given the family's interest in art and their regular visits to exhibitions, that it might have been directly inspired by Turner's painting 'Cottage Destroyed by an Avalanche' (later called 'Fall of An Avalanche in the Grisons') which had been on view at the Turner Gallery at Marlborough House (1856) and discussed by Ruskin in his accompanying *Notes*. Hopkins had also had the opportunity for first-hand observation of mountain landscape, having toured the Rhineland with his father and Cyril in 1857. (In the summer after he had written *The Escorial*, Manley took him on another tour through Southern Germany.)

Storm, shipwreck, physical and moral endurance—nature and man in extreme circumstances—these were popular Victorian themes, and ones that fascinated Hopkins as an adolescent. He once, for example, had an argument about the amount of suffering seamen could endure (backed up, no doubt, by knowledge gleaned from his father who later published *The Port of Refuge, or advice and instructions to the Master-Mariner in situations of doubt, difficulty, and danger*), and wagered sixpence against ten shillings that he could survive without liquids for a specific number of days. It is said that towards the end of the experiment his tongue had turned quite black, and Dyne swooped down and forbade the wager to continue.

Luxmoore recalled (in a letter written after Hopkins's death) that when Gerard was moved to a new dormitory at Highgate, he was initially ridiculed by the other boys because he read the New Testament every night—thereby keeping a promise made to his mother. He was not, however, deterred, and they soon decided to stop hindering him. Luxmoore remembered him as a boy 'with his face always *set* to do what was right'.

He was nicknamed Skin—presumably an anagram of the last syllable of his surname rearranged to describe his physical slightness (cf. skin and bone). But his build did not prevent him from being tenaciously pugnacious if he felt that Dyne was treating him unfairly. He would never willingly submit to the headmaster's threats and bullying in order to avoid being beaten, and liked to entertain his friends with quick cartoons and satirical rhymes about the school and staff. An idea of how unpleasantly severe the head-master's rule was is contained in an article Marcus Clarke wrote after he had left school and emigrated to Australia:

When I was at school I was flogged twice a week, and did not like it. The gentlemanly headmaster—he was cousin to an earl, a D.D., and strictly orthodox—was noted for his use of the birch, and used to smack his lips over flogging with intense glee. He was a left hander (there was a legend extant to the effect that he had broken his right arm in flogging a boy, but I always doubted it myself), and the way he used to 'draw' the birch was astonishing. He used always to stop after ten strokes, if the victim cried out, but as I was under the impression that he flogged me from purely personal motives, and wanted to show my indifference ... I would have died rather than whimper. So the worthy man, his thoughts, perhaps, busy with the Greek particle or the state of the funds, would 'flog' away unconscious, waiting for the customary howl. I remember once I was flogged a second time for laughing ... and as by a superlative chewing of indiarubber I did *not* howl, I was regarded as a small hero by the whole of the fourth form, and when my particular friend picked out the buds [of the birch twigs] with his penknife that night, and related a complimentary remark made by Bluggins ma., head of the sixth, and a triton among schoolboy minnows, I felt almost happy.

(The Australasian, 24 July 1869)

'My particular friend' is probably a reference to Cyril Hopkins, and the 'triton' just may have been Gerard. For reasons of pride, boys seldom expressed their sense of outrage—as opposed to their defiance—at being flogged, but Dyne, like so many schoolmasters of his day, clearly far transgressed the bounds into indecency and cruelty.

One of the few surviving letters from Hopkins's pre-Oxford years, was written in 1862 to Luxmoore, who had by then left Highgate and had apparently written accusing Gerard of giving him 'the cut'. Hopkins elaborately denied the charge and then ironically chided his friend for an inaccurate classical reference. This was followed by a summary of incidents culminating in a row with Dyne (the immediate cause of which is not revealed) which had led to Hopkins becoming a day-boy. Luxmoore had asked if he was 'still cock of the walk at Elgin'—the schoolhouse at which they had both boarded—and is told how all his study privileges had been withdrawn (a quiet room, fire, candle) until the situation became untenable, since he was trying to work for a Balliol College scholarship examination. Dyne had on one occasion 'blazed into me with his riding-whip' after Hopkins had been provoked to cheek him 'wildly'. Marcus Clarke had been included in the row, and he too was flogged as well as being struck off the confirmation list and fined £1. Clarke's biographer, Brian Elliott, suggests that the conflict may have been 'upon some point of religious orthodoxy'. Clarke was drawn to the occult and the mysterious, and Elliott relates how when Gerard became a Roman Catholic he wrote to Cyril Hopkins

> that he considered the Roman Catholic 'the most picturesque and splendid form of belief', which he had once [and the reference must be to his schooldays] been tempted to adopt himself, although he had not done so because he rather 'inclined to the mystical in religion'. By 'mystical' Clarke seems to mean mysterious; if the reference was to schoolboy occultism or any form of 'Roman' experimentalism Dyne would certainly not have approved of it.

Returning to school after walks across Hampstead Heath on dark evenings, Clarke used to enjoy frightening his friends with macabre stories, and one of his narratives, 'Prometheus', was copied out and illustrated by Gerard. The manuscript does not survive, but sketches which he made to entertain his brothers and sisters display a certain relish for gothic spookiness. Cyril recalled that the story concerned a medical student who endeavoured to use an ancient German formula to 'impart to a lifeless body the vital principle'—presumably inspired by Mary Shelley's *Frankenstein, or the Modern Prometheus*. When Clarke left England, he gave Gerard a volume of Poe's poems. Clarke had a reputation at school for being eccentric, and was described as 'a human butterfly'; Gerard is alleged to have called him 'a kaleidoscopic, particoloured, harlequinesque, thaumatropic being'.

In the letter to Luxmoore, there is a hint of the emotional rivalries that took place at Highgate, as at any other school. Hopkins explains how he had summoned a boy called Alexander Strachey to the dormitory for an end of term talk. It seems that Strachey had told Marcus Clarke that he was no longer a friend of Hopkins on account of the fact that Gerard never invited him to go for walks.

Hopkins quotes to Luxmoore the diary entry he recorded after the incident, in which he complained somewhat righteously that Strachey had been most unjust, and that he had only been avoiding him because Strachey seemed to want it that way, and that he had made himself feel wretched as a result. When Strachey came to the dormitory, Hopkins informed him that although he might find friends who were more liberal than he was, he would find few willing to make a similar sacrifice. But they were interrupted by the other occupants of the bedroom at this stage, and Strachey decided 'with a cool smile' that in any case there would have been nothing further for him to say. Hopkins wrote in his journal—and repeated to Luxmoore—'Perhaps in my next friendship I may be wiser'. He appears to have talked to his mother about Strachey, too, for he told Luxmoore that she considered it would be polite for him to write to tell Strachey that he had been successful in getting a Balliol exhibition. However, Strachey did not reply, and when Hopkins returned to Highgate for the summer term, Strachey would only say a cold 'How do you do?' It was, wrote Hopkins, his 'misfortune to be fond of and yet despised by' him.

There is a directness about the way he relates these matters which indicates that he was accustomed to candour. The Victorian tendency for evasion through prolixity seldom touched him; his prose, like his poetry, is not simple, but invariably it has a veracious edge to it.

It would seem that he was used to discussing his friendships with his mother, since she advised him to write to Strachey, and the letters which he wrote to her when he first went up to Oxford the following year indicate that he was particularly close to her. Their relationship may well have been strengthened while he was living at home during his final terms at Highgate. This is especially likely as Cyril had already left school and was studying in Europe, while Arthur had been sent to Lancing College in Sussex.

Gerard did not go up to Oxford until April 1863, over a year after he had won his exhibition. This gave him a period in which he was not under too much pressure at Highgate, although Dyne forced him to sit the 1863 Easter examinations in which, Hopkins pointed out, he had nothing to gain, but his prestige to lose—especially as a Balliol tutor, Edwin Palmer, was to be one of the examiners. During this time he developed his writing and drawing, read a great deal, visited art galleries and went to the theatre. Everard, the last addition to the family, was only two years old, and Kate and Grace were still of nursery age, so there must have been a full complement of domestic staff for his mother to organise, and since his father was extremely preoccupied at this time, Gerard may briefly have experienced the feeling of being the eldest male in a household, with its attendant responsibilities and advantages.

The reasons for Manley Hopkins's preoccupation are worth going into in some detail, as they give a clear illustration of the religious and moral climate in which Gerard grew up. Since 1856 Manley had combined with his usual professional duties the post of Consul-General in London for Hawaii. This appointment was due to his brother Charles, who worked for the legislature in Hawaii and was a close friend of King Kamehameha IV and Queen Emma. When the king had visited England he had been very impressed by the Anglican Episcopal Church, and had subsequently used the Episcopalian ritual at his own wedding. Now he and the queen were anxious to establish an Episcopalian church in Hawaii and had offered to donate a piece of land on which it might be built.

In December 1859 the Hawaiian Minister of Foreign Affairs, Robert Wyllie, wrote to Manley Hopkins instructing him to confer with leading Church authorities in the hope that assistance for the king's proposal would be forthcoming. In a private letter, Wyllie told Hopkins that the king and queen preferred 'that the Episcopal Clergyman, for the proposed Chapel or Church, should have a family of his own, and be eminently liberal in all his principles and ideas'. This was in order that he might clearly be seen to support a faith whose priests themselves celebrated family life and were humane and cheerful, and thus be clearly differentiated from the members of the French Roman Catholic Mission, who were celibate, and the American evangelical mission, who were strict and dour. It was hoped that the American Episcopalians, however, would support the new venture.

Manley Hopkins accepted the task with enthusiasm, recognising in it 'a deep responsibility' which would 'require much earnest thought and exertion'. He was given support by the powerful Bishop of Oxford (Dr Samuel Wilberforce—who had once complained that Hurrell Froude was 'so fierce against him' when he married, and who had now earned the nickname Soapy Sam on account of his rather unctuous rhetoric), and between them they played a prominent part in establishing the Episcopalian Church in

Hawaii. The depth of Manley's involvement can be seen by a remark from a letter he wrote to Wyllie in March 1862:

> When it was suggested to me that an account of the Islands should be written and published to enlighten the British public about them and interest them in the subject, I commenced one without loss of time, rising before daylight for months, and all through the winter that I might accomplish my task.

The result, *Hawaii: The Past, Present and the Future of its Island-Kingdom*, was published that year. Considering that he never visited Hawaii, it shows remarkable empathy.

The following extracts from the book are quoted at length because their style and content give such a clear indication of Manley's personality and ethical position. The phraseology suggests a man who enjoyed literary execution, and they display the slightly self-satisfied philosophy of one who had come to terms, to his own satisfaction, with the theme that was to haunt Gerard's life: the conflict between sensuality and purity.

> The fatal gift of beauty, a delicious climate, which rendered clothing unnecessary ... an indolent and pleasure-loving constitution ... and the absence of adverse public opinion, are among the prevalent causes of a general absence of chastity among the Hawaiians. Till taught otherwise by the missionaries, the natives had no conception that aphrodisiac indulgences were even wrong or hurtful; they had not even a word to express chastity in their language. ... The American missionaries, and the native government actuated by the missionaries, threw themselves unenquiringly and at once into a crusade against the prevailing licentiousness of the people. Fines, imprisonment, severe labour, and informers, were the weapons of their warfare. A great apparent change was rapidly effected. They clothed and converted the natives, and they produced, not, alas! a regenerated people, but a nation of hypocrites. It is no difficulty to the Hawaiians to dissemble ... In fact they are admirable mimics. The missionaries' gesture and intonation, their soft feline style of approach, their very seat in the saddle, the sunburnt black suit, all were exactly counterfeited—nothing escaped them!
> ... It is to higher influences we must look for the possible salvation and regneration of the Hawaiian nation. The instrument

must clearly be the inculcation of a pure and gentle religion; a holy and exalted doctrine, illustrated and made living by the Christian conduct and self-denying lives of its professors and its teachers. Such influences have already had some weight; but there has been about former efforts of the American missionaries a 'hidden want', which shows that vital power is lacking, the loving power which works by assimilation,—the leaven which must permeate the mass and take hold of the affections and will of the natives, and convert them, not into hypocrites, but Christians. . . . To take the young Hawaiian girls at an age so early that even they have not been contaminated, to keep them as in a parental home, to watch them by day and night, and screen them from sights and sounds of impurity, to teach them to control transmitted passions, and to fill their minds with interesting subjects of thought, to befriend them always, and finally to see them married respectably—these are the means by which the nation must rise in true morality. . . . The sentimentalist may exclaim against this change of natural habit, instincts, picturesque attitude, this assimilation of the wild and the beautiful to the thoughts, manners, dress, and expression of a hackneyed Europe. Well, something must be sacrificed. We may have to forsake the temple of art, to dwell in the temple of God.

For Manley Hopkins, Christian married life provided the solution to the temptations of the flesh, and although on occasion 'we may have to forsake the temple of art, to dwell in the temple of God', it was for him an eminently satisfactory solution.

During the two years prior to the publication of his book, he had organised a committee to collect money for the proposed mission, and approval had been obtained for it to be headed by a bishop rather than a clergyman. Concerning the appointment of such a bishop, Hopkins wrote to Wyllie:

I feel deeply the responsibility of procuring a suitable person to act at the head of the Mission. He must be truly earnest in the Christian cause, and be of a liberal habit of mind, so as to endear and not to estrange other workers in the Vineyard.

The Reverend Thomas Nettleship Staley was finally selected, and a Royal License granted by Queen Victoria to the Archbishop of Canterbury for the consecration of a 'bishop of the United Church of England and Ireland in Hawaii'; the ceremony took place at

Lambeth Chapel on 15 December 1861—the day after Prince Albert died. (A month later Manley suffered a personal tragedy when his brother Marsland died, leaving an expectant wife and two small children.)

Earlier, a move had been made by the American Episcopalians to influence the choice of leader for the mission. In 1860 they told the Reverend William Ellis, a prominent English misisonary who had worked in Hawaii, that the type of man they wanted was

> a man of evangelical sentiment, of respectable talents, and most exemplary Christian life. A High Churchman, or one of loose Christian habits, would not succeed. He would not have the sympathy and support of the other evangelical ministers at all, but rather opposition, as you well know from personal observation

and asked if he could help to guide the selection. Ellis duly called on Manley Hopkins to see what he could do, but was not at all satisfied with the outcome. He reported back to Hawaii:

> Mr Hopkins . . . handed me a sort of circular, which he had prepared, and by the names attached to which I perceived that he was associated with that section of the Church of England from which the greatest number of perverts to Popery has proceeded, and between whom and the Roman Catholics the difference is reported to be slight. I left Mr Hopkins under the impression that any interference on my part was by him deemed unnecessary, and would not be welcome.

From this remark it can be seen that the climate of prejudice that had been inflamed by the Tractarians had by no means abated; and nowhere were the issues more alive or more openly debated still than in Oxford itself, where the forces of critical reason and religious orthodoxy were warring as strongly as ever. Manley Hopkins presumably was aware of the complex mental and moral climate that was shortly to absorb his eldest son, but would no doubt assume that his united family background and sound Anglo-Catholic faith would stand him in good stead. There would be anxieties. Benjamin Jowett, Regius Professor of Greek and the most influential of Balliol's tutors, was at the centre of an uproar about a collection of articles, *Essays and Reviews* (1860), to which he had contributed. The aim had been to produce a volume 'in which theological subjects should be freely handled in a becoming spirit'.

Jowett's contribution 'On the Interpretation of Scripture' was a plea for reason, arguing that the scriptures should 'be interpreted like other books, with attention to the character of its authors, and the prevailing state of civilisation and knowledge. . . .'. The essays caused increasing waves of wrath—particularly from Dr Pusey and Dr Wilberforce—which culminated in Jowett being summoned for prosecution in the Vice-Chancellor's Court two months before Gerard went up to Balliol. The case was in fact dismissed, but Oxford was humming with the controversy. Two years earlier, in Janauary 1861, when Manley Hopkins was involved with the Hawaiian mission project and in contact with Wilberforce, the latter had written in the *Quarterly Review* that 'the attempt of the essayists to combine their advocacy of such doctrines with the retention of the status and emolument of Church of England clergymen is simply moral dishonesty'. One feels that the issues must have attracted Manley's notice, but it is interesting that by 1865, after two years at Balliol, Gerard had still not read either *Tracts for the Times* or *Essays and Reviews*, as they both appear in a list of 'Books to read' in his diary.

The conflict between sensuality and purity which was to dominate so much of Hopkins's work has already been mentioned, and something should perhaps be said of the prevailing climate of opinion on this complex subject before focusing on Hopkins's own experience.

The moderate view was to be well expressed by Jowett in some jottings he made in his notebook under the heading 'Control of Passions' in 1867—the year Hopkins graduated. 'A man is not a man,' Jowett notes, 'who does not control his passions.' Then he goes on to say:

(But there are great difficulties about this: marriage is deferred generally for 15 or 20 years after the passions are strongest and is sometimes impossible altogether without loss of rank. Then there is the concealment which takes place about vice. We speak as though this was the exception and yet with the Upper and Middle classes at least it is the rule. And we speak as if there was one rule and one guilt for all. Whereas the degrees of temptation may be absolutely different.)

Note the subtle admixture of good and evil in the passions. Energy has a great deal to do with strong passions. Ideals of good have a certain connexion with love and lust. There seems also to be a natural feeling of remorse about sins of impurity . . .

. . . It has been imagined by Sceptics that all the more intense forms of religion are really bastard or illegitimate results of the relations of sexes. Whether this is true or not, it is plain that there is a close connexion between them and an easy transition from one to the other. Hence an important question. The right use or the right regulation of the passions in religion. How to kill the sense or lust and leave the ideal or aspiration ? . . .

His opening sentence—'A man is not a man who does not control his passions'—is central to Victorian morality. Masculinity was associated with self-control and continence, whilst effeminacy was associated with sexual licentiousness. William Acton, the medical moral mentor of the day, claimed that it was not the

strong athletic boy, fond of healthy exercise, who thus early shows marks of sexual desires, but your puny exotic, whose intellectual education has been fostered at the expense of his physical development.

With his slight stature and dislike of games, Hopkins no doubt became conscious that he did not live up to the Victorian ideal, and one of the first things he reported to his mother when he arrived at Oxford for his second term was that 'Nurse did not pack my dumb-bells'. However, there was no overt pressure in his family for boys to become 'hearties', and he always had like-minded friends at both Highgate and Oxford. It is of coincidental curiosity that the word so often used by Victorian moralists—'manly'—to describe their masculine ideal, should be, in pronunciation if not spelling, Gerard's middle name. Being also his father's name, it may have provided him with a subconscious strengthening of that ideal. 'We Englishmen like manliness, openness, consistency, truth,' Newman had stated in his attack on the Roman Church. In the year before he died, Hopkins was to accuse Keats's poetry—which had once so intoxicated him—of 'abandoning itself to an unmanly and enervating luxury'; while George Herbert, whose 'fragrant sweetness' was to remain dear to him, was once claimed by Coleridge to use diction that was 'pure, manly and unaffected'. 'Savages,' Freud remarks in *Totem and Taboo*, regard a name as an essential part of man's personality . . . and children are never ready to accept a similarity between two words as having no meaning; they consistently assume that if two things are called by similar-sounding names this must imply the existence of some deep-lying point of agreement between them.

As a child Gerard may or may not have regarded his name in this special way. But the prosperous, middle-class society in which he grew up—questing, artistic, devout and vital—was one in which a non-exaggerated ideal of manliness would be valued; though without too much concern that a highly intelligent, small-statured, non-games-playing boy would be in danger of becoming 'your puny exotic'.

CHAPTER TWO

'Dear Poet'

IN THE late summer of 1862, when he was eighteen years old, Gerard was alone at Oak Hill, except for the servants. The other members of the family—apart from Cyril who was abroad—were staying at Epsom and Croydon, so he had the house to himself and an opportunity to order what he liked for meals. On 3 September he toyed with the idea of going down to Thurloe Square in order to persuade one of his cousins to accompany him to an art exhibition, but 'a stupid book' which he read while eating his dinner continued to absorb his attention. When he finally laid it down he decided to stay at home and answer a letter from his one-time school-friend, Ernest Hartley Coleridge. He had received the letter a week earlier, and had read it 'luxuriously in the garden' for he considered his friend's letters to be 'always great treats'.

The main subject of their correspondence was poetry. Hopkins addressed Coleridge (who was the grandson of Samuel Taylor) as 'Dear Poet', and entreated him to enclose some of his recent poetry in his next letter. He in turn copied out for his friend a prodigious amount of his own work: some lines he had translated from Aeschylus's *Prometheus Bound* (160), *Il Mystico* (77), *A Windy Day in Summer* (78), and *A Fragment of Anything You Like* (79). In addition he reported that he had written two-thirds of 'Linnington Water, an Idyll'; was planning 'Fause Joan'—a ballad; had begun the story of Corinth; and was writing descriptions of 'sunrises, sunsets, sunlight in the trees, flowers, windy skies etc. etc.' It is the slightly swaggering yet workmanlike report of work-in-progress of one aspiring poet to another, and it illustrates Hopkins's capacity for study and his irrepressible creative energy.

Coleridge was two years his junior, and was completing his schooling at Sherborne, having been at Highgate from 1858–60 when they became close friends. Gerard enquired what he was doing at Sherborne 'in the way of classics', and implored him to read the poems of Theocritus and Moschus. He particularly recommended *Thalusia* and *Hylas* by Theocritus, and *Elegy for Bion* by Moschus. (The quotation from Theocritus which prefixed *The Escorial* was from *Thalusia*, so the poem was clearly a very well-established favourite.) He admitted that he had probably recommended these before, but felt he could not do so too often because there was not 'anything so lovely in the classics'. These pastoral idylls, with their precise, joyous descriptions of nature and unashamed delight in passion, in some ways seem much closer to the heart of Hopkins than the waves of Tennyson and Keats which also flooded his imagination at this time. *Thalusia* describes the meeting of three men with a goatherd, Lycidas, who has great poetic talent. Lycidas sings of his love for a boy, Agenax, and one of the men reciprocates by telling of the love between a certain Aratus and the boy Phillinus. The travellers then leave Lycidas and continue on their way to a feast, where they recline beneath poplars and elms, on couches of fresh-cut leaves, and listen to the thrushes, larks, goldfinches and bees, while pears, apples, damsons and wine are offered in profusion. Theocritus provided a complete contrast to the pale ladies and unrequited loves of so much nineteenth-century poetry, and posed something of a problem to his translators with his celebrations of adoration and attraction between men and boys as well as men and women. The Reverend J. Davies remarked in an introduction to his own prose translation (published in 1853 under a pseudonym):

> There are blemishes to his Idylls, which certainly render an expurgated edition of them a desideratum ... [but] ... We cannot forego the charms of the whole, because our delicacy is offended, our purity shocked, by one or two Idylls, which, while they illustrate the darkest traits in the life of a heathen, only make us the more thankful that Christianity has at least gone far to banish one of the worst forms of human guilt and degradation.

In the 'metrical version' by J. M. Chapman which accompanied Davies's literal translation, the sex of Lycidas's loved one is not mentioned, while Phillinus is transformed neatly into Phyllis.

Hopkins remarks in his letter to Coleridge that he found most Greek tragedy to be 'stilted nonsense'; but in the pastoral poets he appears to have found a mirror for his own emotional joy in physical beauty of all kinds. There is little vapid poetising in Theocritus: the objects of delight are very real. But despite his stricture about Greek tragedy, Hopkins did admit that he had found *Prometheus Bound* 'full of splendid poetry'—a little of which he had translated—and recommended reading it alongside Shelley's *Prometheus Unbound* which was 'as fine or finer', if rather too fantastic.

Coleridge had sought an explanation of Tennyson's *The Vision of Sin*, which Hopkins confessed he found a mysterious poem—though 'not so much as your grandfather's poems'. He expounds the theme of the poem—that of a youth who is tempted into a palace of sin, where he indulges himself to the full and goes on to become 'a grey and gap-tooth'd man' seeking alcoholic oblivion—but does not give an opinion on it. Its tone is quite opposite to the spirit that had pleased him in Theocritus: the youth's debaucheries take place in an environment somewhat resembling the more exaggerated psychedelia of the late 1960's. Tennyson described the music as a 'nerve-dissolving melody' and dancers pant 'hand-in-hand with faces pale' amid 'Purple gauzes, golden hazes, liquid mazes'. There is also an undeniably phallic fountain which 'spouted, showering wide / Sleet of diamond-drift and pearly hail'. The poem ends with three voices that discuss the youth's demise, the first of which says, 'it was a crime / Of sense avenged by sense that wore with time'. Hopkins explains to Coleridge that the speaker feels the sensual crimes of youth have been atoned for by 'the terrible reaction' that sets in when the senses are 'worn out' and can no longer attain pleasure. (The Victorians, as well as claiming that sexually active men were effeminate and unmanly, also believed that each man had but a limited stock of virility and sensual enjoyment, so that one who was 'free-spending' in this area would achieve sexual bankruptcy.)

Hopkins passes straight from Tennyson to recent news. He has seen the farce *Our American Cousin* at the Theatre Royal, and found it 'truly admirable'. Cyril had been fetched from Esslingen in August and taken to a *pasteur* near Rouen, where he would stay until Christmas; he was reported to have shaved twice (despite having 'not a vestige' of facial hair), to be 'mad about the army', and to smoke furiously. (In a later letter to Coleridge, Hopkins said he hoped they might be able to meet some time well out of the way of Cyril 'and other pomps and vanities of this wicked world'. Cyril was to be the only one of Manley's sons to follow him permanently into the family business.)

Coleridge had enquired whether Gerard admired Tennyson's *St Simeon Stylites* since he had never heard anyone speak about it.

Hopkins retorted that he either could not have been listening properly to conversations, or the people he talked with were lacking; for himself, he considered the poem 'magnificent'—an adjective it would be rather hard to apply today. Simeon is pictured in gruesome detail atoning his sins on top of his pillar, and awaiting death: the dew has rotted his thighs, an iron collar grinds his neck, he has suffered 'coughs, aches, stitches, ulcerous throes and cramps', etc. etc. There is a certain relish about Hopkins's enthusiastic reaction— and, indeed, adolescents might still find the macabre tale quite exciting—but it lacks the intensity implied in his response to Theocritus.

He apologised for not having enough time to draw a picture for Coleridge, but copied out the 142 lines he had thus far written of *Il Mystico* (77)—a poem supposed to be in imitation of Milton's *Il Penseroso*. The metre comes from Milton, but there is more of Tennyson in the general substance. The poem represents the struggle of the writer's spirit to rise above gross sensual desire and inhabit a sphere which seems to hang suspended between heaven and earth, and from which the ecstasies of nature may be safely observed and appreciated. The lines of conflict could not be more clearly stated: the earthly senses (which are rank and reeking) condemned to grovel in a slimy, filthy hovel, and the spirit soaring like a lark amid the exquisite tints of a rainbow.

This is immediately followed by *A Windy Day in Summer* (78) which shows how Hopkins was beginning to attempt to turn his observations of nature into verse, and *A Fragment of Anything You Like* (79) in which a sorrowing lady is compared to the moon when it rises late and wanders aimlessly in broad daylight. Hopkins sought his friend's opinion on all the verses he had enclosed.

This long letter is like a prelude to his later correspondences with Robert Bridges, R. W. Dixon and Coventry Patmore, in which poetry was to be the meat, motivation and inspiration of their relationships. By then he had become a Jesuit, and very personal epistolatory exchanges were not always possible; but it can be seen from what he chose to write to Ernest Coleridge, a schoolboy of whom he was fond and with whom he had plenty of more everyday gossip in common, that poetry could easily become his prime concern. And through poetry he was exploring and expressing his intellectual and emotional needs. Theocritus, Tennyson, Keats, Milton and Shelley were relevant and absorbing, and he embarked enthusiastically on the apprenticeship that would eventually equip him to approach their ranks. He was always a conscious and conscientious craftsman, and even though the language in some of these early poems is over-precious and too rich to be exact, it is seldom sloppy and never insipid.

Three months later, at Christmas time, he wrote *A Vision of the Mermaids* (2), whose major influence was Keats at his most lush. It is worlds away from the botanical and emotional exactitudes of Theocritus, being frenziedly poetical, and reminding one that years later Hopkins was to confess to R. W. Dixon that 'crimson and pure blues' had once had the power to draw tears from him, they seemed so spiritual and heavenly. And indeed *A Vision of the Mermaids* is written as though the imagination of the poet were looking at its fantasy through deep-stained panels of glass—particularly shades of rose, garnet, crimson and blood. It is the sensuality of colour *in extremis*, and despite its exaggerations it has a feverishness that makes it seem real—at any rate for the writer. Tennyson's palace of sin, with its fountain and coloured lights, is not very convincing; but Hopkins's hectic sunset and colour bath is a recognisable reminder of aspects of youth. The poem also contains an image of Summer with 'lusty hands' tearing at the 'rosy foam' blossoms of his sister Spring, deflowering the coronals, 'a glorious wanton', which directly foreshadows later poems in which Hopkins was to compare the freshness and sweetness of spring, of Eden before the Fall, with the cloyed souring of over-ripe summer. But at eighteen his thoughts were more unbridled, and he produced what is in some ways his most actively virile piece of imagery: as Summer 'crushes and tears' at Spring's blossoms he boasts 'I have fairer things than these' and proceeds to blind the air with petals. The images in the poem spring from a mind which cannot help but revel and rejoice in the sensuality of words, spilling out phrases such as 'throbbing blood-light' and 'dusk-deep lazuli' in an attempt to recreate the actual visual impact of 'crimson and pure blues'.

In the circular pen-and-ink sketch which he drew to illustrate the poem, the turbulent sky and light-reflecting sea are convincingly dramatic, though the groups of mermaids, with their heads and shoulders above water, do not attempt a parallel pictorial description of the words. They are, in fact, distinctly odd and original mermaids, with a crest 'of tremulous film' down their backs that continued over their heads and drooped from their brows 'like

Hector's casque'—and, indeed, the one nearest the foreground of the picture does rather give the impression of a burly, helmeted soldier. In the poem they are so wreathed and chapleted in silver skirts, corals, shells, rosy weed, sea anemones, amethyst and silver film, and crystalline feelers, that any mental picture of their form quickly becomes camouflaged. Holidaying in the Isle of Wight the following year, Hopkins recalled the poem and decided to try a chaplet of sea anemones for himself: 'I thought I would look strikingly graceful,' he wrote ironically to a friend. He was somewhat chagrined to receive a painful sting on his forehead with its accompanying circular red mark.

Illustration, as well as painting and sketching, was a subject that particularly interested the Hopkins family, and both Arthur and Everard were to become professional artists and earn a major part of their living from magazine work. Manley Hopkins subscribed to a journal called *Once A Week* which had been launched partly in order to involve the greatest artists of the day in illustrative work, and it was here that Gerard's first published poem appeared. In the issue of 14 February 1863 it shares a page with the conclusion of a light-hearted piece about the trials of being shy and diffident, and is opposite the beginning of 'an historiette' by Harriet Martineau with an illustration by Millais. The poem is called *Winter with the Gulf Stream* (3), and it remained popular enough with Hopkins for him to revise it eight years later. It contains a description of a winter afternoon, starting with bare boughs and lightly frozen leaves, and finishes with this sunset:

> the emblazon'd west,
> Where yonder crimson fire-ball sets,
> Trails forth a purfled-silken vest.
>
> Long beds I see of violets
> In beryl-lakes which they reef o'er:
> A Pactolean river frets
>
> Against its tawny-golden shore:
> All ways the molten colours run:
> Till, sinking ever more and more
>
> Into an azure mist, the sun
> Drops down engulf'd, his journey done.*

* This extract is from the unrevised version.

It is an eminently tidy poem compared with *A Vision of the Mermaids*; one written, perhaps, with an eye to publication. It fits smoothly into the world of his father's style of verse: fluid, harmonious, but lacking anything to distinguish it from countless other peoms emanating from artistic households. Taken along with the various works sent to Ernest Coleridge, it shows that Hopkins, at the start of his career, was trying everything: conformity, translation, imitation and emulation, as well as involuntary passages of exuberant creativity.

CHAPTER THREE

'This is my park, my pleasaunce'

HOPKINS'S RESPONSE to Oxford was ecstatic: he adored it. He apparently went up on Friday, 10 April 1863, accompanied by his father, who remained for a few days, helping to superintend his initial financial needs and commitments. By the beginning of May, Gerard declared in a letter to his mother that he was 'almost too happy' and apologised if that sounded unkind, but the fact was he had so many friends and so much liberty that he could not help being content, despite being away from home.

His rooms were high up in the roof, and he found running up and down stairs between lectures exhausting, but by way of compensation he had the best views in Balliol, and the best college scout on his staircase. Indeed in that first flush of newness everything was best: Balliol was the 'friendliest and snuggest' college, and had the best cricket eleven; canoeing on the Cherwell supplied 'the summit of human happiness'; Edwin Palmer's lectures showed amazing heights of scholarship; and the Balliol chapel contained 'the finest old glass in Oxford'. Hopkins seemed at times to be almost bursting with delight; his only real complaint was that he could not keep his hands cool.

People invited him to breakfasts and to 'wines' (it was not done to refer to the latter as 'wine parties' and he was eager to demonstrate to his mother that he was quite *au fait* with Oxford parlance). On his first Sunday, Courtenay Peregrine Ilbert, a distinguished Balliol scholar, called up the staircase to ask whether he felt inclined to go for a walk. They went up the hill past Bagley Wood, and Ilbert, who was in his third year, no doubt put Hopkins at his ease by chatting about the college. Jowett was to be Hopkins's tutor, and he was famed for allowing embarrassing silences to occur; this could be extremely unnerving for new undergraduates, themselves shyly tongue-tied, and many anecdotes circulated concerning such encounters. Ilbert told Hopkins that one of these, if not exactly true, certainly was so in essence. It may have been the one included by Martin Geldart, a contemporary of Hopkins, in his loosely-disguised autobiography (published under the name Nitram Tradleg . . .), *A Son of Belial*:

> It is said he [Jowett] once walked from Belial [Balliol] gate to Maudlin [Magdalen] bridge [a distance of half a mile] with an undergraduate who had remarked on starting, 'It is a beautiful day.' On reaching the latter point in their peregrinations, Jewell [Jowett] turned suddenly upon him with the question, 'What's that you said?'
>
> 'Oh, I only remarked it was a beautiful day.'
>
> 'Ah! yes,' was the rejoinder; 'rather a weak remark that of yours.'

Hopkins decided that Ilbert was not only the cleverest man in Balliol (and therefore in the University), but also handsome and a veritable Admirable Crichton. By contrast, the two open scholars from his own year were decidedly poor specimens. One of these was Martin Geldart, and Hopkins described him to his mother with harsh adolescent scorn. Poor Geldart was dreadful and ghastly, full of haggard hideousness, shuffled, had goggle eyes and a scared suspicious look. Hopkins would not, he declared, change places with him for twenty Balliol scholarships. (A scholarship carried more value and prestige than an exhibition.) The other scholar, Alfred Barratt, was dismissed as looking commonplace. Hopkins would no doubt have shuddered at these dismissive judgements, reeled off light-heartedly to his mother, a few years later, but they show that in his early Oxford days he was as callow, bigoted and snobbish as the next man—and also perhaps harboured a little jealousy that he had not been awarded one of the scholarships himself.

He was invited to breakfast with Jowett and found him amusing when he did talk, but embarrassing when he didn't. Jowett advised him that his success would depend largely on his weekly essays (alternately in Latin and English), and told him not to get into debt. Besides the weekly essay, Hopkins had to prepare a paper in mathematics and a question paper known as 'catechecs'. This was short for catechetical, and was set every week to ensure that the undergraduates had listened to the divinity lecture delivered each Sunday afternoon instead of a sermon. These lectures were given by Edward Woollcombe (described by Hopkins as a 'pinch-faced old man' although he was only forty-seven), who was a well-liked, gentle Tractarian. Jowett, however, did not think much of him, nor of Henry Wall, Bursar of Balliol and Professor of Logic, and Hopkins once reported that he went to evening chapel in order to hear Wall speak and 'see Jowett laugh'.

As well as the controversy over the publication of *Essays and Reviews*, Jowett was at that time the centre of another dispute. His Regius Professorship of Greek was worth only £40 a year, and despite recommendation to the appropriate authority that the endowment should be increased, Jowett being one of the most conscientious and skilful teachers within the University, no positive action had been taken. The difficulty lay in the fact that for historical reasons the authority concerned was the Dean and Chapter of Christ Church, not the University itself, and Christ Church did not wish to seem to support Jowett's liberal theological views by raising his stipend. Pusey, who was still a Canon of Christ Church and leader of the High Church faction in Oxford, was chief among Jowett's opponents—but on religious grounds, not monetary. He thought responsibility for his salary should be transferred to the University and that the amount should be increased; but he could not agree to Christ Church increasing it, and thus directly helping the promulgation of views which he believed would lead to irreligion and the destruction of the Church. As far as the general members of the University were concerned, it simply appeared that Pusey was deliberately obstructing Jowett from receiving a living wage, and was thus behaving spitefully. In his book, Geldart recounted that

> as for the sons of Belial, they were, man for man, on the side of their Professor. All shades of opinion, High, Broad, Low, and No-Church, united in denouncing the meanness, the malignity, the crooked perversity of the orthodox tactics ... Even my Ritualistic [High Church] friend, Gerontius Manley [Hopkins], acknowledged what he called the 'purity' of our hero ... as something which struck him more in Professor Jewell than in almost any other.

Geldart, who had been brought up as an Evangelical, became friendly with Hopkins despite the latter's adverse first reactions, and he gave a warm account of the mixed opinions and beliefs which he found at Balliol, and which had recently been broadened by a reform which permitted dissenters to become undergraduates:

Never in all my life before or since was I among a company of men so young and ardent, yet so utterly devoted to plain living and high thinking. Never was I in an intellectual atmosphere so fearless and so free. I never knew what true tolerance without indifference was till I came to Bosphorus [Oxford]. It was a new experience to me altogether—to me, who had been brought up to regard Ritualism and Rationalism as the two right arms of the devil, to find myself suddenly launched among a lot of men who were some of them Ritualists of the deepest dye, some of them Rationalists, some of them Positivists, some of them Materialists, all eager in advancing their respective views, and yet all ready to listen with courtesy to their opponents.

It was not long before Hopkins's religious inclination, and combative disinclination, became known. An undergraduate called Augustus Secker, whom Hopkins described as disputing 'for the palm of ugliness with Geldart', failed to persuade him to join the Oxford Rifle Corps; and twelve days after his arrival he walked to Littlemore with William Edward Addis to see the church where Newman had preached his last sermon—'before the exodus', as Hopkins put it. Addis and he were to become very close friends, though unfortunately their correspondence has not survived.

By Monday, 4 May, Hopkins could claim to his mother that it appeared likely he would 'know all Oxford' soon, and that he had not breakfasted in his own rooms for ten days. He wrote the letter from the Union, and announced he had 'just been wining' with one Arthur Jebb. The letter is breathless, youthfully boastful, and utterly happy. Its main item of news concerns Frederick Gurney, who was in his third year at Balliol and already known to the Hopkins family. After chapel on the previous evening he had invited the college's High Church contingent (among whom Hopkins 'humbly' hoped 'to be enrolled') to wine, and had included Gerard in the invitation; Addis was also there. Someone came and 'played the piano gorgeously', and then Gurney asked Hopkins to accompany a group of them to go to hear Henry Parry Liddon give a lecture (on the first epistle to the Corinthians). This was Hopkins's initiation into the general Sunday evening practice of Oxford's High Church undergraduates: they attended the lecture, and were then given coffee and tea, and chatted to by Liddon. (Geldart called it 'Canon Parry's tea-and-toast and Testament'.) Hopkins explained carefully to his mother that Liddon was Pusey's 'great *protégé*', and that he had been introduced to him and would in future go to the lectures and meetings every Sunday.

At that time Liddon held no specific office, but lived in Christ Church and concentrated on pastoral work among the under-graduates—over some of whom he had a very strong influence. Geldart describes him as a 'gaunt, cadaverous-looking man' with 'a sweet, somewhat sickly smile, especially when indulging in sarcasm'; when preaching, he said he 'crouched in his pulpit in a catlike attitude ... ready to spring on his adversary'. Liddon's own summing-up of his character was: 'A heart of iron to myself, a heart of flesh to my neighbour, and a heart of fire to my God.'

However, it was the social, as much as the spiritual, side of that first evening which impressed Hopkins. He and Gurney were invited to go to the rooms of William Sanday, whom Hopkins reported to be probably the most popular person in the college, and whom Gurney considered 'the most charming man' he knew. When he finally arrived back in his own rooms he was in a high state of excitement, and became alarmed by the sound of what sounded like someone walking over the roof. It was probably only a noisy cat, but he prudently left his candle burning when he finally went to bed.

His letters to his mother are spattered with the names of all the people he walked, talked, wined and breakfasted with: of his popularity there can be little doubt. There was a touch of childish-ness about his enthusiasm that was probably charming to many, and though Geldart described him as a 'gusher' he found it an acceptable trait because Hopkins always meant what he said. Indeed to many of his contemporaries the intellect and intuition that lay behind the gushing words were well appreciated. At the end of his first term he passed the examination known as Smalls (or Responsions), and was whirled off to the Mitre Hotel with two other successful candidates where they 'proceeded to booze'.

One of his closest friends, who was not part of the High Church group, was Alexander Baillie, a Scottish Presbyterian whose rational mind gradually led him to become an atheist. Baillie acted as an affectionate mental sparring partner for Hopkins, and they remained friends until Hopkins died. Then Baillie wrote:

It is impossible to say how much I owe to him. He is the one figure which fills my whole memory of my Oxford life. There is hardly a reminiscence with which he is not associated. All my intellectual growth, and a very large proportion of the happiness of those Oxford days, I owe to his companionship . . . Apart from my own nearest relations, I never had so strong an affection for anyone.

During the summer vacation of 1863, Hopkins sent Baillie two long, teasingly critical letters, the first opening with the statement, 'Yes. You are a Fool', which he proceeded to prove in the form of a syllogism. He had tried on one occasion to show his *Prometheus Bound* translation to Baillie, and was dispirited when he offered no opinion on it, though Hopkins admitted it was awkward being asked to criticise friends' poetry. Imaginative criticism was important to him, both as a student of other writers and as a poet himself, and he wrote to Baillie that the main fault of most critics was that they tended to 'cramp and hedge . . . the free movements of genius'.

Hopkins sent the letters from Manor Farm, Shanklin, in the Isle of Wight, where the family summer holiday was spent. He praised the island's beauty and fair weather, and seemed very content to be with his family—walking, bathing, drawing and studying, and enjoying everything except the 'odious Fashionables'. Many of his sketches from the holiday survive, together with some by an unidentified member of the family. They obviously spent much time together, since the subjects and dates concur.

Hopkins hoped that Baillie would appreciate some of the sketches from 'a Ruskinese point of view'. He explained how he became obsessed from time to time with a particular type of tree or plant form, which, when thoroughly observed, became part of 'my treasury of explored beauty'. His current passion was the ash, and he made a study of sprays of ash-leaves which showed how a line drawn joining the tips of the leaves on one spray formed a trefoil, and this no doubt made a link in his mind with the tracery of church windows. A few of his Shanklin sketches—many of which were unfinished—are accompanied by meticulous verbal notes, and indicate how he used drawing as a means of visual research, sometimes finding it easier to complete the observations in words. It is just after this holiday in September 1863, that the entries in his first surviving diary begin, the first two of which are concerned with relationships (both etymological and aural) between words. Together with the holiday sketches and notes, they demonstrate his increasing interest in studying the nuts-and-bolts of both writing and drawing.

It is tempting to extract at least the significance of coincidence from the two groups of words that open the diary—though it is only chance that this particular notebook should be the earliest to survive, and its opening pages are missing so that the first entry is curtailed. It is concerned with growth, fruitfulness: the word 'mead', in the sense of both drink and meadow, is linked with 'meat'—all words of nourishment; then it is linked with maid, and subsequently virgo (virgin) is linked with virga (green shoot). And, having associated the young female with a tender shoot, he remembers the phrase from the Psalms: 'That our sons may grow up as young plants.' So, in this abbreviated entry, the organic connections between nature and man, purity and fecundity, are dispassionately noted by means of word association. The second journal entry stems from the word 'horn'. Whereas the first had had the femininity of nourishment, virginity, and sapling growth, the second contains many masculine words and phrases: 'projection', 'climax', 'badge of strength', 'spiral', 'something to thrust or push with'. It encompasses other links too, including (in telescoped sequence): horn—corn—crane—heron—herne—corns on the foot—grin (because of the way the mouth curves up like a horn), and continues, via corn and grain, into a sequence which contains the words: grind, grate, crush, crash. This gives a foretaste of Hopkins's free-wheeling ability to gather clusters of words around a theme or meaning, and shows his interest in onomatopoeia.

*

When he returned to Oxford in the autumn, he had a better set of rooms—larger, and with a sitting-room overlooking the Garden Quad so that he could lean out of the window and talk to passing friends. By the following term the rooms had been re-papered, and the mantelpiece covered with a cloth 'the colour of stewed pears' whose fringe of white china-headed nails resembled 'nobs of cream'. His scout sold him two pairs of candlesticks to replace some broken ones, and Hopkins felt that these gave the mantelpiece a decidedly 'distingué air'. He made a note in his diary to bring from London various portraits for his rooms (they included Raphael, Tennyson, Shelley, Keats, Shakespeare, Milton, Dante and Dürer), but it was some time before he could afford to have them framed. Later in his diary he planned a scheme for displaying statuettes on brackets backed with cardboard covered with green, or green and purple, silk. But how could he make them? Perhaps, he decided to himself, he should write home for some. Manley Hopkins took responsibility for his major expenses (such as the valuation deposit payable on his rooms), and Gerard evidently wrote to him, perhaps expectantly, about the sad state of the carpet in his sitting-room; but on the whole he had to balance his budget within his allowance and was always glad of extra tips from his grandparents. He forgot his sister Milicent's fourteenth birthday in October, but when apologising said that he would not in any case have been able to afford a present for her.

The appearance of his rooms was important to him, and, judging from entries in his diary, he worked out his breakfast party guest lists with some care. The domestic and social sides of university life were serious matters; in the marvellously detailed notes to *The Journals and Papers of Gerard Manley Hopkins* (edited by Humphry House and completed by Graham Storey) there is a quotation from a letter written by J. A. Symonds to his sister in 1860 which describes the complicated business of giving a breakfast:

> I find these breakfasts formidable things; for there is a succession of meats, all of which I have to dispense, to change plates, and keep people going with fresh forks and knives, etc. It is not the custom for any scouts to be in attendance, so that the host has to do all the menial offices. You would be amused to see these intellectual men begin with fried soles and sauces, proceed to a cutlet, then taste a few sausages or some savoury omelette, and finish up with buttered cake or toast and marmalade.

Hopkins was no longer, so he informed his mother, the smallest person in Balliol, and some of his friends seemed to think he had 'grown decidedly'. Nor does he seem to have been quite so dizzily ebullient. He was drawn more and more into the Liddon circle, and the proposal was made that he should join the Oxford High Church society known as the Brotherhood of the Holy Trinity. The aims of this society had once been to help undergraduates 'from pious homes and well taught at their schools' to conduct good lives, but they became rather more specific under the leadership of Pusey, who suggested that members 'should rise early, use prayer, public and private, be moderate in food and drink, and avoid speaking evil of others'. His proposals that they should also either walk around with their eyes turned to the ground, or wear a flannel girdle around their loins as a token of self-restraint, were not, however, accepted. Several of Hopkins's friends—including Gurney—were already members, and among those proposed and seconded at the same time as himself (8 December 1863) were Addis and Robert Bridges (who had just come up from Eton to Corpus Christi College). Addis and Bridges were duly elected members on 28 January 1864, but on 23 January Hopkins wrote in a longish, chatty letter to his mother (prefacing the remark with 'And this is private') that he had consulted Gurney and Addis and they both agreed it better for him not to join the Brotherhood for the moment. A few days later he noted in his diary that he had received a reply from 'Mamma' saying she was glad about his decision and adding that he could always join the society later when he had had more time to weigh the matter well. It appears that Hopkins may have talked privately with her during the Christmas vacation, and that she had voiced doubts about the Brotherhood. These he perhaps relayed to Gurney and Addis—possibly with some of his own—and they advised him to defer a decision rather than go against his mother's wishes. But whether the deferment was mainly to avoid family disquiet (it would seem that Hopkins had not felt able to discuss the matter with his father—or, perhaps he had done so and had aroused direct opposition), or because the Brotherhood did not quite meet his own needs, is unclear. However, when he went home for the Easter vacation he wrote a letter to Baillie which gives the first real sign that he could become impatient with his home background.

This impatience was caused as much by social trivia as by the clash of opinion. His aunt *would* insist on referring to 'parties' instead of 'wines'; the only papers to hand were *The Times* and *Saturday Review*; the church (that graceful Georgian church) was 'dreary'; and people *would* talk about Oxford as though it were Bothnia Felix. By way of compensation for the dreary church in Hampstead, he had been twice to St Alban's in Holborn, a new church well-known for its ritual.

Much derision has been aroused by the obsession with details of ritual that so concerned adherents to the High Church in the mid-nineteenth century. That a lawsuit should have been needed to maintain the sequence of coloured frontals on the altar of St Barnabas, Pimlico, and that a riot should have been caused elsewhere

by the use of a chasuble, seems absurd now. But the objectors were
unnerved by what appeared to them to be insidious Roman influence: a mumbo-jumbo of incense, silk vestments, and precious
chalices; while for the adherents these symbols identified the beauty
and the mystery of their faith. The Eucharist lay at the heart of the
mystery, and Hopkins revealed the intensity with which he now
regarded the ceremony of Holy Communion when he wrote to his
old schoolfriend, E. H. Coleridge, on 1 June 1864. Only the end of
the letter survives, and in it he expressed the hope that Coleridge
would soon come up to Oxford since he did not appear to be 'very
Catholic', but would be bound to undergo a change of mind once he
was at 'the head and fount of Catholicism in England and the heart
of our Church'. Hopkins warned his friend against doing what he
had once attempted: that is to try to 'adopt an enlightened Christianity' and to endeavour to become 'a credit to religion'. Such a view,
if logically developed, could lead to lack of faith. The main object
of belief, and the main aid to such belief, was the doctrine of
the Real Presence: that is belief in the actual presence of Christ's
body and blood in the Eucharist. Religion without such belief,
he wrote, was 'sombre, dangerous, illogical'; but with it, religion
became 'loveable'.

The faith he had been taught at home had been called by his
father 'winning, persuasive, holy, and altogether lovely' and had
been said to contain 'dignity, beauty, tenderness, and amiability'.
These were, perhaps, the descriptions of an 'enlightened' Christian,
one who attempted to be 'a credit' to his religion by singing its
praises and widening its sphere of influence. They were the expressions of someone who served God in an active manner. By calling
his religion 'loveable' and renouncing all ambition to be 'a credit',
Hopkins indicates acceptance and passivity, a channelling of his
impulses into ritual worship and away from active pious achieve-
ments that might please or impress people. He was just twenty years
old, of an age to pay homage and be compliant in love.

No direct evidence remains of any other objects which might have
attracted his devotion at this particular time and been rejected in
preference for spiritual worship, though, as will be discussed later,
various inferences may be drawn from his poems. The letters and
diary entries together give a general picture of his ordinary day-to-
day absorptions. He walked with friends to outlying churches to
observe and sketch their architectural detail, and he made notes on

C

the various trees, flowers and creatures which he saw—including a rather comic little drowned rat, which he drew floating along, tail uppermost, in the Isis. The lists of word relationships continued, and by the beginning of the summer vacation he had started a number of poems, some of them fairly ambitious. These were written piecemeal, in fits and starts, and often left unfinished.

He arranged to spend part of the vacation reading in Wales with two Balliol friends, Edward Bond and Alfred Erskine Gathorne-Hardy. The latter was son of the Earl of Cranbrook and one of the Balliol High Church group; Bond, a Hampstead neighbour, was not particularly religious. When Hopkins wrote to Baillie during that holiday, he reported that he was finding it difficult to resist being contaminated by 'the bawdy jokes and allusions' of his companions. He added (but obliterated with a piece of stuck-on paper) a remark to the effect that Hardy was always talking about debauching and introducing himself to young ladies. At this time Hopkins was interested in the pre-Raphaelites, and the poems he was writing reflect their concern with idealised love—the antithesis of undergraduate bawdiness. He had met Christina Rossetti and Holman Hunt (and George Macdonald and Jenny Lind) at a gathering at the Gurneys' just prior to going to Wales, and was working on a poem which was in the form of a reply to Christina Rossetti's *The Convent Threshold*. The latter is about a young woman, shortly to become a nun, who begs her ex-lover to repent, using extremely violent, guilt-ridden imagery. Hopkins's reply, *A Voice from the World* (81)—which he never fully completed—is written from the point of view of the rejected lover, who is racked with misery and anger at losing his beloved, but would like to repent and to receive God's forgiveness. The lover claims he is not 'spent so far' that he cannot energise the 'penetrative element' within himself and with it 'unglue the crust of sin'—the imagery of sex is grafted on to a moral resolution. And yet . . . if he does repent, he still cannot bear the idea of not reliving his sweet memories: how, he asks, can he possibly transform his 'passion-pastured' thoughts?

It is difficult to believe that Hopkins had not experienced some kind of passionate love before he wrote this poem. That he should have been moved by Christina Rossetti's verses to identify with the rejected lover, and have used this identification to illustrate the near impossibility of banishing pleasurable memories of love from the mind in order fully to repent, indicates he well understood the guilt of a man who loves, believing the love to be wrong. The next chapter will show that Hopkins could apparently be strongly attracted to people of his own sex, and it may be this was the source of the knowledge of guilt indicated in *A Voice from the World*. But during the summer of 1864 he also wrote poems implying his appreciation of the charms (and pitfalls) of the opposite sex, and it could be argued that his sexual orientation was, at this stage, equivocal. These latter poems include the fragment *She schools the flighty pupils of her eyes* (82) (which, of course, could apply to men's eyes just as well as women's), *The Lover's Stars* (83) and *Miss Story's character!* (94).

The last-named gives an indication of the jokey tenor of the period spent with Bond and Gathorne-Hardy, and shows that—despite his squeamishness about bawdiness and talk of debauchery—Hopkins could enter unprudishly into a teasing, slightly flirtatious, relationship. Staying at the same house in Maentwrog as he and his friends were three sisters—the Miss Storys—and their companion, Miss Louisa May. He described their presence to Baillie as being 'a great advantage'. *Miss Story's character!* was apparently written at Miss May's request. One might gather from it that Miss May thought Hopkins was attracted to Miss Story and wanted to see what he had to say about her. Certainly the poem contains a good deal of cheerful bitchiness that shows he had observed Miss Story's behaviour closely, and was by no means disinterested—though whether he actually found her attractive is another matter. It is written by someone who obviously thinks he understands women's self-deceptions very well. Miss Story, he declaimed in heroic couplets, over-estimated her own will-power, liked to succeed and to be flattered yet could not take compliments gracefully, was capable of strong—if misplaced—affection, was patronising and witty and tactless, thought she was religious but was not, would make a 'sweet and matchless' wife but would lead a 'misdirected life' if she remained single. Besides this, Hopkins wrote other fragments of comic verse and epigrams in order to amuse his companions, and one gets the feeling that he thoroughly enjoyed the opportunity to show off to a group of young ladies. Four months later he made a note of Miss Story's address in his journal, so perhaps he kept in touch with her, or at any rate planned to send her a Christmas or New Year greeting. In private he was concerned with very different matters: continuing to work on *A Voice from the*

World and also *Pilate* (80)—in which Pontius Pilate plans his own
crucifixion in order to try to atone for his guilt. His moods must
have swung between fairly hectic sociability and solitary concern
with guilt and suffering.

Before he went to Wales he had written some verses that illustrate
the dichotomy of his feelings. The first two of these were no doubt
directly inspired by *A Convent Threshold* (and influenced by
Tennyson in their sound). Originally entitled *Rest*, they were
renamed *Fair Havens, or The Convent* and finally became *Heaven-
Haven* (9, RB 2) and subtitled 'A nun takes the veil'. But, when first
written, *Rest* probably applied as much to his feelings about himself,
as to his idea of the image of a would-be nun:

> I have desired to go
>   Where springs not fail,
> To fields where flies no sharp and sided hail
>   And a few lilies blow.
>
> And I have asked to be
>   Where no storms come,
> Where the green swell is in the havens dumb,
>   And out of the swing of the sea.

The two verses which follow these in his diary give the opposite
view. (They were not published by Bridges, and appear among the
fragments in the collected poems (88).) In them, the writer yearns
for infinite adventure: he must follow the dictates of his heart, must
reach as high as the eagle, as far as the green seas near the arctic
pole. People have tended to think that *Heaven-Haven* represents an
early and simple wish on Hopkins's part to submit to the cloister.
But the separated last verses carry equal weight.

One of the outcomes of the reading party in Wales was that he
ventured to show his poems to Edward Bond. He was immediately
elated by the way Bond both praised and criticised with boldness,
and it helped Hopkins to have confidence in retaining the hope of
his future as an artist. (He still included painting as well as poetry
in his ambition.) Baillie was perhaps a little jealous that Bond had
proved such a ready and helpful critic, for Hopkins had to reassure
him that he was wrong to assume himself 'not such a pleasant
critic to keep as Bond'; the trouble with Baillie was that he was too
reticent in his remarks, and Hopkins needed reactions he could get

his teeth into. Baillie was a traditionalist by temperament and not very receptive to new verse, so his reticence was no doubt based on a wish not to hurt Hopkins's feelings. From the phrases Hopkins used towards him in his letters—'my dear friend', 'goose'—they were apparently fond of one another in an easy, uncomplicated sort of way.

Besides studying, writing and socialising, Hopkins was able to report to Baillie from Maentwrog that he had also had an adventure. He went walking alone in the mountains and became lost in a rainstorm. It was, he wrote, exactly like the story-books said: the dried stream beds turned to swollen torrents. Luckily he found a shepherd's dwelling and was invited to stay the night. That, he decided, was what self-satisfied old gentlemen meant when they told people of his age that they must learn to 'rough' it—always claiming that they had had to do so when they were young. The term arose, he speculated ironically, from the texture of the blankets proffered in such emergencies. Not that he had lacked hospitality: the shepherd and his family had 'gorged' him with eggs, bacon, oatcakes, and curds and whey.

It was in September, after the stay in Wales and while he was spending some time with his grandparents at Blunt House, that Hopkins included in a letter to Baillie some ideas for an essay that were to become well-known almost a century later. They contain his description of what he called the 'Parnassian' in poetry: that is verse of high technical competence, which could only be achieved by poets of stature, but which lacks real imaginative energy. He cites Wordsworth and Tennyson (and Milton and Spenser elsewhere) as being all too capable of slipping into Parnassian, and Shakespeare as being virtually exempt. The greatest poetry, he claimed, is written in a state of 'mental acuteness' and can never be imitated or anticipated: it is truly original. It becomes clear that Hopkins felt that to fall back on Parnassian when the language of inspiration was unforthcoming was just not good enough. And this was perhaps one of the reasons why he lacked the will to complete the long poems he had embarked on during that summer—which include *Richard* (107) and *Floris in Italy* (102), as well as *A Voice from the World*.

The first two fragments of *Richard*, which were all that were completed during 1864, set the scene for an Oxonian pastoral idyll. Richard, a shepherd 'of the Arcadian mood', whose sheep are as nebulous as the clouds above the downs, is drawn towards Oxford, to exchange the tinkling of the herd's bells for the 'much music' of the towers and spires, and to find a 'sense of gentle fellowship'. This idea of gentle fellowship was uppermost in Hopkins's mind now, and was entirely centred upon Oxford. The eager ability during his first terms to be dazzled by reputations and personalities had been replaced by a fervent admiration for moderation. He told Baillie how he winced at the excesses of writers in the *Church Times* who displayed irreverence and injustice in their vulgar support of the Church, and beside whom Newman and Pusey—despite their apparently extreme positions—were moderate men. Good taste and moderation, he felt, had an 'indescribable' 'prestige', and he was aware he had often sinned against them. He instanced Addis as an example of someone who combined balance, heartiness, sincerity and greatness to a remarkable degree. He was beginning to search, it would seem, for that indefinable 'moral taste' in which Keble had once instructed the passionately despairing Hurrell Froude. And Oxford, as the 'fount of Catholicism' and the harbour of gentle fellowship, would surely provide what he wanted. In *To Oxford* (12), written the following year, he described how his love for the place grew 'more sweet-familiar' every term, and stated emphatically that 'This is my park, my pleasaunce'. Here he had found friends who shared or understood his difficulties and desires; who tried, in the pursuance of religion and art, and the practice of friendship and worship, to discover what path they would choose in life which would enable them to fulfil their moral and professional aims. They usually exercised reticence in their gossip and conversation, and when they did not do so—just as when he indulged in laziness, lack of concentration at prayer, or over-indulgence at dinner—Hopkins felt that he had acted badly. Such lapses were later recorded in his diary, but already they were among the type of behaviour he tried to avoid as he grew to admire the ideals of moderation and good taste. That he should have named Newman and Pusey as moderates may at first appear strange, but his admiration for them was based on the opinion that their theological positions, however extreme they might appear to middle-of-the-road churchmen, had been reached through a rigorous combination of intellect and devotion, and on the fact that they did not practise the sort of empty, exhortatory rhetoric that he so hated.

At Oxford he was among people who regarded High Church

development and procedures to be of absorbing interest; when he was at Oak Hill he found he got out of touch with Church matters. His parents' interest in religion presumably did not extend to detailed discussion of contemporary eccelesiastical events, and they may have wished not to encourage too much talk from their eldest son regarding his religious views. He had always shown a tendency for excess (such as when he wagered he could go without liquids), and they probably hoped he would return to a frame of mind more easily assimilable into the general habit of the family.

However, a young man with so much intellectual and emotional energy was not going to be content to dabble here and there, to indulge in a few excesses, and then to end up as an ordinary clergyman or gentleman artist. Hopkins had to reach for some sort of perfection, though for the moment he would briefly be content to try to make it the perfection of moderation and good taste, turning his back on all undergraduate passion and folly. Yet passion and extremes were what by nature enthralled him. In a letter to E. W. Urquhart, curate of SS Philip and James in Oxford, written on the day of Epiphany 1865, he remarked that the only two people in the whole of history for whom he had 'a real feeling' were Savonarola and Origen, and a brief list of some of the facts and legends associated with each of these famous Christians is quite instructive.

Savonarola (b. 1452), a Dominican monk, decided as an adolescent that he could not suffer 'the blind wickedness of the peoples of Italy'. He thought that humanistic paganism was corrupting the country, and that the church must be scourged before it could be renewed. Having prophesied the overthrow of the Medicis, he tried to found the City of God in Florence. His authority was demonstrated when citizens voluntarily burned lewd pictures, ornaments, cards and gaming tables during carnival. When he was finally overthrown he was tortured and hanged.

Origen (b. *c*.185) was the most influential and seminal theologian of the early Greek Church. His father was martyred, and from the age of seventeen he had to provide for his mother and six younger brothers. He earned his living by teaching, and legend has it—although there are no facts to support this—that he castrated himself in order to be able to work freely among young women. Certainly his chastity and asceticism were widely known. As an old man, he was persecuted, imprisoned and tortured, but survived to live a few more years.

That these should have been the only figures in history to reach past Hopkins's own strong personal identity and create a sense of recognition and curiosity is interesting. He made the remark immediately after reading *Romola*, but it could not be said that he had been bowled over by George Eliot's interpretation: the author of *Romola*, Hopkins claimed, 'being pagan, clever as she is, does not understand' Savonarola. He, of course, felt that he did understand him, and wrote to Urquhart that he could well imagine himself among the company of painters, architects and other artists who so enthusiastically followed the Dominican reformer. His interest in Origen arouses speculation—but it can remain only speculation. Did Hopkins intuitively find appeal in the idea of taking the father's place (just as his own father had done at eighteen), and supporting the mother and younger siblings but with the threat of sexuality quite removed? His letters to his mother reveal that he was very close to her; unfortunately hardly any to his father have survived, but it seems their relationship, on Gerard's part at any rate, tended at that period to fall back on a sort of word horse-play—the Thomas Hood-type puns and jokes that Manley had taught him as a child. As families go, the Hopkinses were united, with Gerard remaining very much within his parents' perimeter when he first went up to Oxford. But like most children he wanted to prove that he and his ways were best, without provoking actual quarrel or bitterness. What could be more convenient, more full of moral rectitude, than a father's martyrdom and the eldest son taking over? Not that he would have formed the thought, but the 'real feeling' for Origen was there.

Origen and Savonarola both suffered martyrdom. People have speculated before (from the poetry) that Hopkins had a lively and imaginative interest in physical suffering and that he may have had masochistic tendencies. Given the regular beatings inflicted by Dyne on his pupils, this is a possibility, although it would be heavy-handed to erect too much around it at this stage.

Oxford, for all its Ruskinesque beauty and comradely fellowship, for all its intellectual discipline and religious idealism, had nothing as overwhelmingly dominant in its appeal as a reforming Savonarola to offer. Not that Hopkins was conscious of any lack, and Oxford certainly did contain all the ingredients for the pastoral idyll, *Richard*, that was continuing to form in his mind. And, from the academic point of view, he was shaping up in a perfectly acceptable way as far as the authorities were concerned, gaining a first in Mods. (Moderations: the first public examination for the B.A. degree). But the only legitimate outlet for his more intense feelings was the symbolism of religious ritual, and this was reflected in several poems which he wrote during 1864, including *Barnfloor and Winepress* (6), published in *The Union Review* the following year. Like much of his religious poetry of that period, it springs partly from his reading of George Herbert, but does not approach Herbert's grace in combining the imagery of nature and Christianity. It links the crucifixion to harvest, to grape-treading and wheat-threshing, in a way which is uncomfortably literal; yet, because it does not take refuge in poesy or sentimentality, but forces through the linking imagery in an almost scientific manner, it gives some idea of Hopkins's ability to find vigour and strength in his belief. The Real Presence had to be real. His own vitality and energy were far too precious to be expended on pious, cloudy, or insipid religious images. 'Youths,' Newman had written some years before, 'need a masculine religion, if it is to carry captive their restless imaginations and their wild intellects, as well as touch their susceptible hearts.'

Hopkins's heart was at a very susceptible stage; and he had not yet found his own finally preferred religion.

CHAPTER FOUR

The Eton Connection

IN FEBRUARY 1865, a short-sighted, seventeen-year-old poet called Digby Mackworth Dolben came to stay in Oxford for a few days. He lodged with his friend and distant cousin Robert Bridges, who introduced him to Gerard Hopkins.

Humphry House has suggested that 'Dolben was closely bound up with [Hopkins's] religious crisis of that March', and speculation has also been made that he inspired some emotional sonnets written a little later. W. H. Gardner, on the other hand, cautions against placing too much emphasis on Dolben, or on Hopkins's ability to become fascinated by the 'physical beauty of choristers and certain of his fellow alumni'. These fascinations are expressed in the unpublished confessional fragments of his journal, which began very shortly after Dolben's visit. Gardner claims there is nothing in them 'to suggest, let alone prove, that Hopkins was tainted with any serious homosexual abnormality'; and he mentions one entry concerning 'the sin of looking a little too long and admiringly at a certain married woman' as establishing 'Hopkins's physical normality'. There is, of course, no need to push such slight evidence to concrete conclusions in either direction. Hopkins's tendency to be fascinated by beauty was an inherent part of his make-up and extremely important to his poetry. But admission and discussion of an involuntary capacity to find men attractive is not to 'taint' him with 'abnormality'. Since he was to become a celibate, and since his life as an undergraduate was apparently very chaste, it may fairly be claimed that his sexual orientation was never conclusively evolved. Awareness of male beauty, palpably expressed, appears in some of his later poetry, but whether it indicates the direction in which his feelings might finally have deepened and expanded under a different life-style is not established. It was remarked some years ago that Hopkins was seen more on the shelves of undergraduates than any other poet, and one of the reasons for this may well have been that such readers found (consciously or unconsciously) echoes in his poetry of the sexual ambivalence many experience at that age.

Certainly one thing his poetry does not contain is any revulsion for, or exclusion of, women. He never gives any impression of shrinking from the female sex in the manner of the 'pork chop' image of Newman's *Loss and Gain* referred to on page 9. Nor, however, is there much indication that he found them exciting.

Since there is no conclusive evidence to answer the question about whether Digby Dolben did or did not have a strong emotional effect on Hopkins, one can only set out what one feels to be nearest to the truth. What cannot be denied is that Dolben was such a romantic, extravagant creature that—if he did not arouse antipathy—he would very likely hold a susceptible new acquaintance in thrall.

In order to establish why a seventeen-year-old boy from Eton might create such an impression during a brief visit to Oxford, it is necessary to look more closely at his background. And since it is to Robert Bridges that we owe the survival of Dolben's poetry and an account of his life (from which much of the information in this chapter is taken), the exercise is useful in that it also reveals facets of Bridges's character—and that of Vincent Stuckey Coles, a friend of Hopkins at Balliol and another old Etonian.

Bridges's memoir of Dolben was published, together with the poems, in 1911. While writing it, he was faced with a difficult task: how was he to present in a sympathetic, but truthful, light, a young poet who had had extravagant Romanist tendencies and whose life had been governed by a passion for a fellow pupil at Eton? On the whole he found it easier to rationalise the latter involvement than the former: Bridges developed a strong distaste for the Roman Catholic church.

Dolben went to Eton in January 1862—eighteen months before Bridges, who was three years older, left. In order to discharge his duties as a distant relative (he had not previously met Dolben), Bridges enrolled him 'among my fags, and looked after him'. He describes him as

tall, pale, and of delicate appearance, and though his face was thoughtful and his features intellectual, he would not at the time have been thought good-looking . . . His short sight excluded him from the common school-games; and though the dreaminess which it gave to his expression came to be a characteristic and genuine charm, it was, until it won romantic interpretation, only an awkwardness.

The phrase 'until it won romantic interpretation' remains un-explained. Who provided the interpretation—general opinion among their set, or Bridges himself? Certainly he appears to have been captivated by Dolben, as these long-remembered details, recalled almost half a century later when he was a circumspect sixty-six-year-old, demonstrate:

> ... if we both had work to do, he would sometimes bring his to my room, but more often I would go uninvited to sit with him. The clearest picture that I have of him is thus seated, with his hands linked behind his head, tilting his chair backward as he deliberated his careful utterances: or sometimes he would balance it on one leg, and steady himself by keeping the fingers of his outstretched arms in touch with the walls. There was moreover a hole in the boards of the floor, and if the chair-leg went through and precipitated him onto the carpet, that was a part of the performance and gave him a kind of satisfaction. The bureau-lid lay open before him as a desk, and in the top drawer on the right he kept his poems. His face whether grave or laughing was always full of thought ... When he spoke it was with a gentle voice and slowly as if he pondered every word.

> One evening I remember his exhibiting to me how he escaped the necessity of going to the hair-dresser, by burning his hair when it got too long. It was then rather curly rough hair that stood off from his head. He set it alight with the candle in one hand, and when it flared up, he put it out with the other, gravely recommending the practice on the professional theory of sealing the ends of the hair.

Bridges—handsome, athletic and purposeful—states that he had two prime interests in common with Dolben: poetry and religion. 'We were in fact both of us Pusey-ites ... [and] neither of us at that time doubted that our *toga virilis* would be the cassock of a priest or the habit of a monk.' There was a small group of boys whose religious tastes were similarly inclined, and Dolben made friends among them. One of these was Vincent Stuckey Coles, a plump, unctuous boy, 'who served him with kind offices and sound advice on many occasions when he sadly needed it'. The cause of Dolben's sad need was Martin Le Marchant Gosselin, a fellow-pupil with whom he was passionately in love. Bridges disguises Gosselin under the name 'Archie Manning' (did he borrow Cardinal Manning's name in view of the fact that Gosselin later became a Roman Catholic?) and describes him thus:

> He was a little older [three months] and taller than Digby, but practically his contemporary, with features of the uncharactered type of beauty, the immanent innocence of Fra Angelico's angels ... He was naturally simple and modest ... full of fun, and affectionately attached to Digby, though he never to the last had any suspicion that his friend was making an idol of him ...

Bridges sticks to his declaration that Gosselin never knew of Dolben's love, which continued without diminishment to the end of his short life, and is the subject of many of his poems. Indeed, he is said to have described Gosselin as 'his only poetry'.* Gosselin was also one of the High Church group, and while at Eton he and Dolben both contemplated becoming Roman Catholics. (Gosselin finally took the step in 1878, and Dolben would have done so before his death in 1867 were it not for his family's opposition.) Dolben's devotion to religion, like his devotion to Gosselin, was extravagant. The weekly 'Sunday-questions' period at Eton, Bridges writes, 'gave him a grand opportunity of airing his mediaeval notions; and he must have enjoyed exercising his malicious ingenuity in dragging them in'. He played truant to visit High Anglican and Roman Catholic establishments—the final straw being a visit to some Jesuits, and he was removed from school before the end of the summer term in 1863. After much deliberation his father decided that he might return for the following term. Dolben wrote to Bridges:

> Of course I shall be very discreet, and generally unexceptionable (I hope) but, alas, who can tell? The frailty of human nature is so great. Isn't it? My last frailty was to go to see a Catholic chapel at Bangor, and as a low mass was just beginning, can I be blamed if I remained on my knees until it was concluded.

Early in 1864, he managed to obtain an introduction to the controversial Father Ignatius (born Joseph Leycester Lyne) who had begun the observance of the Rule of St Benedict and presided as Abbot over a small community of monks and nuns. He somehow arranged secretly to join the Third Order and to take the title

* Typescript of a paper 'An Unknown Eton Poet', by H.M.P., in the Northamptonshire Record Office.

Brother Dominic. His handwriting underwent a change too, as he endeavoured to imitate—without too much success—the script of Savonarola. (This was a year before Hopkins was commenting on *Romola*.) Dolben hoped that Bridges would follow him into the Order, but Bridges reports that he found Father Ignatius's style of 'commonplace rhetoric' (as revealed in a letter to Dolben) chilling, although the fact that Dolben could be affected by it 'shows his simplicity of heart'.

> It was difficult to take Ignatius as a prophet in touch with humanity; and I knew him only by a *carte de visite* portrait with extravagant tonsure and ostentatious crucifix. But Digby's father was, no doubt, really distressed, and unwittingly supporting his son's folly by the seriousness of his opposition. As for Ignatius, he was, I suppose, delighted to have caught a live Etonian, while Digby, furnished with a correct habit, imagined himself a medieval monk.

A letter to Coles reveals that Dolben was in a highly nervous and excitable state, imploring his friends to join the Order, deploring Eton as a place from which he could serve God: 'It is full of mental temptations that you know nothing of, and you know it is well nigh impossible to attain anything of the Saintly Life there.' He was writing a great deal of poetry, nearly all around the theme of penitence, as in the following lines:

> Thus by the loving touch
> Of thy cool priestly hand restore to me
> The weary years the greedy locust ate.
> (from *The Prodigal's Introit*)

Bridges remarks:

> The reading of these poems makes one see why schoolmasters wish their boys to play games, and one is forced to confess that writers, whose books can lead a boy of 17 to think in this vein of false fancies and affected sentimentality, are as poisonous as simple folk hold them to be.

The chief culprit among such writers was Frederick Faber, the late Superior at the Brompton Oratory and one of Newman's most fulsome and exasperating followers, 'of whose works,' Bridges wrote, 'I have nothing to say, except that a maudlin hymn of his, when Digby showed it me, provoked my disgust'.

Towards the end of the summer term, Dolben played truant once more to a religious establishment, and Coles reported to Bridges:

> Dolben gave me a full account of his meeting with Father Ignatius and Dr Pusey. It was at Ascot Priory near Windsor, where Miss Sellon has a convent . . . Dolben slept in an outhouse with Ignatius, and was wakened by Dr Pusey 'thumping at the door' . . . He said offices with them & Miss Sellon. She gave him a solemn audience, sitting in her chair with her pastoral staff at her side—she is an ordained Abbess.—All this took place when he had leave for the Harrow match.

Bridges comments wryly:

> To sleep in the outhouse of a nunnery when you were supposed to be in Chesham Place, and to be called in the morning by the great Dr Pusey himself 'thumping at the door', must have been very satisfactory to the truant . . . It was, I suppose, the occasion of his admission into the 'Second Order of St Benedict', and it served, with similar excitements, to make his conscience at ease in the Anglican fold.

Forty years before it had been Pusey who was suffering guilt for sometimes placing his obsession for Maria Barker above his love for Christ; now she had been dead for twenty-five years, and the High Church establishments and confessional opportunities which he instituted attracted similarly guilt-ridden young people. The convents in particular were the subjects of virulent attack by those suspicious of Pusey, and some of the attacks were well-founded. Undue chastising and punishment of an unpleasant kind did take place, and Father Ignatius and Priscilla Sellon were both involved in such practices.

Dolben was finally taken away from Eton at Christmas. It was decided that if he was ever to gain a Balliol scholarship—as his father hoped—he would need to study with a private tutor. On the day after he left Eton he wrote some verses which, on the manuscript, are dedicated to Gosselin. They begin:

> On river banks my love was born,
> And cradled 'neath a budding thorn,
> Whose flowers never more shall kiss
> Lips half so sweet and red as his.

A tutor, the Reverend Constantine Prichard, was found for him in Lincolnshire, and Dolben wrote despairingly to Bridges from his home in Northamptonshire:

> I am about to go to a most dreary tutor, with grey hair, situated in the midst of a vast ploughed field, with a young wife, one other pupil, and endless Greek grammar. But I have got leave first to come up to Oxford for a few days.

Unfortunately by 1911 Bridges had 'but a hazy remembrance' of the visit. He recalls that Coles was away, Gosselin was still at Eton, and the only people Dolben really knew were himself and his friend Lionel Muirhead.

> It was at this visit, and only then, that he met Gerard Hopkins: but he must have been a good deal with him, for Gerard conceived a high admiration for him, and always spoke of him afterwards with great affection.

What did Dolben and Hopkins talk about? Perhaps Dolben's plan (hatched at Eton) that one day it would be possible to form a new Brotherhood among his friends, with Bridges at its head. (Bridges remembered how Dolben would scheme to 'make a monastery of his father's house' and 'rejoice openly if any of the "Brothers" had prospects of wealth; it added to the many mansions of his ideal establishment'.) Hopkins must have found affinity with Dolben's active penitence, and shortly afterwards he started to confess to Liddon and to note down his 'sins' in his journal. Poetry, certainly, was discussed, and they each made copies of the other's work. Did they discuss Gosselin? It seems unlikely that they would have done so in specific terms, though as Dolben was very pre-occupied by his feelings, and was such an impulsive, transparent character, it seems inevitable that the emotional atmosphere in which he lived must have spilled over and communicated to Hopkins in a potent manner, however undefined.

Shortly after the visit was over, Hopkins made a fairly formidable list in his diary of 'Books to be read'. The ones on religious subjects included *Tracts for the Times* and *Essays and Reviews*, and among others Malory, Bacon, Ruskin, Browning, Wordsworth, Matthew Arnold, Meredith and Dickens jostled for his attention. Nor had he given up on George Eliot, despite her being pagan, since *Silas*

Marner and *The Mill on the Floss* were included. The list shows that if Dolben had affected his life, it was in a stimulative way, throwing him with renewed ambition and energy into a broad programme of study.

He was also continuing to write poems, and one, *Easter Communion* (11), written between 2 and 12 March, is explicit in its celebration of forms of Lenten self-chastisement that lead to spiritual rewards at the Easter altar. It contains the kind of phrases and fervour that represent what many found distasteful in the High Church's more advanced practices: the penitents have experienced 'breath-taking whips' and 'ever-fretting' shirts, but 'God comes all sweetness' to their lips at Communion. When Dolben—or Coles— wrote verses on penitential themes, the actual message was smoothed by a sort of lulling blandness, but Hopkins was beginning to sharpen and develop the physicality of his poetry. It is not, perhaps, a poem acceptable to many, but it sets down very concisely images of scourge followed by divine ease of a type which these young men savoured in their imaginations, and which are now open to sexual interpretation. Not that explicit physicality was original to Hopkins (though his way of expressing it came to be). Tennyson's *St Simeon Stylites*, which he had once described to his schoolfriend Coleridge as 'magnificent', contains descriptions of a most lurid kind. And it must have lingered in Hopkins's mind, for the phrase 'crust of sin' which he used in *A Voice from the World* (see p. 54) is taken from its second line. It is difficult now to see the poem as a serious influence, containing as it does lines like

> On the coals I lay,
> A vessel full of sin: all hell beneath
> Made me boil over.

Nor indeed did Hopkins always treat its subject with reverence, and once put a comic drawing of a skeletal figure perched on a stile high among the stars and labelled 'Simeon the Stileite' at the bottom of a letter to Baillie. But by the time he came to write *Easter Communion* the knife-edged balance between jokiness and serious-ness which had been characteristic of his earlier years, was giving way to a much more dogmatic commitment.

Sunday, 12 March, he noted in his diary, was 'A day in the great mercy of God'. This is the first of his few recordings of a personal intimation of a sign from God, and it must have flooded his mind and imagination. It was presumably in the form of either forgiveness or revelation, and confirmed some element in the development of his religious life. It has been suggested that it was his first mental step towards Roman Catholicism. The next diary entry reveals that Addis, whose opinions and character he seemed almost to revere, had warned him against basing his arguments too much on personal feeling. Hopkins duly noted that this was a tendency he must repress. The balanced and sincere Addis perhaps felt that his friend was acting too much under the influence of Dolben, and possibly urged him to develop his beliefs in a more rational manner.

Miscellaneous diary jottings show that the surface of his life was continuing in a normal manner. He remembered Cyril's birthday, paid a shilling subscription to Liddon's Hexameron Essay Society, noted he owed Addis sixpence, gave a penny to a beggar, and put down brief phrases about the sun and moon and pussy-willows—'palms dotted with silver'; it was nearing Palm Sunday.

Then on Saturday, 25 March, the Feast of the Annunciation, he made his first confession to Liddon. He could not have chosen a more appropriate day than one which celebrated a divine combination of fertility and virginity, an ideal which was to occur in so much of his poetry. It was from that date that he started to note down the faults and 'sins' which he had committed. These particular diary entries have a pencil line drawn through them, and apart from a few brief mentions have not been published. They are often repetitious and demonstrate the meticulousness with which he tried to apprehend any falling-down in his conduct. Inattentiveness at chapel, eating or drinking too much, getting up or going to bed late, dawdling and gossiping with friends, wasting time, not working hard enough, are the minor misdeeds that recur. There are also mentions of yielding to old and unclean habits at night which probably refer to masturbation, and he confessed to looking up bad words in the dictionary. The latter activity is usually connected with quite young schoolchildren, and reveals how curbed, and easily excited, his feelings were.

Specific mentions of people show that he talked to Liddon about Jowett in a way which he felt had been impertinent; he once allowed Lionel Muirhead to stay late in his room; he talked for too long to Addis on a dangerous subject; he got irritated with Urquhart; ate too many of the Master's biscuits; wasted time chatting to Baillie; had evil thoughts about a pastor's boy, and looked at another boy

standing in a shop doorway. He also chided himself for having evil
thoughts while writing about Christ's Passion on Good Friday, and
this may confirm that he became excited by pain and suffering and
tried to suppress this particular reflex.

After Easter he made a note in his diary of Dolben's address at his
tutor's. (Five months later he mentioned to Bridges that he had
written Dolben 'letters without end' but had received no 'whiff of
answer'.) After the address, and written between 25 and 27 April,
comes the sonnet *Where art thou friend* (13), and immediately after
the sonnet he mentions that he drifted on to a forbidden subject
while in Coles's room; a few days later another entry indicates that
certain queries about Dolben were classed as an evil and forbidden
subject. The sonnet has been taken by Humphry House to refer to
Dolben, though W. H. Gardner suggests it might just as easily be
addressed to some 'fascinating stranger' since in September 1866
Hopkins was to mention in a letter to Bridges that he had seen a man
at St Alban's church whose face had been intriguing him for some
time: 'I generally have one fascination or another on'. It is possible
that the forbidden subject he referred to concerned Dolben's
Romanist tendencies rather than his physical ones, though Coles
did not apparently avoid discussing the less acceptable aspects of
friendship. In a memoir (published in 1930), G. W. Borlase recalled
that while still at Eton Coles developed

> what Bishop Gore in a notice in *The Times* calls 'his enormous
> capacity for friendship, and his unforgetting faithfulness to his
> friends'. His love for his friends throughout his life was remark-
> able for its intensity, tenderness, and catholicity. Stuckey's
> friends were of every age and class, for he was capable of as great
> affection for a ploughboy as for a peer. However, he soon realized
> that this beautiful and ennobling love for his friends might
> co-exist with much that is faulty and ill-regulated, and even with
> much that is corrupt, and that, like all passionate enthusiasms, it
> has untold capacities for good but also carried within it possibi-
> lities for evil. While still a schoolboy Stuckey set himself the task
> of sanctifying his friendships, and thought out a philosophy of
> conduct in these matters.

After reading which, it is not entirely surprising to find that Hopkins
had to admit to quarrelling with him on 17 May. When Geldart
excused Hopkins for gushing (in *Son of Belial*) because he meant

what he said, he also named Coles as another gusher and did not mitigate the charge.

Where art thou friend is almost impossible to construe with any certainty. As already mentioned, Gardner suggests

> that it was addressed to an actual unknown, some 'fascinating stranger', male or female—the woman, for instance, whom Hopkins, but for 'God's dear pleadings', might have loved and married

and House surmised that it was addressed to Dolben. Trying these, and one or two other, interpretations, it is easiest to make House's fit. Then the sonnet seems to say:

> Friend, whom I am either not going to see again, or who has gone away until some vague, future time, when I try to grasp you with my mind, I fall short of my object. You of all people may be sure you have contributed to my joy. You like something about me—perhaps even the fact that I have chosen such a weak statement with which to plead. If God's pleadings have not yet made you change your position, and because of the virtues I have already found in you which indicate that if I knew you more thoroughly I would totally accept you, for these reasons, please let every virtue grow in you—but let them be for Christ, who has always known and loved you.

Was the poem the result of Coles telling, or hinting, at Dolben's love for Gosselin, and was it a private attempt on Hopkins's part to express his understanding, love and guidance? It seems a reasonable guess.

Meanwhile Dolben was not, apparently, listening too carefully to God's pleadings, since one afternoon in April he sat down and wrote the poem which follows. Bridges did not include it in his selection, and it is therefore printed in full.

> From DMD in an armchair in the diningroom of Luffenham Rectory, To LMG in a seat in the playing fields of Eton College.*
>
> I'm taking, dear, an after dinner nap,—
> At least they think so,—& in confirmation
> Of this idea, I keep my eyes fast shut,
> And give you something of the conversation.

* MS in the Northamptonshire Record Office.

They, talking of the war beyond the sea,—
'When will it end? with all its shocking slaughter'—
Or else, 'Poor Mrs Smith! she's left, you know,
'Quite unprovided for, with thirteen daughters.'

'Restored your Church?'—'Yes, out of my own purse.'
'Dear me! how sad, with such a wealthy squire!'
'Gave but a five pound note, which scarcely paid
'To gild the cock's tail on my noble spire.'

'Jemima Jones—gone to America
'With that mere boy! I fear he'll badly treat her'—
'And Widow Brown—married within three months!
'She never cared for B.'—'They say he beat her.'

'That Church—the Bishop's sure to interfere'—
'You mean, of course, the Rev. D. Scandel's,'—
'They use, (I speak on best authority)
'At least six crosses and a dozen candles.'

. . . . . .

O was the sweet sweet spring time made for this?
Not so, not so we thought, a year ago,—
When leaving book or boat, linked arm in arm,
Through newly daisied fields we used to go.

Or else, beneath the grand old chestnuts, watch
Their cloudy green against the western light,
And hear the rugged music of the rooks,
And read the poet of the Isle of Wight.

If easy-chairs had wings instead of arms
I soon would find you in the dear old place,
And with you, find the dearest of old joys,
The sweetest spring, while looking in your face.

. . . . . .

'Another glass of wine?'—'No more.' 'You're *sure*?
'Suppose then, we adjourn to Mrs. P.
'A *quiet* game of cards before they go,
'A *little* music, and a cup of tea.'

Can one believe that this was not intended for Gosselin's eye? Perhaps, though barely. Or perhaps, given the contemporary popularity and acceptance of Tennyson's *In Memoriam* written in memory of his friend Arthur Hallam, the correct interpretation is that the verses were sent and received as an admissible token of friendship. Either way, they demonstrate a rather more earthy side to Dolben than is shown by Bridges in his memoir. Indeed Dolben could be said to have had the best of both worlds, with his ability to embrace a monk's habit *and* an all-consuming human passion in such a dramatic way. Hopkins on the other hand was struggling at Oxford to repress faults which varied from eating too much of Coles's pudding and making a dirty joke, to gazing at a man whom he found tempting. He too was expressing grief over a love affair in poetry—and here he had the edge on Dolben since he channelled the drama of his life into a real development of quality and feeling in his writing. The poem in question is a series of three sonnets called *The Beginning of the End* (14), plus the fragment written at the same time, *Some men may hate their rivals*, printed among the notes on p. 250 of the collected poems. They are about an ill-omened, desperate passion which is beginning to lessen, and have been interpreted in various ways. One explanation is that they are an exercise inspired by Meredith's sonnet sequence *Modern Love* (1862) and based on no personal experience. Another that they are addressed to an unknown lady—and indeed at a later date the copies of the first and third verses in Bridges's manuscript collection acquired the subtitle 'a neglected lover's address to his mistress'. To support this theory, the fragment *Some men may hate their rivals* is explicitly concerned with a lover who is so consumed with shame that he does not envy his rivals, since any man 'she sets higher' will be preferable to himself. A third explanation is that they were inspired by his feelings for Dolben, and this has been animated by Bridges's own note on his manuscript copy which reads, 'These two sonnets must *never* be printed'.

The verses contain a good deal of not entirely successful artifice, so they might be just an exercise. However the sheer desperation in some of the lines indicates a base in experience, and certainly the third verse fits the psychology of a brief, flaring obsession. The final image where the fading of the passion is compared to the 'sceptic disappointment' a boy feels when his once-favourite poet becomes 'less and less sweet' as he re-reads him, perhaps fits rather better a brief obsession with Dolben than an unknown girl (for whom there is no evidence whatsoever), but the matter remains inconclusive.

Bridges said that Dolben's dreamy expression, caused by short sight, 'won romantic interpretation'. In 1878, when Hopkins wrote his first letter to R. W. Dixon—whose work he started to read at Oxford—he said that a line from Dixon's poetry had given him more 'extreme delight' than any other single line had ever done. It reads:

Her eyes like lilies shaken by the bees.

It could recall the thick-lashed, fluttering, luminous eyes of someone who but dimly perceived the everyday shapes and shadows of the real world. It could have reminded Hopkins of Dolben. But that is just an intuitive guess.

Whatever their involuntary feelings for other people, Hopkins and Dolben both soon admitted in their poetry that they would find resolution of their needs only in Christ. Hopkins tried hard to continue to bind the complexity of his feelings into sonnet form. In *Myself unholy, from myself unholy* (16) written in June, he compares his own 'unholy' self with the characters of his friends. They have many less faults than he, but they are still not perfect, and he knows he can only serve perfection—i.e. Christ. Dolben's conclusion was the same, though expressed in more commonplace poetry.

Hopkins's love affair with Oxford itself did not abate. The week after Easter he had written two sonnets, *To Oxford* (12), and sent them to Addis, and in June he wrote a third (119), which he sent to Coles. The latter contains a reference to 'Meadows . . . inexplicably dear' which were unknown to the author, but from which news was apparently as sweet to some as was news from Oxford. The meadows are almost certainly those of Eton, and the poem explains that among them the initiate experienced 'their best and undivulgèd love'. Hopkins appears to feel some regret that he must remain an outsider to this charmed circle. The phrase 'best and undivulgèd love' might seem to indicate that he knew about Gosselin, and confirm that Dolben's love remained undeclared, or it might refer to other friendships mentioned by Coles.

In the end Dolben's obsession became part of Eton's mythology, for William Johnson (alias William Cory, author of *The Eton Boating Song*) and one of the College's most beloved and notorious masters, copied out his poems, while at the same time supposedly muttering: 'Newman's nothing to him.' And when Cyril Connolly went to Eton over fifty years later, he was dispirited to be given some of the more sentimental verses to translate into Latin.

In the summer holidays of 1865, Robert Bridges tried to arrange for Coles, Dolben and Hopkins to visit him at his home in Rochdale. Hopkins was unable to go, though he said he could think of nothing more delightful. It was then he mentioned that he had written 'letters without end' to Dolben. When the latter wrote to Bridges about the projected visit, he made no reference to Hopkins, and it seems safe to say that he had not impinged very far into Dolben's imagination. It is also safe to say that Dolben's romantic fervour (whether towards boy or God or both) had given impetus to Hopkins's journey into Catholicism. In September he expressed to Baillie his feeling that only Catholicism (he still meant Anglo-Catholicism) could alleviate what he called 'the sordidness of things'. This sordidness presumably included the discovery that beautiful faces, bodies, minds, all had their negative side, the side which belied the breathtaking initial attraction and offered decay, lust and evil thoughts. Someone like Dolben both intensified the possibilities of friendship and love, and increased their dangers.

CHAPTER FIVE

'My sap is sealed'

As HOPKINS tried to develop a love for Christ which was all-absorbing, and as he tried to become worthy of the love he believed God to have for him, his scrupulosity increased. But just as he noted and checked his behaviour, so spontaneous thoughts and feelings of an unspiritual nature continued to proliferate.

In July 1865 he went to stay with Martin Geldart at his home near Manchester. Here he could not resist looking at Martin's younger brother when he was naked, or at the choirboys in church, and he was much distracted by what he considered bad habits at night. Five weeks later he was staying with Frederick Gurney and his young wife in Torquay, and here it was Mrs Gurney who aroused his thoughts. In between these visits he had walked in Devon, staying at Tiverton and Chagford and looking up the place called Manley where his grandmother was born and which he was surprised to find was "but a farmhouse". He called on acquaintances of the family and reported these doings in precise detail to his mother, including the fact that two third cousins, the Miss Patches, were very charming: one with a pretty figure and beautiful eyes, the other with cherry lips. On the day he wrote the letter, though he appeared unaware of the fact, Queen Emma of Hawaii, on a visit to London, was able to put in her diary that 'At 3 drove off to Manley Hopkins's Oak Hill to lunch & it was excellent lunch & very sociable'.

While in Devon he observed sunrises and sunsets and other natural phenomena with the 'empathic cognition' which Geoffrey Grigson describes in his vigorous and perceptive essay on Hopkins, *A Passionate Science*. Hopkins tried, he says, 'to let each object exist *per se* in his apprehension of it, in the most sheer language entirely and accurately correspondent to the sum of the qualities of the object'; and so, after the grandeur of bronze stormclouds over Dartmoor, a butterfly is preserved for ever on a summery cinder road 'pinching' or 'wagging' 'his scarlet valves'. Also the patterned effect of combing is seen to apply to the way the hair lies on the breast of a horse, as well as to ribs of water and mealy clouds across a moonlit sky. The scrupulosity of these observations contains praise; but when it is turned to his confessions of bad behaviour there is terse self-blame. Yet the same muscularity lies in both. There is no maundering.

Earlier in the year he had summarised—partly in Latin, presumably to disguise and distance the entry—the number of nocturnal emissions he could recall having had over a period of several months. Against some of the dates he remarks that he had been unwell and was almost, or completely, unaware of the occurrence. The contrast between this entry, with its endeavour to rationalise his body's rebellious behaviour by reference to illness, and his joyous response to less dangerous natural phenomena, demonstrates his dilemma. Already—he was just twenty-one—he had virtually chosen the path of chastity, but his biology made it difficult for his intellect to condone this choice entirely convincingly. After the observations on the 'combed' effects to be found on the surfaces of sky, water and steed, he wrote a fragment of six lines: *Mothers are doubtless happier for their babes* (123). In this he says that mothers are presumably happier if they have babies and grown sons, but at least the childless do not experience the agony of seeing their children die (perhaps he recalled the death of his brother Felix) which may be compared to the followers of Christ who suffer loss and pain but at least do their suffering in His domain among the lilies. The likening of a childless woman (often an unwelcome condition after all) to a celibate reveals that right from the beginning Hopkins subconsciously had mixed feelings about renouncing his own fertility. Certainly he never appeared disgusted by healthy fecundity. Three years earlier he had written how Summer

> Plashes amidst the billowy apple-trees
> His lusty hands

and twelve years later the exuberant rebirth of spring would be celebrated by mention of the humblest plants:

> Nothing is so beautiful as spring—
> When weeds, in wheels, shoot long and lovely and lush
>
> (33, RB 9)

His exact observation of the way things grow—the development from the vague 'billowy' to the specific 'weeds, in wheels'—never desiccated his emotional response, it intensified it. So when, in September 1865, he wrote a fragment of verse (127) stating that trees are appreciated by their fruits, whereas for him 'my sap is sealed', his root dry, and he would bear no fruit, he is remarking a real loss.

(127) is a terse fragment: he can have no fruit, nor does he have an inner life either, except for one of sin. Yet—might there not be someone to dispute this? Might not He, if He searched, find . . . Here the fragment breaks off. Might not Christ find something worthwhile, perhaps; something on which to build?

Two poems he wrote the following month, *Let me be to Thee as the circling bird* (19) and *The Half-way House* (20), show him striving to move out of this arid mood towards a positive relationship with God. They are love poems, and at the time of writing them he made a note in his journal to the effect that if he ever left the 'English Church' he would have to reconcile this with the example of Provost Edward Fortescue, a well-known High Anglican and ritualist (who did, in fact, become a Roman Catholic six years later). He also copied into his journal Newman's famous, if pallid, verses, *The Pillar of Cloud*, which begin: 'Lead, Kindly Light.' He was clearly attracted by Newman, and towards the end of the summer vacation, when he was back at Oak Hill, he chided himself for talking about him at dinner in a way that might cause unhappiness. He was quite frequently impatient within the family circle, speaking ungraciously to his mother and harshly to Cyril, and relieving his feelings towards his father by imitating his pompous behaviour at the office. But while he sought some comfort in Newman's conventional lines, his own poems (19) and (20), which he wrote on returning to Oxford in October, show the need of a young man who desired love of the most ideal and overwhelming kind.

In *Let me be to Thee as the circling bird* he developed a musical metaphor, concluding that Love was the dominant note of his life— love for God, and God as Love; this was the only 'strain' which he could approve, and he admitted to having found such 'authentic cadence' late in his life. *The Half-way House* shows how difficult it was for him to find this Love, how the established church had not fulfilled his needs, and how it was only the revelation of the Real Presence at communion that enabled him to 'o'ertake Thee' and not be stranded and left behind as Love swept by on wings.

Before returning to Oxford, he had written to Baillie (10–12 September) the letter in which he claimed that Catholicism relieved the pain caused by the '*sordidness* of things'. The tenor of the letter seems to have been prompted by an admission on Baillie's part that he was beginning to approve a Catholic point of view. (If this is so, it was not an approval which ever developed into specific faith. Perhaps he briefly tried to share Hopkins's Catholicism because he was so fond of him.) Hopkins apologises if his own outspokenness in the past might ever have stood in the way of Baillie perceiving the validity of the Catholic principle, and urges him particularly to consider its capacity to mitigate sordidness—a capacity which, he felt, might alone lead people to Catholicism. His actual brief statement of how this is achieved is interesting in its relation to Jung's theories on the Roman Church. Hopkins states that Catholicism objectively intensifies, and then subjectively destroys, this all-pervading sordidness. Jung thought that the disturbing symbolism of the unconscious was effectively objectified in the ritual and dogma of the Catholic church, thereby placing any psychological conflict outside the individual—and thus subjectively removing it, if not actually destroying it. Of all the ritual, the fact that salvation could be offered every day through the Real Presence, the presentation in objective form of God become man and man become God, was, Jung felt, the most subtle psychological technique.

Hopkins announced to Baillie that he was 'teeming' with ideas, but he forbore to develop them further since they mainly concerned metaphysics—a subject which did not appeal to his friend. He did, however, mention he was 'amused' to find that recent advances in science and thought by no means all infringed against Christianity. Jung was to remark in *Psychology and Religion*:

A scientific theory is soon overtaken by another; dogma endures for centuries. The figure of the sorrowing God-man must be at least five thousand years old, and the Trinity is probably even older.

and

Taken in itself, any scientific theory, no matter how subtle it may be, is of less value, I should say, from the point of view of psychological truth, than religious dogma, for the simple reason that a theory is necessarily abstract and exclusively rational whereas dogma always expresses an irrational whole in its images. This guarantees a far better rendering of an irrational fact like the psyche.

While Hopkins was at Oxford, the gossip which surrounded undergraduates' religious waverings was as rife as speculation about love affairs at a matrons' tea-party. He felt it was wrong to gossip in such a way, but frequently found himself drawn into joking and tittle-tattle with Coles which would afterwards make him angry. Nor could he resist speaking deprecatingly about the curate Urquhart, who seemed to provoke much laughter. (At this period Urquhart was referring to the Church of England as 'Our poor dry branch' and had told some undergraduates that 'he thought Rome was right'.) There was so much opportunity to linger and chat in people's rooms, and so often the conversation seemed to take a course which Hopkins afterwards regretted. He appeared to feel that to talk of his doubts about the Anglican Church was to show a lack of faith in God's purpose—which presumably would reveal itself in due course.

On 6 November he both received a letter from Dolben and made a resolve in his diary 'to give up all beauty' until God indicated that he should do otherwise. We do not know what the letter was about, but it caused Hopkins to write: 'Glory to God.'

It is difficult not to see his resolve as sad, if inevitable. The objects that caused him joy, that made his blood rise, both literally and metaphorically, must be put aside, away from his fascinated gaze. Lips, hair, vital expressions, the stance of a body, must not be allowed to absorb his capacity for adoration. He must not allow himself to stray into what he considered to be dangerous territory. Which may seem absurdly exaggerated now, but territory is dangerous when it tempts one to break the taboos of the age. Self-excitement at the glimpse of a pretty head across an aisle, or in a doorway, was not acceptable to a pious follower of Christ in 1865. And nor were the lesser, more furtive, peeps which he could not resist at things which contained subject matter of a dubious nature —dubious because they transgressed conventional good taste, and doubly dubious because they excited him: a Blake drawing, something in W. S. Landor's writings, a report in a newspaper. Here the 'sordidness of things' broke in like a dirty tide, and perhaps it was difficult to keep it completely separate from the exhilaration aroused by more acceptable images of beauty. So they too must be eschewed until God made the boundaries absolutely clear.

But it was difficult to wait for God's intervention when the presence and stimulus of friends prevailed so much of the time. Four days after receiving Dolben's letter, he found himself gossiping with Bridges in what he thought was a foolish manner, and it appears that the name of Gosselin was mentioned. Also he was flattered by the attentions of a rather ambivalent character who haunted Oxford, Henry Oxenham, then in his mid-thirties. Oxenham had been ordained in the Church of England, but became a Roman Catholic in 1857; however, he still believed in the validity of his Anglican orders and did not change the style of his clerical dress. It was said of him that

> No one had a happier faculty of endearing himself in the manliest and simplest fashion to young men. All the sealed fountains of his own nature seemed to be unlocked by their society, and they were often surprised by his recollection of birthdays, and by Christmas books and cards.

Hopkins defended Oxenham to his friends, but admitted to himself that it was unwise to talk to him too much on certain subjects.

The effect of all this self-criticism and spiritual enquiry was to separate him further from his family. On Christmas Day he wrote the fragment *Moonless darkness stands between* (129) in which he describes the partition between his past and his future: a future into which he would be led by the star of Bethlehem. He spent part of the holiday with Aunt Kate, Marsland Hopkins's widow, and found her more easy to talk to than his mother, with whom he tended to get irritated—indeed, once he almost reduced her to tears in an argument about the saints. Aunt Kate was very High Church, and extremely good-looking, and on one occasion he confided in her with a lack of reticence which he afterwards regretted, just as he used to regret his gossipy sessions at Oxford. Not only did he talk about himself, but he told a story against some acquaintances. It was a struggle: suppressing the effervescent, slightly malicious side of his nature that liked to entertain and be good company.

When he returned to Oxford he wrote an accomplished, deceivingly assured, poem about control of the senses and the increased satisfaction that would be gained thereby. It is called *The Habit of Perfection* (22, RB 3) and the first verse celebrates the claims of silence:

> Elected Silence, sing to me
> And beat upon my whorlèd ear,
> Pipe me to pastures still and be
> The music that I care to hear.

Then the lips are asked to find eloquence in muteness:

> Shape nothing, lips; be lovely-dumb:
> It is the shut, the curfew sent
> From there where all surrenders come
> Which only makes you eloquent.

The eyes are urged to 'Be shellèd' 'And find the uncreated light' which lies beyond the everyday surface of things. The virtues of fasting are impressed upon the palate:

> Palate, the hutch of tasty lust,
> Desire not to be rinsed with wine . . .

The nostrils are assured of relish from incense burned within a sanctuary, and the limbs must not fear restriction:

> O feel-of-primrose hands, O feet
> That want the yield of plushy sward,
> But you shall walk the golden street
> And you unhouse and house the Lord.

In the final verse, self-denial is chosen as a bride, recalling Matthew 6, verse 28: 'And why take ye thought for raiment? Consider the lilies of the field, how they grow; they toil not, neither do they spin':

> And, Poverty, be thou the bride
> And now the marriage feast begun,
> And lily-coloured clothes provide
> Your spouse not laboured-at nor spun.

The graceful tone of this poem, implying the possibility of simple yet infinite spiritual achievement, demonstrates the mood often connected with Hopkins at this period. But that is because the poem is well-known; during Lent of the same year he wrote the despairing *Nondum*, whose tone is more like that of the so-called 'terrible' sonnets he wrote towards the end of his life, but it is not nearly such a successful poem as *The Habit of Perfection* and therefore less frequently published. It is based on the Isaiah text 'Verily Thou art a God that hidest Thyself' and shows that the rewarding asceticism proclaimed in *The Habit of Perfection* was not easily achieved. It contains an almost melodramatic image of Hopkins quelling despairing sobs, walking a 'tomb-decked' path towards death and pleading for patience with which to overcome his doubts until God chose to lead him 'child-like by the hand'. In the last verse he likens the moment when God will finally speak to him to the moment when a mother speaks to a startled infant, causing a smile to break across its troubled face. It was written during Lent, while he was trying to follow a programme of self-denial concerning his diet and general comforts. Then at Easter he wrote a conventionally joyful, but nevertheless dull, hymn (24) urging a mood of gladness and praise.

Towards the end of April, he moved into lodgings with Addis, whose character he so admired and who was also entertaining doubts about the Anglican Church. Addis was on a month's fast which had made him unwell, and he lapsed into hysterical laughter at a meeting of the Hexameron society which was held in their rooms and at which he read out an essay on the Franciscans. It was an exceptionally cold spring, the leaves of the chestnut trees being limp with frost on 2 May, and Hopkins's face was chapped and his lips cracked by the east wind three weeks later. But despite the cold there were many welcome signs of spring for him to observe on his frequent walks: creamy drifts of cowslips, voluptuous green meadows, dog violets, new beech leaves edged with minute silver fur, and blue and purple swallows with amber-tinged breasts.

Walter Pater was to be his tutor for the first time, and he walked with him on a bitterly cold, fine evening, describing him with a line from one of Charles Turner's sonnets: 'Bleak-faced Neology in cap and gown.' Pater in fact wore no cap or gown, but was, as far as fervent Hopkins was concerned, 'very bleak'. This was the year after Pater had first visited Italy, and had shed the remnants of a Keble-inspired High Anglicanism (while still enjoying the aesthetic qualities of church services). The inspiration which he had received from seeing examples of Renaissance art at first hand was—during the year he first taught Hopkins—ignited by reading Otto Jahn's biography of the German art historian, Johann Joachim Winckelmann. In his own essay on Winckelmann, written the following year, he indirectly used his recent experience of early Renaissance art to help to describe what Winckelmann must have felt when he saw Greek sculpture for the first time:

Hitherto he had handled the words only of Greek poetry, stirred indeed and roused by them, yet divining beyond the words some unexpressed pulsation of sensuous life. Suddenly he is in contact with that life, still fervent in the relics of plastic art. Filled as our culture is with the classical spirit, we can hardly imagine how deeply the human mind was moved, when, at the Renaissance, in the midst of a frozen world, the buried fire of ancient art rose up from under the soil. Winckelmann here reproduces for us the earlier sentiment of the Renaissance. On a sudden the imagination feels itself free. How facile and direct, it seems to say, is this life of the senses and the understanding, when once we have apprehended it! Here, surely, is that more liberal mode of life we have been seeking so long, so near to us all the while. How mistaken and roundabout have been our efforts to reach it by mystic passion and monastic reverie; how they have deflowered the flesh; how little have they really emancipated us! Hermione melts from her stony posture, and the lost proportions of life right themselves. Here, then, in vivid realisation we see the native tendency of Winckelmann to escape from abstract theory to intuition, to the exercise of sight and touch.

Pater no doubt felt that Hopkins was a student who would understand very well the pleasures of this kind of sensuous aestheticism. Though how far he tried to share them, given his pupil's increasingly devout religious activities, we do not know. Pater's most famous injunction (written in 1868 in his short essay which would finally form the conclusion to *The Renaissance* (1873)) sums up the attractions and dangers—to those less controlled than he, such as Hopkins —of his creed:

Not the fruit of experience, but experience itself, is the end. A counted number of pulses only is given to us of a variegated, dramatic life. How may we see in them all that is to be seen in them by the finest senses? How shall we pass most swiftly from point to point, and be present always at the focus where the greatest number of vital forces unite in their purest energy?

To burn always with this hard, gemlike flame, to maintain this ecstasy, is success in life.

They were in some ways like chalk and cheese: Pater expressing a pagan yet refined sensuality in serene sentences, and Hopkins

D

striving for Christian asceticism while developing a form of poetry that crammed pulses and vital forces into volatile expression. One of the essays which he wrote for Pater was on 'Pagan and Christian virtues', and in it he makes a statement about self-abasement and humility. These have no moral value in themselves, he says, and man has no right to depreciate himself; it is only in a comparative relationship with God that the soul is humble, and this is where humility becomes a virtue. He then goes on to say that although those without leisure or education to reason out their beliefs must rely on the impulse of faith, it is imperative that everyone else's beliefs are grounded 'on the same kind of truths' as those which Plato and Aristotle explored. In an essay on Plato, also written for Pater, he mentions the way in which love, like all strong emotions, can colour everything and so develop a logic of its own, to illustrate which he quotes from Shakespeare's *Sonnet No. 98*:

> Nor did I wonder at the lily's white,
> Nor praise the deep vermilion in the rose:
> They were but sweet, but figures of delight,
> Drawn after you, you pattern of all those.

In another essay, 'On Representation', which was not written for Pater, he writes in favour of widening the franchise to include women, and concludes that a larger franchise should entail a more general moral education (to encourage political intelligence and political morality); he believed the latter to be of greater importance than literary education.

The notes which he made in his journal during the summer of 1866 exemplify Geoffrey Grigson's description of his approach as 'a passionate science'. Grigson reminds us that Hopkins

was born five years after Cézanne, four years after Thomas Hardy, a year after Henry James. The scientific mind had slowly formed, slowly extroverted itself on to nature, and at an even slower rate the concerns of the artist had moved in the same direction, at least outwardly. The process had already known its phases and varieties. A being and a personality had been ascribed to nature; some artists had been pantheists, some nature-drunkards. Passionate emotions declined to an easy, popular sentiment about nature; poets and painters then corrected themselves by looking carefully at its select details.

At no time did Hopkins look more carefully than during that chilly early summer; but although the forefront of his mind was scientifically recording details of landscape and weather, the middle area— so to speak—was responding with emotion to the beauty of nature's proliferation, while the deepest, over-riding response of his mind was a philosophic one—a desire to find unity. In an essay on Plato ('Plato's view of the connection of art and education') which he wrote for Pater, he comments with apparent approval on Plato's wish to 'preserve unity in the distracting multiplicity of life'. The aim of education was therefore to express the underlying law and order of things so that the presence of such unity would emanate from all experiences 'like breathing a wholesome air'. In his daily walks around Oxford, either alone or with friends, Hopkins was thirsting for that unity. It was almost achieved, it seems, as he stood in the Garden Quadrangle of Balliol and watched the sunlight through chestnut trees, and considered the satisfaction, when indoors, of glimpsing squares of green through a window or a garden door. The lilac was in full bloom, and the mulberry tree in bud: but something clouded his responses and made him record that matters seemed 'sad and difficult'. Once he went boating with Horace Dugmore, who had been at Highgate School and was a member of the Brotherhood of the Holy Trinity, and outwardly it was an harmonious occasion. The day for once was a warm one, with a white-grey sky, and the spring foliage brilliant in the shielded light. A cuckoo contributed its notes of hope and urgency, but the whole day, he felt, lacked a canon to harmonise and round-in its different elements, a canon made not of music, but of feeling.

On 13 June he attended the Commemoration Day celebrations in the Sheldonian Theatre—a traditionally rowdy occasion. Matthew Arnold, who was Professor of Poetry, delivered an oration which included a eulogy of Keble, who had died in March, but his respectful words were scarcely heard for the uproar from the undergraduates in the gallery. Hopkins was among them, but his observations of the occasion were very detached and painterly: the black coats and white shirt fronts of the audience, repeated hundreds of times, with all the heads looking in the same direction, revealed a pleasing order in which he found 'a sort of beauty'.

Two days later he set out on a tour with Addis, travelling first to Glastonbury to see the Abbey and to look out over 'Avilion' from Glastonbury Tor, and then walking on to Wells. They spent the next morning visiting Wells Cathedral, and then set out to walk over the Mendip Hills to Bristol. The following day was wet and windy, and the coldest summer one that Hopkins could remember. They visited St Raphael's, a chapel near the docks well-known for its ritualism, and heard the choir sing 'a delightful Gregorian'. There were showers the next day when they took a boat across the Severn estuary to Chepstow and walked up to Tintern Abbey, and it became too wet to go further. The weather improved on the following day, and they walked from Tintern to Ross-on-Wye, via Monmouth. The countryside was lush with oaks and orchards, and they particularly enjoyed a sunken grassy path which led to a ferry between bushy banks which filtered the sunlight. After booking into a hotel in Ross, they walked by the rushing river Wye, streaked with moonlight, and Addis said that he regarded 'fondness or friendship' to be a matter of feeling, not of kind acts. They talked of a one-time friend of his, who had associations with Herefordshire, and he said it made him feel sad to be in the area. They seemed to agree that this would not apply if a friend were dead, but only when there had been a breach. Hopkins jotted down (inaccurately) the line from Newman's *David and Jonathan*, 'He lives to us who dies, he is but lost who lives'.

Addis walked to Hereford the next morning (about twelve miles) while Hopkins caught the train—his feet were sore, despite having borrowed a pair of kid boots from a cousin. They visited the cathedral together, and then separately went to the Roman Catholic Benedictine monastery at Belmont, two miles up the river. Here they were both courteously received—almost certainly by Dom Paul Raynal, who became the most influential Benedictine in England—and shown around the buildings. Writing in 1909, Addis said that this was probably the first time Hopkins had spoken to a Roman Catholic priest. He recalled that Raynal told both of them of the 'doubtful validity' of Anglican orders, and said that until this doubt was cleared up by the authorities it was 'unlawful' to take part in the Anglican Communion. They were, claimed Addis, both very impressed by Raynal, and probably 'from that time our faith in Anglicanism was really gone'. They returned to Ross by train, and mulled over their immediate reactions separately. The indefatigable Addis walked on to Gloucester (about twenty-five miles), while Hopkins strolled by the river and then caught the train.

Addis was very melancholy the next morning as they visited

Gloucester Cathedral where, according to one account, the services had 'a cold propriety' and lacked 'poetry and affection'. Hopkins does not seem to have shared Addis's gloom, though as the train took them back to Oxford, and the stormy sky cleared a little over Cumnor Hurst, he thought he could 'partly feel' his friend's mood. There was a fine sunset, the soft clouds wedged with fleshy rose, but then thunder and lightning and hard rain enveloped the town. It cleared by the next morning, and Hopkins went home to Hampstead where the haymaking was coming to an end and the cottage gardens were bright with irises.

He stayed at Oak Hill for most of the next three weeks, visiting the Royal Academy, the Society of Painters in Water-Colours, and an exhibition of French and Belgian paintings; he also dined with a Mr and Mrs William Holland of Harley Street and met George Street, the architect and devout Anglo-Catholic who had designed SS Philip and James where E. W. Urquhart was curate. Throughout this period he continued his intricate observations of natural detail, and when he went to Croydon for a brief visit he noted that his grandparents' carnations had 'tongue-shaped petals powdered with spankled red glister' and their copper beech's buds were like 'soft vermilion leather'.

During this time he was planning a reading party with two Oxford friends, William Garrett from Tasmania and William Macfarlane, an accomplished musician from Edinburgh. There was some correspondence as to where they should stay, the one imperative factor being that it must be near a church where they could receive communion. In the end they chose West Sussex, Hopkins spending a day on his own walking from Midhurst to Petworth, before catching a train to Horsham where he met Garrett. The two of them found lodgings in an ugly farmhouse near beautiful parkland.

On either 17 or 18 July, their second or third day at the farmhouse, Hopkins 'saw clearly the impossibility of staying in the Church of England'. He resolved to tell no one until the end of the Long Vacation, and to do nothing about it until he had taken his degree the following year. He kept neither decision.

Macfarlane joined them on 19 July, and five days later he noted in his diary, 'Walked out with Hopkins and he confided to me his fixed intention of going over to Rome', while Hopkins tersely noted that he had spoken to Macfarlane 'foolishly'. He at some time also told Garrett. Macfarlane recorded that he 'did not attempt to argue with him as his grounds did not admit of argument', and that he had to wait for his tea until eight o'clock in the evening 'owing to non appearance of Garrett and Hopkins not providing eggs'. It was not an entirely happy holiday for Macfarlane; he and Garrett had already had to chide Hopkins 'about his manners, etc.' after Hopkins had abruptly left them during a walk, and the local church services were not always satisfactory. However, they usually held prayers together in the evenings before going to bed, and managed to get their picture taken by a photographer in Hythe. It shows Hopkins had grown a small moustache, and he grasps his bowler hat and cane, and leans on the shoulder of the seated Macfarlane, in a posed manner just slightly reminiscent of Charlie Chaplin.

On the day Hopkins stated his intentions to Macfarlane, he also replied to a letter he had received from Bridges. It seems that at some stage he had told Bridges he might go north to the Lake District, and Bridges had invited him to extend his visit and stay with him in Rochdale. He had apparently written to ask whether this was likely to happen, and Hopkins had to explain that he had changed his plans and after the Horsham excursion was over he was going to the Isle of Wight to join his family on their usual summer holiday. Bridges persisted, however, and replied immediately asking whether Hopkins could not come after the Isle of Wight— holding out the prospect of Dolben as a fellow guest. Hopkins wavered, but said he was so behind with his work he could not possibly take any further holiday. Bridges replied that he might certainly study should he go to Rochdale. Hopkins wrote from Oak Hill on 28 August, having just returned from the Isle of Wight, that he would travel up to Birmingham that Friday, stay overnight, and arrive in Rochdale on Saturday.

On the same day he wrote his first letter to Newman at the Oratory which he had established in Birmingham. He told him that he was 'anxious to become a Catholic' and asked, with scrupulous politeness and reverence, whether he might see him for a short time when he was in Birmingham on Friday. He explained that he had no doubts about his conversion, but was suffering great anxiety about his immediate duty and course of action. By way of introduction he mentioned that he was a close friend of Addis, who had once visited the Oratory and was, Hopkins felt sure, soon to become a Catholic. Newman was abroad, and unable to reply until 14 September.

The fact that it was to Newman that Hopkins turned for advice is an indication of the influence he had on the minds and imaginations of young converts—particularly those based in Oxford. And it is interesting that Hopkins appealed directly to him, not to any Roman Catholic intermediary. There is, perhaps, a touch of egotism and romance in such an appeal: like a would-be poet who writes to the leading poet of his day for advice, rather than attending his local writing group or evening class. Newman represented the chief mentor for someone in Hopkins's position, and with his blessing he would feel strong and safe.

Hopkins went to Rochdale without having heard from Newman, to find that Dolben was unable to be there. The latter wrote to Bridges:

At any rate you must know that neither are my pleasures so various nor my chances of seeing my friends so many, but that I would have given a month at least of ordinary existence for a week at Rochdale. The fact is that my father likes me to be with him all the time that I am at home . . .

To begin with Hopkins did not tell Bridges of his conversion. He later explained that he felt it would have been dishonourable to do so while staying with Bridges's mother and stepfather—who would have disapproved, the latter being Vicar of Rochdale. They settled down to their studies, reading Herodotus together, but Bridges found that Hopkins

was so punctilious about the text, and so enjoyed loitering over the difficulties, that I foresaw we should never get through, and broke off from him to go my own way.

Hopkins found some relief at being with Bridges during this time of uncertainty, but he must often have been tense and preoccupied, and on one day in particular, when they filled an aquarium together, he felt great anxiety. In due course a reply came from Newman cordially agreeing to see him, and since this meant that he decided to travel home via Birmingham, he felt that he could no longer conceal the reason from Bridges—who was a little hurt he had not confided in him earlier.

Hopkins must have been in an elated, nervous mood, staying at Oak Hill while his parents visited France, and privately going over the details of his successful visit to Newman. After repeated questioning from one of his brothers—we do not know which one, though it was possibly Arthur—he admitted to him that he was to become a Roman Catholic. Newman had asked him to state his argument for his change of faith, and when he had done so Hopkins concluded that he could see no alternative. Newman had laughed, saying: 'Nor can I.' Hopkins found him helpful and sensible, and not at all solemn. Apart from the difficulties it would cause with his family, Newman saw no reason why he should not be received into the Church at once, though he did not recommend any undue urgency. He advised him to read certain books and then, after what was a thorough and unhurried interview, went to find one of his staff (discovered playing football) to look after him. This was John Walford, who had known Bridges and Dolben when a junior master at Eton, and who told Hopkins that he had heard that Dolben had recently been mobbed in Birmingham for walking around barefoot in his monk's habit. Hopkins remarked to Bridges that he did not know whether to be more amused or moved by this report. In a letter to Bridges, Dolben wrote:

> I was in Birmingham on my way home from Wales and made acquaintance with our Third Order Brothers there. They are exceedingly nice, and might be called 'earnest young men' (if it did not suggest such unpleasant persons)—for their quiet earnestness is a very remarkable contrast to the noisiness of the Bristol Brothers. My habit and bare feet created some astonishment in the choir at S. Albans—but on the whole I made great friends with the clergy etc. . . . I visited the Oratory. Newman was away, but Father Ryder was most civil, and not at all contemptuous.

Hopkins wrote to E. W. Urquhart about his conversion, and appears to have implied that he expected he would very shortly follow him. Urquhart apparently replied that he was shocked by the news, and raised many points and objections for Hopkins to consider. Alexander Wood, a friend from Trinity College, on the other hand wrote to Hopkins full of perplexities about his own faith, and on receiving a reply to the effect that Hopkins was now a convert, promptly decided to become one too. By chance Wood bumped into Addis shortly afterwards, told him what had happened, and Addis went that very evening to be received by a priest at St Mary of the

Angels, Bayswater. Garrett too was influenced by Hopkins's conversion, and was confirmed by Henry Manning at Bayswater
on 8 October.

On about the same date Hopkins returned to Oxford and wrote
to his parents about his decision. On 15 October he reported to
Newman that their replies had been so 'terrible' he could not read
them through more than once. They begged him to wait until after
he had taken his degree, but he felt it was quite impossible to wait
that long, and since he could not meet their wishes it seemed useless
to delay his reception at all. He therefore asked Newman if he should
travel to Birmingham within the next few days to be received at
once. The main reason for this hurry was that he had just learned he
could not, as a Roman Catholic, take communion with non-
Catholics at the College Chapel.

He wrote a long letter to his father explaining this last point, and
begging him to understand the futility in asking him to delay. It was
God who called him to His Church, and if he died before he was
received he would have no excuse for not being saved. (Addis, too,
it seems, worried before his reception on this latter point, and was
said by William Bright, the leading Anglican and close friend of
Liddon, to have 'longed for an external oracle, and trembled lest,
if attacked by cholera, he should die out of the Church'. Presumably
bumping into Wood, and hearing about Hopkins, acted as such an
oracle.) Hopkins had no power, he told his father, 'to stir a finger';
his decision had been made entirely by God.

The core of his belief, he went on, lay in the Real Presence, and
without it he would become an atheist. But the doctrine could only
be held by Tractarians and Roman Catholics, and he had seen the
Tractarian arguments 'broken to pieces'. He denied a charge made
by his father that he was acting hastily, or that he had been influenced by 'fancy and aesthetic tastes'—adding tartly that the
accessories of Catholicism were often in bad taste. His conversion
was, he said, due to argument, common sense, reading the Bible,
and knowledge of the Catholic system.

In answer to a plea by Manley Hopkins to consider the family
estrangement his conversion would cause, he replied that he had
had months to think over everything and launched into a fervent
polemic begging his father and mother to approach the Catholic
point of view just once and cast themselves into 'His sacred broken
Heart and his five adorable Wounds', saying that people who did not

pray to 'Him in His Passion' prayed to God but not to Christ. After this peroration he claimed to feel 'lighter-hearted' and signed off affectionately. To Manley Hopkins the letter seemed 'hard and cold' (and presumably fanatical) when he sat down to reply two days later. He pointed out that when Gerard decided to become a Roman Catholic, he had not turned to Liddon or Pusey for reasoned discussion but had gone straight to Newman. And he also feared that he had been on the point of being received without even informing his family, and had only been prevented from such a cruel insult by the entreaties of Edward Bond, not from his own good feeling. He concludes the letter:

> All we ask of you is for your own sake to take so momentous a step with caution & hesitation; have we not a right to do this? Might not our love & sorrow entitle us to ask it? & you answer by saying that as we might be Romanists if we pleased the estrangement is not of your doing. O Gerard my darling boy are you indeed gone from me?

Manley had written to Liddon begging him to intercede—which he was already in the process of trying to do, after hearing news of Hopkins from Coles. He had written to Hopkins on 16 October:

> From what Coles tells me I fear that you will consider my approaching the subject with you somewhat in the light of an impertinence; and yet, after our intimate friendship with each other, I cannot bear to be silent, even though you should not be willing to listen.

He wrote further letters, but to no avail. Hopkins had in fact informed Pusey of his decision and had asked whether he would like to see him before he wrote to his parents; in reply to a second letter Pusey wrote:

> I thank you for the personal kindness of your letter. It would not be accurate to say, that I 'refused to see' you. What I declined doing was to see you simply 'to satisfy relations'. I know too well what that means. It is simply to enable the pervert to say to his relations 'I have seen Dr P, and he has failed to satisfy me', whereas they know very well that they meant not to be satisfied, that they came with a fixed purpose not to be satisfied. This is merely to waste my time, and create the impression that I have

nothing to say. It has, in fact, when done, been a great abuse of
the love I have for all, especially the young.

I do not answer what you say, in a note, because it would be
still more useless. You have a heavy responsibility. Those who
will gain by what you seem determined to do, will be the
unbelievers.

On 20 October Hopkins wrote to his mother from the Oxford
Union. It was a very different letter from the first he had written
to her from there in May 1863, when he had boasted gaily that he
had not breakfasted in his own rooms for ten days. Now he remarked
that his father seemed to think he was off his head, but that in fact,
both at Horsham and since, his mind had been quite cool. He again
went over many of the facts and arguments relating to his decision,
and said that he had never intended to be received without warning
his parents, though admitted he had intended a last-minute warning,
which was wrong of him, but his intention had been to give the least
pain. The next day, Sunday, he was going to Birmingham and would
be received by Dr Newman. There was no point in her hoping for
a change, and he was incapable of bearing any more letters from
home that made him break down. His parents, he claimed, tried to
make it sound as though all the love was on their side and that he
held none for them. This was simply not true, but the more they
repeated it, the more difficult it was to write anything that would
convince them.

There is no descriptive record of his visit to Birmingham and his
reception into the Roman Catholic Church. A fortnight later, on
Sunday, 4 November, he was confirmed by Manning at St Mary
of the Angels, together with Addis and Alexander Wood.

On 7 November he wrote a courteous, well-reasoned letter to
Liddon, thanking him for his kindness and trouble, and endeavouring to convince him that his decision had been most carefully
considered and was caused by no supernatural illumination 'or even
an unusual access of grace'.

To the agnostic, writing a century later, it seems an inevitable
decision—an act of individuation whereby he stepped into a new
territory of his own choice and separated himself from the compass
of his parents. He had been influenced along the way by many
indefinable moments of argument, subjective feeling, and psychological need, and the shadowy presence of Newman in Oxford

(through his writings and reputation—he had not visited the city for over twenty years) provided a model and authoritative point of reference. Hopkins's type of dedication to Christ, however, was probably nearer to Froude's than Newman's: he was a perfectionist, and he was very romantic, and love excited him extremely. If his actions leading up to his reception by Newman remind one of anything, it is an elopement. But it was an inevitable elopement, with Christ as the only possible object for his love; not the kind of elopement that ends in tears and retracing of steps a few months later. Which is not to say it proved a scatheless match.

CHAPTER SIX

'Resolved to be a Religious'

NEWMAN INVITED Hopkins to spend Christmas 1866 at the Birmingham Oratory should it prove awkward for him to remain at home. However, Kate and Manley must have adjusted with reasonable parental flexibility, for on 6 December Newman wrote to Gerard:

> I am glad that you are on easier terms than you expected with your friends at home . . . I proposed your coming here because you could not go home—but, if you can be at home with comfort, home is the best place for you.

Hopkins did visit the Oratory after Christmas, and discussion took place about his future, during which he indicated he did not wish to become a schoolteacher. Newman—always in need of teachers for the somewhat erratically-run Oratory School—said nothing. But when he heard that Nicholas Darnell had asked Hopkins to join his private coaching enterprise, he stepped in:

> When you said you disliked schooling, I said not a word. Else, I should have asked you to come here for *the very purpose* for which Mr Darnell wishes for you. It is quite uncertain how long Walford stays, and we could give you work independent of him.
> I think you would get on with us, and that we should like you: Since then it was only delicacy which prevented my speaking when you were here, I have no hesitation in asking you to accept the invitation which we make to you.
> You will find it much better for you to be in a religious house, than with Mr Darnell in the country.

The tone of his final paragraph was no doubt influenced by the fact that Darnell had once been headmaster of the Oratory School and had left after a long-drawn-out row—in which Oxenham, then also a master at the School, had taken Darnell's side. Oxenham may, perhaps, have introduced Hopkins to Darnell. It was settled that Hopkins should go to the Oratory School in the autumn, after he had taken his degree; Newman had already advised him that 'your first duty is to make a good class. Show your friends at home that your becoming a Catholic has not unsettled you in the plain duty that lies before you'.

A letter written to Urquhart, who had moved to a curacy in Bovey Tracey, Devon, shows that Hopkins was still intent on developing his writing. He was making some slight revisions to *Barnfloor and Winepress*—which Urquhart greatly admired—but had decided not to do any more work on *Beyond the Cloister*. The reason for the latter decision was a moral one; he had started the poem two and a half years ago, and no longer completely approved of its theme. He had given up all idea of attempting to get it published, though once in the past had submitted it, unsuccessfully, to *Macmillan's*. However, he did defend what Urquhart had found to be unnecessary licence in the actual technique of the poem; and here started Hopkins's long struggle for acceptance of his irregular, personal rhythms and word formations. The mode of his defence shows, perhaps, the height of his ambition. He said that beginners were just as likely to use eccentricities as established artists, naming Shakespeare, Keats, Millais and Tennyson as doing so at the start of their careers, and Milton, Turner and Beethoven in their maturity.

He decided to stay in Oxford with Garrett for most of the Easter vacation, and they invited Macfarlane to join them for a few days. On 13 April he wrote to his mother, conveying thanks for £20 which his father had sent, and claiming to have been extremely busy —his final examinations were looming. Much of Balliol was 'a wreck' because of demolition and restoration work being done by Alfred Waterhouse, who was replacing a pleasant eighteenth-century building with an out-of-scale Scottish-baronial façade, and demolishing a fifteenth-century gate-tower; Hopkins particularly mourned the latter. He informed his mother, a little tentatively, that he would be spending a week at the Benedictine monastery near Hereford which he and Addis had visited the previous summer. Then he would go home to Oak Hill on Easter Monday. He felt it would be better if he returned straight to Oxford from Hereford, but if he did that, he would not see his parents before the summer. Whether it would have been 'better' because he had so much work to do, or because it was not easy to be at home, is not clear: perhaps the former.

He gave up all versemaking while working for the examinations, and according to Bridges he sat them having 'not read more than half of the nine books' because of his painstaking thoroughness with each text. Nevertheless Bridges's tutor, Professor Wilson, who was one of the examiners, told him that

'for form' he was by far the best man in the first class. 'Form' was an all-pervading esoteric *cliché* of that hour.

Almost certainly Hopkins aimed for a first and would have been disappointed had he not got one. It is with the confidence of a man who knows his own worth that he stated to Bridges, just before the latter took his final examinations, that he expected him to get a second. He was proved right.

He had two months of vacation to fill before he was due to arrive at the Oratory School, and he proceeded to plan a series of visits. The first was to Paris for a week with a Christ Church friend, Basil Poutiatine (*né* Putyatin), whose father, a Russian admiral and diplomat, was in Paris at the same time. They paid five visits to the Universal Exhibition at the Champ de Mars and did a considerable amount of other sightseeing. Hopkins travelled home alone and enjoyed a rough Channel crossing, noting meticulously the colours and formations of the waves. He shared a railway carriage back to London with a Norman housemaid.

A letter had been waiting for him since the day of his departure. It was from Coles, and it reported that Dolben was drowned on Friday, 28 June.

On 1 May, Dolben had been to Oxford to matriculate, but had fainted during the examination and been thrown out. He stayed at the Randolph Hotel, and only Coles knew of his visit. After this failure it had been decided he should return to his former tutor, Constantine Prichard. The following extracts are taken from the memorandum which Prichard wrote for Dolben's family:

The last poem he construed to me was the speech of Ajax taking leave of the world before his death. On my asking him whether it was not beautiful, he said, 'Very beautiful' emphatically. I remarked that one could have been content if the play had ended there. He said 'yes': and then added with a smile—'In the *Persae* which I read with you when I was here before, there were some hundreds of lines at the end, with little but "alas! alas!" in them.'

These were the last words I heard him say in a lesson: I rather think the last I heard him speak. Our life was very even and uneventful during this fortnight. He seemed *quite* happy; much more so than when here before, though then he was not unhappy. But now there was a continual play of mind, as if he was at peace, and had leisure for such enjoyments as his studies and books and conversation gave him. He knew and felt that we all loved him. His playfulness in conversation and quiet perception of humour were great... His gentleness, sweetness, delicate courtesy, graceful manners, quickness of mind, his docility, modesty and humility—his playfulness and tenderness and affection—made his presence in our quiet home a constant delight. And now it seems as if an angel had been among us.

He had been used to bathe almost daily when here before with Edgell [a friend from Eton] and I knew he was accustomed to swimming. Walter [Prichard's son] had begun to learn to swim last year in Herefordshire, but could only just lie on his back, and could not swim. Dear Dolben only took him, to please Walter himself, and out of kindness . . .

On questioning Walter and the men who were in the fields: it appears that on getting to the spot, dear Dolben and Walter undressed. The former got in first—then Walter with a sash round his waist, by which Dolben was to hold him. Strange to say, the place was out of their depth—out of Walter's certainly. After a minute or two either Walter asked, or Dolben proposed that the latter should take him on his back (he had intended to take him by the sash in one hand, swimming with the other) to try if he could swim with him. On a former day, it seems, Walter had asked him if he thought he could do this, he did not ask him now, but dear Dolben proposed it, Walter tells me. On his getting on he said it was quite easy, and Walter says contrary to his own expectation, he swam across the river with him. Walter felt nervous on the way, not having expected that he would do more than swim out a little and back. They rested on the opposite bank—and Walter said 'Are you tired?' Dolben said 'Not at all, but only out of breath': and then, after a minute or so, told him to get on his back again. His face had no expression of fatigue or distress of any kind, but he seemed happy, and as usual. On their way back Walter spoke, and he said 'Do not speak to me'. Soon after, when within two or three yards of the bank to which they were returning, he sank. It was from sudden cramp the surgeon says. Walter sank with him, but rising, turned on his back. He felt, while under the water, dear Dolben's hand on his shoulder, and then taken off again. Whether he saw him rise once, or not, I cannot clearly make out. After lying still some time, Walter remembered the mowers whom they had passed in the field, and cried out. At first they thought it was in play, but on hearing it again, they ran to the bank—they were perhaps 100 yards off or more. They saw Walter, his face just above the water. He was praying earnestly, but making no effort to get nearer the bank. He must have sunk in another minute or two in human probability. They told him to try to get nearer, and he struck out, still lying on his back, and after some struggling, they drew him to the bank by a pitchfork put round the lily stems. One of them says his head was supported by the lily leaves. They could not swim, and they never saw dear Dolben. Walter was extremely agitated, and seemed to have almost lost his senses. While they were rubbing him, he kept exclaiming about his companion . . . Some days after he had a severe illness from nervous agitation.

Dolben's body was not found for several hours. In his desk there was a paper asking that, should he be taken seriously ill or have an accident, his promise to his father not to become a Catholic should be absolved, and a priest sent for. There were also several poems, from one of which the following verses are taken:

> I saw no sun in any place;
> A ghastly glow about me spread,
> Unlike the light of nights and days,
> From out the depth where writhe the dead.
>
> I passed—their fleshless arms uprose
> To draw me to the depths beneath:
> My eyes forgot the power to close,
> As other men's, in sleep or death.
>
> I saw the end of every sin;
> I weighed the profit and the cost;
> I felt Eternity begin,
> And all the ages of the lost.

He was nineteen when he died. Six weeks after hearing of his death from Coles, Hopkins wrote to Bridges:

I have kept the beginning of a letter to you a long time by me but to no purpose so far as being more ready to write goes. There is very little I have to say. I looked forward to meeting Dolben and his being a Catholic more than to anything. At the same time from never having met him but once I find it difficult to realise his death or feel as if it were anything to me. You know there can very seldom have happened the loss of so much beauty (in body and mind and life) and of the promise of still more as there has been in his case—seldom, I mean, in the whole world, for the conditions would not easily come together.

Bridges quoted this letter in his memoir of Dolben, saying:

No one ever wrote words with more critical deliberation than Gerard Hopkins, and I am glad to have preserved the letter which he wrote, having met Dolben but once, for it must give some idea of the grief which his more intimate friends suffered at his death . . .

After returning from Paris, Hopkins spent five weeks with his family. At one time he had expected to be invited by Pater to join a reading party in Sidmouth during August, but the invitation was not confirmed. He went to art exhibitions and museums, accompanied Lionel to Harrow where he tried unsuccessfully for a place in the School, and went on the river at Richmond with Cyril. On 28 July, his twenty-third birthday, he thought the timbered countryside around Oak Hill 'looked finer' than he had ever seen it: the blue-silver sky of the day was followed by a gold-edged sunset that lit bright sprays along the tops of the dark, velvety poplars.

On 23 August his parents and his sister Milicent set off for a holiday in Brittany, and he went to call on Mrs Cunliffe, a cousin of Baillie's and a 'most engaging lady', at whose house he had once met Christina Rossetti and Jenny Lind. He was still very preoccupied with the former's *The Convent Threshold*, and had been translating two of its most dramatic stanzas into Latin. Mrs Cunliffe was out, and he walked to Hyde Park where he took particular note of a fine chestnut tree. He left the park and went to pray in the chapel of the Poor Clares-Colettines in Ladbroke Grove, Notting Hill. There he 'made my resolution "if it is better" ', which has been taken to mean* that he then decided to destroy his poems if that

---

* See House's Appendix V, *The Journals and Papers of Gerard Manley Hopkins* (1959).

turned out to be appropriate to his final choice of vocation. He spent the evening with Aunt Kate.

Three days later he went to stay with Urquhart in Bovey Tracey, and it was from there he wrote to Bridges about Dolben. He may have done so in the summerhouse at the top of Urquhart's 'mountainous' garden, where they sometimes spent the mornings looking out over a commanding view. Urquhart's mother, whom Hopkins liked, and his sister, whom he did not, were also visiting. He was taken around the local sights, on social calls, and to the Horticultural Society's annual show. The latter was interrupted by a thunderstorm which ruined a taxidermist's exhibit for, as Hopkins wrote to his mother, 'the rain melted the birds off their perches and they were found twice dead'. It was arranged that he could attend mass at Ugbrooke Park, home of Lord Clifford, on his first Sunday, and on the second he walked over to Newton Abbot. After the service Father Kenelm Vaughan gave him breakfast and drove him in a mule cart to a nearby Augustinian convent. There he told Hopkins about how he had recently been assumed to be dying from consumption, but he went to say mass one (rainless) Sunday and a shower of water fell on him and the altar; ever since he had been quite cured. In a letter that Hopkins wrote to Urquhart at the end of that year, continuing their intense debate about the respective claims of the Anglican and Roman Churches, he regretted that Urquhart did not discuss these matters with a qualified theologian, and said he would surely benefit from meeting Vaughan who was good and charming, and had 'an extraordinary devotion to the Blessed Sacrament'.

On 10 September he left Devon to go to Birmingham. The clocks in Bovey Tracey were slow and he missed the local train to Newton Abbot and had to tear in by foot to catch his connection. As a result, his back was sore for several days.

The back strain was a monitory symbol for life in general at the Oratory School, which was to cause stress to Hopkins's health and mental energy during the two terms he remained there. Although at first responsible for only seven children, he had to rise at 6.15 in the morning, and his teaching duties often continued until ten at night. He liked the boys—whom he found innocent and backward—but became exhausted by the lack of privacy and opportunity for personal study. He felt cut off and longed for his friends to correspond and visit, yet had little inclination or time to write letters himself and thus stimulate replies. Part of his difficulty may have been due to moving from a very established university, anchored in tradition, to a small school barely twenty years old, which was still on trial as far as the Catholic authorities were concerned. Newman was in an almost permanent stage of cat-and-mouse siege with his superiors on many matters, and Hopkins may subconsciously have missed being in the mainstream of English upper middle-class life. He did not see Newman very often, and his fellow teachers he at first described to Urquhart as the dregs of Great Britain, then corrected himself and said he meant the sweepings, because— including him—they were drawn indiscriminately from all parts. There were diversions, such as a string quartet in which Newman played the violin, and the countryside was 'really very good for so near Birmingham'; but on the whole there was nothing to see, seldom anyone interesting to talk to, and he was always tired.

He spent the first three weeks of the Christmas holidays with his family, staying with Aunt Kate and his grandparents as well as at Oak Hill. Among several social engagements and entertainments he included a visit to Crystal Palace with an uncle and saw the Beni Zoug-Zoug Arabs in a performance advertised as 'marvellous and daring'. For the last week of the vacation he stayed in Shropshire with his mother's sister, Laura Hodges. She and her husband lived in Edgmond Hall, near Newport, and their three-year-old daughter, Mildred, intrigued Hopkins with her babytalk and the way she always referred to herself in the third person. After being teased she exclaimed: 'Sissie not mock Baby! Baby good mind to cut Sissie,' and called her little scissors 'baby-cuts'.

Schoolteaching did not improve on further acquaintance, and on 12 February Hopkins wrote to Baillie that if it were not for the presence of Henry Challis, a one-time member of the Brotherhood of the Holy Trinity, at the Oratory School, the place would be virtually unbearable. He did add that the boys were 'very nice indeed', but it would appear that intellectually he was starved, while physically he was overworked. He was, he confided to Baillie, almost certainly going to take minor orders. The only trouble being that his mother had claimed this would cause her much grief, and this preyed on his mind and made the future seem 'quite black'. He recalled his one-time ambition to be a painter, and said that even if he were able to fulfil it he would not do so now because it might place an unsafe 'strain upon the passions'. Writing would be compatible with being a priest, but probably not poetry: only work which would serve his religion. Philosophy remained the one interest in which he felt himself 'quite free to indulge'.

The only poem he is known to have written during this period in Birmingham is *The Elopement* (135), which appeared in a short-lived, handwritten school magazine called *The Early Bird or The Tuesday Tomtit*. It is about a girl sneaking out of the house at night and going to her lover, but breaks off before the actual meeting occurs. It contains lines written in his journal two years earlier, and in parts has a personal ring about it, as though it were not just written light-heartedly for the magazine. Perhaps the girl's experience has links with the day he rose early and left Oxford to go to Birmingham to be received—though that may be fanciful. The last verse describes how the girl planned to meet her lover by a brook at a point where it stopped making a noise as it ran over small flints, but her heart is beating so loudly she cannot distinguish the silence. It is a haunting image.

On Palm Sunday, 5 April, Hopkins went into retreat for five days under Father Henry James Coleridge, the Jesuit editor of *The Month* and frequent visitor to the Birmingham Oratory. He was an old friend of Newman—who, unlike many Catholics, was sympathetic to the Jesuits. A week later Hopkins left the Oratory for good and went home to Hampstead. On 29 April he went into a privately-arranged retreat at Manresa House, the Jesuit Novitiate at Roehampton, in order to try to settle his future. Exactly how the retreat was conducted, we cannot know: whether Hopkins was introduced then to the *Spiritual Exercises* that form the backbone of Jesuit training, or whether he was instructed less specifically. The director of the retreat would himself be under the Society's rule not to try to persuade him towards becoming a Jesuit, though critics have said that this very detachment and reserve leads young men who are in a state of emotional religious doubt to make that choice more quickly than any amount of encouragement would do.

During the retreat, on 2 May, Hopkins decided, with some hesitation, that he would need to carry out his tentative resolution of the previous August to destroy his poetry. Three days later he 'Resolved to be a religious'. And on 7 May he returned home still undecided as to whether he should join the Benedictines or the Jesuits.

He soon made his decision, for on 14 May Newman wrote to him:

> I am both surprised and glad at your news. If all is well, I wish to say a Mass for your perseverance. I think it is the very thing for you. You are quite out, in thinking that when I offered you a 'home' here, I dreamed of your having a vocation for us. This I clearly saw you had *not*, from the moment you came to us. Don't call 'the Jesuit discipline hard', it will bring you to heaven. The Benedictines would not have suited you.

This letter seems to indicate that Newman had had no inkling that Hopkins had been considering becoming a Jesuit. It also reveals that Hopkins had decided to prefer what he deemed their 'hard' discipline to what is generally considered to be the humane rule of St Benedict. It was a very crucial decision.

The date of his final, irrevocable choice was probably 11 May, for that is the date he recorded in his diary 'Slaughter of the innocents', which House has convincingly argued refers to the burning of his poems.

This burning was the most significant symbol available to Hopkins to demonstrate his dedication to God. The poems represented his love of beauty, his fine sensitivity, the rhythms of intellectual and physical excitement—the whole developing synthesis of his creativity and skill. But when he read them over he must have realised that many of them did not reflect the virtues which he was now planning to embrace: they had that element of dangerous attraction which he was trying to avoid. They also represented the possibility of future fame and honour in the secular world of art, and he had to prove that he was willing to turn his back on that. As he wrote to Bridges three months later, he destroyed them because he thought they could interfere with his 'state and vocation'. He did, however, keep a few copies of verses such as *For a Picture of St Dorothea* (10, RB 1). He was not destroying the poems in order to remove all evidence of his early aspirations but in order to clear a path in his own life. So the original drafts in his journals remained, as did copies owned by his friends.

Hopkins presumably partly chose the Jesuits because he was attracted by the rigour of their training and the purposefulness of their mission. In doing so, he was defying the widespread unpopularity of the Society, which was described in an article on *The*

Training of a Jesuit by R. F. Clarke,* published in the *Nineteenth Century*, July 1896:

One of the curious phenomena of the modern world is the mystery that hangs around the name of Jesuit. There is a general consent that the Jesuits are a body of men who exert a considerable influence in the world. This at least is conceded to them alike by friends and enemies, by Catholics, and by those outside the Catholic Church. But the secret of their influence, the source whence their power arises, is a matter on which the widest possible opinion prevails ... A large majority of non-Catholics impute to them an unscrupulous readiness to avail themselves of any means, good or bad, by which they think that their cause can be served. Not a few believe them to be a secret and perfectly organised society, ready to occupy any position, or to fill any office, inside or outside the Catholic Church, in which may be seen an opportunity of carrying on their work of unscrupulous propagandism. They are fully convinced that Jesuits are to be found in her Majesty's Service, in the various learned professions, in the commercial classes, among domestic servants and those who labour with their hands, and even in the ranks of the Anglican clergy. Some among the more zealous Protestants believe in the existence of 'female Jesuits', who, in the garb of domestic servants, nurses, and governesses, find an opportunity of instilling into the minds of the young children committed to their charge the principles of Popery ...

This belief, like all other popular superstitions, has an element of truth in it. In the days of persecution, when Jesuits were hunted up and down the land, and were mercilessly butchered simply because they were members of the proscribed Society, their only chance of escaping the hands of the pursuivant was to be 'Jesuits in disguise' ... Even when other priests were tolerated, they were not, and in the present day they still remain an illegal corporation, who are liable at any moment to be expelled from

* One of the reasons that extensive use, both here and later, has been made of Clarke's article is that he was a contemporary of Hopkins. He became an Anglican priest in 1864, and was a Fellow of St John's, Oxford, until 1869 when he was the last Fellow of a College who had to resign to become a Catholic. He became a Jesuit novice in 1871, and was at St Beuno's, the Jesuit theological college, with Hopkins. He became editor of *The Month* in 1881, and founded Clarke's Hall—ancestor of Campion Hall.

England if the existing laws were put in force. All this engendered a certain policy of caution and concealment, the traces of which linger on even when the necessity of it has happily passed away.

No doubt this element of being beyond the pale supplied a not unpleasurable ingredient of adventure to Hopkins's dedication; uniting, perhaps, the 'I must hunt down the prize' (88) side of his nature to the *Heaven-Haven* one.

On 19 May he went to see Father Alfred Weld, Provincial of the English Province of the Society of Jesus, in order to apply for admission as a novice. Clarke gives this description of the procedure of application; we do not know how strictly it was followed in Hopkins's case.

When any one applies for admission to the Society, he has first of all to satisfy the Head of the Province that he is a likely subject; and he is then handed over to four of the Fathers to be examined by each of them separately. This examination is no mere form; the candidate for admission has to answer the most searching questions, and is submitted to a somewhat rigorous scrutiny. He is asked about the age, health, and position of his parents in the world; whether they are Catholics; whether they are likely to need his help in their old age. He has also to give a full account of himself; whether he suffers from ill-health or other infirmity, hereditary or acquired; whether he owes money, or is under any other obligation; what studies he has made and what are his literary attainments, whether he has lived a virtuous life; how long he has been entertaining the idea of entering the Society, and what is his motive for wishing to do so; whether it has been suggested to him by any one else or springs entirely from himself. The examiner has meanwhile to try and ascertain from personal observation what talent he possesses; what is his natural disposition; whether he seems to be a man likely to persevere, and to prove a useful member of the Society. He is not admitted if he has any notable bodily defect or mental infirmity; if he is deficient in intelligence; if he is in debt; or if he has worn the habit of any other religious body, even for a single day. Each of the four examiners has to write out at length his report on the above points, and to state in writing his opinion as to whether it is expedient to admit him or not, with any further remarks that he may choose to add. The four reports are sent in to the Provincial, who after carefully reading them decides whether the candidate is to be accepted or rejected.

Eleven days after seeing Weld, Hopkins learned that he had been accepted. The process of being carefully examined before being pronounced suitable to join an apparent élite quite probably appealed to him.

Three months were to elapse before he actually entered the novitiate, but as a result of his decision he quickly gained, so he told Urquhart, the first complete peace of mind he had ever known. His parents accepted his decision in a much more kindly and contented way than he had expected, and he was free to spend these months as he wished. He started to plan a holiday in Switzerland with Edward Bond, and in the meantime visited concerts and exhibitions. He had not realised, until Bond pointed it out to him, that it would be his last chance to see Switzerland, whose laws proscribed Jesuits.

He had been to Oxford at the end of May to receive his degree, and at the ceremony had seen Swinburne and met his friend, Simeon Solomon. It was almost certainly Pater who made the introduction, and on 17 June Hopkins lunched with Pater in London, and afterwards visited Solomon's studio and then the Royal Academy—presumably accompanied by Pater. Hopkins made no comment on the visit to Solomon, but it would provide plenty of scope for an imaginary conversation piece: Solomon the extravagantly flamboyant and outspoken homosexual who had been closely associated with the Pre-Raphaelites, was an intimate of Swinburne, would be arrested on a charge of buggery in 1873 and go on to become a 'waif of the streets' and die an alcoholic in a workhouse in 1905; Hopkins at 'The Convent Threshold', so to speak; and Pater hovering beside this somewhat incongruous duo.

At the Academy, Hopkins was particularly struck by Frederick Walker's painting *The Vagrants*, and he was later to compare Walker's genius to that of Keats (partly because they both died before coming to full maturity). Walker has been described as an artist who 'realised beauty and unity through an almost blind obedience to his own instincts and emotions', and although some of the figures in his paintings were idealised, the effect is more one of innocence and freshness than sentimentality.

On the eve of his departure to Switzerland with Edward Bond,

Hopkins wrote a letter to Father Ignatius Ryder of the Birmingham Oratory, which shows him making a curious, and totally ineffectual, gesture towards earning some money through literary journalism. Ryder had befriended him during his stay in Birmingham, and Hopkins wrote in a very open, easy manner. He claimed not to have sufficient funds both to see him through a month abroad and to settle his affairs before going to Roehampton, and was therefore vaguely seeking advice as to whether the *Dublin Review* might consider an article by him on William Morris's *The Earthly Paradise*. (The *Dublin Review* was edited by W. G. Ward with whom Ryder was engaged in a controversy about the extent of papal infallibility; Hopkins apologised for his own 'levity' concerning this subject.) Ward's sympathies apart, the reason against the likely success of such an article, all mentioned by Hopkins, were overwhelming. He had little time in which to write it; insufficient perseverance with which to complete it; he found the idea of writing for money painful; and he could not get hold of a copy of the book. (It is not clear whether or not he had read it previously: parts I and II had been published together in April 1868.) Besides money, the reason he gives for wishing to do the article is that he would like to sing his 'dying swan-song'.

Why *The Earthly Paradise*? Its cycle of poems telling Greek and medieval stories was enormously popular, offering, as the *Saturday Review* claimed, 'our wives and daughters a refined, although not diluted version of those wonderful creations of Greek fancy which the rougher sex alone is permitted to imbibe at first hand'. It is escapist verse, intended to provide 'balm for the weary mind'. Hopkins liked the work (though he always had reservations about Morris), and that would be sufficient reason for wishing to write about it; but Pater was preparing an article on it, which was published in the *Westminster Review* in October 1868, and one wonders whether he discussed the work at their luncheon together and stimulated Hopkins into considering writing criticism. Their discussion might have continued when they visited Solomon, who had worked with Morris, and perhaps Hopkins had a brief vision of the professional literary life which he was relinquishing before it had even begun. Hence the reference to 'dying swan-song'.

A few hours after completing the letter to Ryder, he set off for Switzerland with Bond. This visit, which lasted four weeks, is recorded in pictorial detail in the published *Journals and Papers*. It is perhaps the most self-contained section of his journals, and provides a full account of their route on what was a typically energetic walking holiday of the period. The highest mountain which they climbed was the Breithorn (13,686 ft.), in the company of a Mr Pease from Darlington and their respective guides, and at its summit Hopkins felt the pressure of trying to appreciate the majesty of the surroundings amid so many people, with their talk of lunch, and spectacles, and cold feet. Even with just one companion, it was almost impossible to feel ecstasy.

They had one beneficial chance encounter, however. Over the border in Italy Bond was sick, and was prescribed effective treatment by John Tyndall, the evolutionist, whom they met when he was about to make a successful assault on the Matterhorn. It was a a Saturday evening, there was no church near, and one of Tyndall's guides refused to climb on the Sunday if he could not attend Mass first. In the end it was specially arranged for one to be held in the local chapel at 2 a.m., and Hopkins got up for it. The guides acted as servers and the noise of a rushing torrent outside accompanied the words of the priest. Hopkins's face was sore and running—the effects of being burned by the wind and sun.

He returned home on 1 August, via the Dieppe to Newhaven crossing. The sea was

> calm with little walking wavelets edged with fine eyebrow crispings, and later nothing but a netting or chainwork on the surface, and even that went, so that the smoothness was marbly and perfect and between the just-corded near sides of the waves rising like fishes' backs and breaking with darker blue the pale blue of the general field; in the very sleek hollows came out golden crumbs of reflections from the chalk cliffs. Peach-coloured sundown and above some simple gilded messes of cloud, which later became finer, smaller, and scattering all away.

Five weeks remained before he was due to go to Roehampton. His friends and relatives were very attentive (his parents apparently delayed their holiday until after his departure), and he was anxious to see them all. Baillie was staying in Hampstead, and they visited an exhibition on one day and walked to St Albans to see the cathedral on another. Bridges came to see him (and got bitten by the family's retriever, Rover); they went into town and walked in Hyde Park and along Oxford Street. He stayed with his grandparents in Croydon

for two nights, and called on Addis on the way home. On
1 September he went to Ely for one night in order to see the
cathedral. In his journal he made his usual precise architectural and
aesthetic notes:

> The nave is not very interesting but it is skilfully and successfully
> designed so as to concentrate and enclose the view up to the
> choir and not through width and scattering in the side arches let
> it loose or escape. The ceiling of the nave painted by L'Estrange
> and after his death by Parry is contributively speaking effective,
> and quiet and good in colour, but the design is babyishly
> archaic. But even this suck-a-thumb is not so bad as the modern
> brasses and the window with the queen in her coronation robes
> and the bachelor and undergraduate and butler and bedmaker.

Privately he must have had thoughts about the Anglican Church of
his heritage.

On 6 September he went with Baillie to call on Mrs Cunliffe;
then he went to say goodbye to Grandmamma, Aunt Annie and
Uncle Charles—who had recently returned from Hawaii. The
following day Horace Dugmore called in the morning to say farewell, and in the afternoon Hopkins set off on his own to Finchley
Road station. However, he had made a mistake over the time of the
train and, having three-quarters of an hour to wait, called on
Grandmamma. She was not very well, but a neighbour came in and
this enabled Aunt Annie to accompany him to the station to see
him off.

Anne Hopkins, a short rather plain lady, keen on archaeology and
eastern religions as well as music and painting, had taught Gerard
in the nursery, watched him grow up and become impatient with
her because she was ignorant of smart parlance (saying 'parties'
instead of 'wines'), and now was inadvertently given the opportunity
to be the member of the family to see him depart from the way of
life with which they were all so familiar. Together they waited for
the train which would take him via Willesden Junction to Richmond
on a hazy, fine and very hot afternoon.

*

The fact of Hopkins becoming a Jesuit has had the effect of
setting him apart, of surrounding him with an aura alien to most
readers today. As we have seen, his conversion to Roman Catholic-

ism was a commonplace within his group, and the taking of orders was not at all rare, but not one of his Oxford friends entered a religious community. It is perhaps worth summarising what happened to some of them in order to demonstrate the variety of their beliefs. Frederick Gurney remained a vicar. Baillie became 'a kind of atheist'. Macfarlane was ordained in the Anglican Church shortly after his stay in Sussex with Hopkins and Garrett, and relinquished his orders in 1893. Addis became a Roman Catholic priest, but renounced his orders after sixteen years and married; then he had an extraordinarily varied collection of appointments and ended up within the Church of England as Vicar of All Saints in Ennismore Gardens. Alexander Wood remained a Roman Catholic, married, and wrote pamphlets on religious matters. Urquhart remained an Anglican vicar. Martin Geldart was ordained in the Church of England (as was his brother), and became a Unitarian with socialist views. Coles became one of the leading priests of the Anglo-Catholic revival. Garrett apparently remained a Roman Catholic and worked for the Indian and Tasmanian Education Services. Challis left the Roman Church and was called to the Bar. Bridges retreated from fervent Anglo-Catholicism into a more personal and pragmatic piety.

Only Digby Dolben would, most likely, have entered a Roman Catholic order. And John Walford, who had taught him at Eton and preceded Hopkins as a master at the Birmingham Oratory, did become a Jesuit, entering the novitiate a year before Hopkins. The numbers of the Society increased significantly during the nineteenth century, as these figures show: 1815:73; 1831:110; 1860:262; 1870:347; 1890:578; 1900:673.

In his book on Hawaii, Manley Hopkins had understood why the Roman Church appealed to the inhabitants of the islands: 'they felt the attractiveness of the forms of worship, and they felt relief at a system of dependence on a conscience not their own'. That this was not, in his opinion, an appropriate form of religion for more sophisticated people, he implied by a quotation from Sir James Stephen's essay, *Founders of Jesuitism*:

Obedience—prompt, absolute, blind and unhesitating . . . such submission, however arduous in appearance, is, in reality, the least irksome of all self-sacrifices. The mysterious gift of free-will is the heaviest burthen of the vast multitude of mankind.

It is this relinquishment of free will that sets Hopkins apart in our imaginations when we think of poets and poetry. But his personal subjugation to vows did not blunt or atrophy his feelings and perceptions.

CHAPTER SEVEN

Obedience

MANRESA HOUSE is named after the town where Ignatius
Loyola, founder of the Society of Jesus, lived for a year in a cave
and first formulated the *Spiritual Exercises* on which the life of the
Order is based. It is a handsome eighteenth-century mansion, taken
over by the Jesuits in 1801, and had large grounds planted with
extremely fine trees. Landscaped walks curved around each side of
the house, and were given the names St Aloysius and St Stanislaus
by the novitiates. It was a setting which provided Hopkins with
many visual riches. He soon noted the chestnuts which shone as
brightly as glowing coals when they first broke from their cases,
although another eight autumns were to pass before these became
the 'Fresh-firecoal and chestnut-falls' of *Pied Beauty*. For—
excepting a few ceremonial religious verses—he wrote down no
poetry during the next seven years. During that long silence, however, rhythms and images and ideas and emotions involuntarily
coalesced towards expression in his mind.

The luggage which he took to Manresa House, like that which he
had taken to Oxford, had been packed by the nurse at Oak Hill.
One of the major surface changes in his life was to be the fact that
the Jesuits employed no servants and took care of most of their own
practical and domestic needs. During the first probationary days he
had a room to himself, but after that he moved to a cubicle in one of
the dormitories. These cubicles could be curtained off, and they
contained an iron bedstead, a washstand, and a chamber-pot.
Everything had to be kept exceptionally tidy.

The purpose of the probationary period, lasting about a week, is
thus described by Clarke:

... the rules of the Society are put into their hands, and are
explained to them; they are instructed as to the kind of life they
will have to live, and the difficulties that they will have to
encounter. They have to study the 'Summary of the constitutions', in which is set forth the end and object of the Society, the

spirit that must animate its members, the obedience they must be ready to practise, the sacrifice of their own will and judgement that they must be prepared to make; in fact, they have every possible opportunity given them of ascertaining what it is that they are undertaking when they declare their intention of serving God in the Society according to its law and constitutions. Of course, there are but few who realise at first all that is involved in the sacrifice they are making; but this must be the case with all who are entering on a new and difficult career. After they have spent a few days in studying the obligation they are going to accept, they are put into retreat for a short time, during which they are kept in perfect silence, and have to spend their time in listening to a series of instructions on the fundamental truths of religion given by the master of novices, each instruction containing a number of suggestive thoughts, on which they have to meditate for an hour after the instruction is finished.

When this time of retirement is over, they are duly received as novices, and are clad in the Jesuit habit. Often one or two fall away during this first probation, discovering that the kind of life is beyond their courage, or requires a higher degree of virtue than they possess.

The habit, an ordinary clerical one, would not be new, but an older Jesuit's cast-off. Hopkins's mother had provided him with hand-knitted jerseys to wear underneath. The Rector and novice master was Father Christopher Fitzsimon, a man described as 'greatly revered by his novices' and 'brimful of fervour'. There were six other new novices, and they were shown around and looked after by two second-year novices (known as 'Angel Guardians'), one of whom was John Walford. One of the new arrivals was called Frederick Hopkins; he had studied medicine and became known as 'the genteel Hop' because of his bedside manner, while Gerard was called 'the gentle Hop'. Another was Henry Schomberg Kerr, an ex-navy captain, and the most commanding member of the group.

Nine days after their arrival, the new novices began a Long Retreat, which would put their vocations to a severe test, and introduce them to Loyola's *Spiritual Exercises*. Clarke writes:

It consists of thirty days occupied exclusively in prayer, meditation, and similar employments. Five times a day the master of novices gives points of meditation to the assembled novices, and

1   Gerard Manley Hopkins in fancy dress, c. 1856

2a Part of letter from Hopkins to C. N. Luxmoore, 7 May 1862

2b Hopkins's illustration for 'A Vision of the Mermaids', 1862

3a Kate Hopkins (mother)

3b Manley Hopkins (father)

4 (*left*) Digby Mackworth
Dolben; (*below left*) Robert
Bridges, c. 1863;
(*below right*) A. W. Garrett,
W. A. Comyn Macfarlane
and Hopkins, 27 July 1866

5   'A Sower' by Hamo Thornycroft

6a   R. W. Dixon

6b   Robert Bridges, 1888

7 Stonyhurst

8   Gerard Manley Hopkins, 1863

they have subsequently to spend the following hour in a careful pondering over the points proposed to them. A regular system is followed; during the first few days the subjects proposed are the end for which man is created, the means by which he is to attain that end, the evils of sin and its consequences, and the four last things, death, judgement, heaven and hell. During the second portion of the retreat the Kingdom of Christ, His Incarnation, Nativity, and His life on earth occupy the thoughts of the novices for a space of ten or twelve days, with separate meditations on the two standards of Christ and Satan, under one of which every one is fighting, in the tactics of the evil one, the choice that has to be bravely made of a life of hardship under the standard of the Cross, and other subjects akin to these. During a third period of four or five days the Passion of Christ is dwelt upon in detail and finally some two or three days of the joyful subjects of the Resurrection, the appearances of our Lord to his disciples, the Ascension, with one or two concluding meditations on the love of God and the means of attaining it, bring the retreat to an end. Three recreation days are interposed between the various portions of the retreat, which are spent in long walks, and in recovering from the fatigue which is caused by the constant mental strain involved in the long time of meditation and prayer. Except during these three days there is no time of recreation, and silence has to be strictly kept throughout.

This month is certainly a trying one, though a very happy and fruitful one for those who are in earnest. It generally has the effect of sending away from the noviceship one or two of those whose aim in life is not sufficiently high, or whose powers are too feeble to allow of their undertaking the yoke of Jesuit obedience, and all the sacrifices that it carries with it. It is indeed a searching process, and generally finds out those who have undertaken a task too difficult for them to accomplish. This is, in fact, one of its objects, as well as of all the other trials of the Jesuit novitiate, which are directed not merely to the formation of the future members of the Society, but also the elimination of those who have no real vocation to serve in its ranks.

Isaac Taylor, an Anglican writer and artist, who in 1849 published *Loyola: and Jesuitism in its Rudiments*, describes the *Spiritual Exercises* as

E

simply a book of drilling; and it is almost as dry, as cold, and as formal as could be any specification of a system of military training and field manoeuvres.

It may be dry from a literary point of view, but one of the modes of drilling laid down—which involves the employment of all five senses—could produce effects which bordered on the melodramatic rather than the arid. This is Loyola's insistence on 'compositions of place', which Taylor describes at some length. The following quotation from his book—which includes extracts from the *Spiritual Exercises*—is given in order to convey some idea of the extra-ordinary commitment to a mental drama, a sort of never-ending serial presentation, that the Ignatian method demands. It also conveys Taylor's revulsion to the *Exercises*—a revulsion which many people have shared. Taylor, who considered Loyola himself to be 'an eminently good and christian man', felt that the *Exercises* were the work of someone with 'an absolute want of imaginative power'—by which he meant poetic imagination. The exercises mentioned below come within the programme for the first week of the retreat.

The prominent characteristic of these Exercises is the endeavour made from time to time, and perpetually repeated, to connect religious meditation with *sensible images* exclusively; that is to say, to pre-occupy the conceptive faculty in every case with sensuous impressions. . . . The subjects of meditation being almost entirely confined to a meagre series of incidents drawn from the Gospels, great pains are taken to give a purely *graphic* direction to the thoughts in dwelling upon each incident. Thus, at the commence-ment, it is said:

'The first prelude is a certain way of constructing the place—forming an image of the scene, for which it must be noted, that in every meditation or contemplation about a bodily thing, as for example about Christ, we must form, according to a certain imaginary vision, a bodily place representing what we contem-plate, as the temple, or a mountain, in which we may find Christ Jesus, or the Virgin Mary, and the other things which concern the subject of our contemplation. But if the subject of meditation be an incorporeal thing, as is the consideration of sins, now offered, the construction of the place may be such as if by imagination we see our soul in this corruptible body, or confined in a prison, and a man himself, in this vale of misery, an exile among brute animals.'

That is to say, care is taken that in every instance the sensuous faculty shall not only be in exercise, but shall *lead the way*. In concluding a meditation, well condensed in its subjects, upon sin, a sensible colloquy is to follow between the penitent and the Saviour—'imagined to be present before me, fixed on the cross'. Much that would be pointed and affecting, if only it were separated from what is mechanical and earthly, might be cited from these Exercises relating to, or intended to produce, compunction for sin. Thus, the emotions that should be spontaneous, are *ordered* at the point where, in due course, they are to be forthcoming; as, for example,—

'The *fifth point* is to break forth into exclamations, from a vehement commotion of the feelings, admiring greatly how all creatures (going over them severally) have borne with me so long, and even to this time preserved me alive; how the angels, bearing the sword of divine justice, have patiently borne with me, guarded me, and even assisted me with their prayers; how the saints have interceded for me; how the sky, the sun, the moon, and the other heavenly bodies, the elements, and all kinds of animals and productions of the earth, in place of the vengeance due, have served me; how, lastly, the earth has not opened and swallowed me up, unbarring a thousand hells, in which I might suffer everlasting punishments.'

... A certain stage on the road of repentance having now been reached, there follows—for the deepening of the emotions already excited—a 'contemplation concerning hell'; and this is so characteristic of these *spiritual* exercises, that it should be cited entire.

'The first prelude is here the forming the place, which is to set before the eyes of the imagination the length, breadth, and depth of hell. The second consists in asking for an intimate perception of the punishments which the damned undergo; that if at any time I should be forgetful of the love of God, at least the fear of punishment may restrain me from sins.

'The first point is, to *see* by the imagination the vast fires of hell, and the souls inclosed in certain fiery bodies, as it were in dungeons. The second is to *hear*, in imagination, the lamentations, the howlings, the exclamations, and the blasphemies against Christ and his Saints, thence breaking forth. The third is to perceive by the *smell* also of the imagination, the smoke, the brimstone, and the stench of a kind of sink, or filth, and of putrefaction. The fourth is, to *taste* in like manner those most bitter things, as the tears, the rottenness, and the worm of conscience. The fifth, to *touch* in a manner those fires, by the touch of which the souls themselves are burnt.'

... Much might be cited, having the same purpose to stimulate the lower faculties; in truth this endeavour is the characteristic of the book throughout. It is in accordance with this intention that frequent directions are given, better befitting the lips of a posture master, than those of a religious teacher. The penitent is directed to set about the allotted contemplation—now kneeling on the ground, and lying on his face, or on his back; now sitting or standing; and composing himself in the way in which he may hope the more easily to attain what he desires.

... As to these Exercises of the first week, we are assured that by the means of them 'Sin *is* abandoned, hated, loathed'. At the conclusion of the painful task the soul finds itself prostrate, and full of anxieties.

Christopher Devlin, in *The Sermons and Devotional Writings* of Hopkins, suggests that

It seems certain that the First Week of his noviceship Long Retreat had contained the profound religious experience which was reproduced much later in the first part of *The Wreck of the Deutschland*.

Hopkins told Bridges that the personal references in the poem were 'all strictly and literally true', and so we can perhaps take Stanzas 2–4 as a description of his terror, mental flight, and final poised submission to God's will during that sensational first week; though it must be remembered that they were written seven years later, and therefore their expression is not that of immediate reportage:

I did say yes
   O at lightning and lashed rod;
Thou heardst me truer than tongue confess
   Thy terror, O Christ, O God;
Thou knowest the walls, altar and hour and night:
The swoon of a heart that the sweep and the hurl of thee trod
   Hard down with a horror of height:
And the midriff astrain with leaning of, laced with fire of stress.

         The frown of his face
      Before me, the hurtle of hell
   Behind, where, where was a, where was a place?
      I whirled out wings that spell
And fled with a fling of the heart to the heart of the Host.
My heart, but you were dovewinged, I can tell,
      Carrier-witted, I am bold to boast,
To flash from the flame to the flame then, tower from the grace
to the grace.

         I am soft sift
      In an hourglass—at the wall
   Fast, but mined with a motion, a drift,
      And it crowds and it combs to the fall;
I steady as a water in a well, to a poise, to a pane,
   But roped with, always, all the way down from the tall
      Fells or flanks of the voel, a vein
Of the gospel proffer, a pressure, a principle, Christ's gift.

The only notes which Hopkins made in his journal at this period
are to do with weather and landscape, and when the retreat was
over he recalled that on one day there had been a brief dawn
thunderstorm in a purple sky, with just one flash of rose-coloured
lightning; on other mornings the early mist resembled still water
that has been clouded by milk or soda. After the retreat, the exhaus-
tion of the novices was acknowledged by the granting of what were
known as 'long sleeps': permission to rise half an hour later, at six
instead of five-thirty.

Their daily routine from then on was along the following lines:

5.30   Rise.
6.00   Very brief visit to chapel.
         Meditation.

7.00   Chapel for Holy Mass.
7.30   Reconsider meditation, write down any thoughts upon it.
7.45   Breakfast.
8.30   Read (at desk) *Rodriguez on Christian Perfection*.
9.00   Instruction on rules.
        Make beds and tidy cubicles.
        Assigned domestic tasks (dusting, sweeping, scrubbing, etc.).
10.15   Learn by heart section of rules or scriptures.
10.30   Free time to walk in grounds, pray in chapel, or read spiritual book.
11.30   Outdoor manual work (chopping wood, sweeping leaves, weeding, etc.).
12.30   Return to house.
12.40   Chapel for prayer and examination of conscience concerning work done that morning, behaviour towards colleagues, and whether silence kept throughout.
1.00   Dinner, during which spiritual book is read aloud.
        Short visit to chapel.
        Domestic and outdoor tasks or (three days a week) a two hour walk with one or two other novices chosen by the master. Occasionally a game of cricket or football.
6.00   Meditation in chapel.
        Vocal prayers.
        Free time.
7.30   Supper.
8.00   Recreation (Latin must be spoken during the first half-hour).
9.00   Prayers in chapel.
        Preparation of meditation for following morning.
        Final examination of conscience.
10.00   Lights out.

Bearing in mind that Hopkins had complained at the Birmingham Oratory of having insufficient time for his own work and reading, and that he had suffered from too much company when climbing with a small group in Switzerland, the regime at Manresa House meant a complete reversal of some of the most fundamental rhythms and aspirations of his being. He had to cast himself into it utterly, be absorbed; to trust that the only way he would find Christ to his satisfaction was through this most demanding of methods, with the guidance and support of his teachers, and the (mainly silent) sharing with the other novices.

There was little opportunity or encouragement for him to communicate with his family and friends, though there was no specific rule that he must not do so, and we know that his brother Lionel at least paid him a visit. In the light of the strict monitoring of daily behaviour within the community, and the fact that Hopkins knew that those outside did not wholly approve his immurement, it was difficult to write letters without being stilted and self-conscious during the brief free time available. It was not until he made his vows in 1870 that he felt able to write more freely. There were long gaps between his letters to his mother, and the most sustained passage in the ones sent during his first novitiate year concerned information about Jesuit exiles after the revolution in Spain. He remarked that it was a 'high distinction' for people to be persecuted 'in a tolerant age'. This echoes one of the best-known of Loyola's teachings, explained thus by Clarke:

He used to beg of God that his followers might always be the object of the world's hatred and enmity. He told them that they should wish to suffer contumely, false accusations and insults, so long as they themselves gave no sort of occasion for it, and no offence is thereby committed against the Divine Majesty. He knew from Holy Scripture and from the history of the Church that this has been an essential condition of success in all great works done for God by saints and missionaries, and a mere process of induction taught him to regard persecution and misrepresentation as a necessary accompaniment of every victory won for the sacred cause of Christianity. I should, therefore, be omitting a prominent feature in the history of my Order if I were to pass altogether unnoticed the reproach which always has been attached, and I pray God may always be attached, to the name of the Society of Jesus.

... we gratefully recognise the fulfilment of the words of Him whose name we bear, and who long since forewarned us: 'If the world hate you, know that it hated me before it hated you. If you had been of the world, the world would love its own; but because you are not of the world, but I have chosen you out of the world, therefore the world hateth you' (St John xv. 18, 19).

Life for the novices was not, however, entirely solemn. Hopkins repeated to his mother a pun made by John Walford: on hearing that A. C. Tait had been enthroned as the Archbishop of Canterbury he had suggested he be called 'Tait de l'église'. There is an account of how Henry Kerr, who had left Winchester at thirteen, had difficulty in exercising the Latin-speaking rule.

Sometimes in moments of extreme difficulty a genuine sailor phrase would escape at the heel of the ponderous Latin, or he would startle and nonplus his companion by suddenly demanding the Latin for 'to cut one's cable', 'get things ship shape', or 'there's a donkey adrift on the lawn'.

Hopkins responded conscientiously to matters of concern mentioned in letters from his mother. One of these was the death of Robert Bridges's sister, Harriet Plow, after an appalling tragedy. In March 1868, she and her vicar husband and their baby had been attacked with a hatchet by the lover of a servant girl whom they had dismissed because of his visits. Anthony Plow and the baby died ten days later; Mrs Plow recovered from her wounds, but died in April 1869. The man was sentenced to death. A fortnight after hearing the news from his mother, Hopkins wrote to Bridges; he said that such sufferings as his sister had borne should be recognised as signs of 'God's particular love'. As Bridges matured, he saw dangers in the kind of fervency he had once shared with Hopkins, Coles and Dolben, and his feelings hardened against dogmatic religion. The type of remark Hopkins made about his sister would seem so out of place when he became a doctor and worked in the Casualty Department of St Bartholomew's Hospital, seeing 30,940 patients in one year. Nevertheless he made distinct if sporadic efforts to keep in touch with his friend. He called at Roehampton once before his sister's death, but was turned away because the community was in retreat. In October 1869 he arranged a specific time to see Hopkins, and the meeting did take place. That there was a deep awkwardness between them may be judged by the fact that they apparently did not communicate for eighteen months after that, and Hopkins made the first move by writing and admitting that he may have 'behaved unkindly' during Bridges's visit. By this, he probably meant that he had been obstinately dogmatic: not in a loud or bullying way, but with his own brand of unwavering persistence. This would be in keeping with the dual aim of the

Society of Jesus—the sanctification of one's neighbour as well as oneself.

There was one specific contact which the novices had with the outside world, and this was the taking of catechism classes. Districts in which these were held included Isleworth, Fulham, Putney and Marylebone. To get to the last, novices had to walk four miles to Hammersmith and then take a train to Edgware Road. The children came unattended and on a voluntary basis, so the novices had both to control them and try to interest and instruct them in Christian doctrine.

Novices could choose to make penances or fast provided they obtained permission from the master. Some, according to one account, still scourged themselves with a lash of knotted cords; others wore a sort of barbed wire garter around their thigh. There is no direct evidence that Hopkins followed such practices; the phrase 'lashed rod' (known to be short for lashed birch-rod) in *The Wreck of the Deutschland* is open to interpretation. During Lent 1869 Fitzsimon would not allow him to fast, but did give him leave for a custody-of-the-eyes penance which lasted from January to July and entailed looking downwards for most of the time, rather than gazing out on to the garden and the park, or looking at other people when he spoke to them. This deliberate relinquishing of the one sensuous pleasure remaining to him is the extreme form of asceticism people find difficult to accept. One could, however, see it as a necessary attempt not to be distracted during a crucial part of his noviceship. He did allow himself to make a few general notes on the weather and landscape during that time.

In September, Fitzsimon became ill through overwork and his place was taken by Father Peter Gallwey—a change which benefited Hopkins. Gallwey approached his teaching duties in an imaginative manner, bringing versatility and humour to his exhortations on the rules of the Society, and seldom relying on notes or repetitive passages of rhetoric. This helped to make more immediate and alive what must sometimes have been a very wearying programme. The amount of mental concentration each novice had to undergo, the continuous process of making abstractions and fictions into the common and real mental furniture of their daily lives, was extremely fatiguing. Hopkins recorded in his journal one instance of listening to Gallwey's points for meditation just before going to bed one evening. In the passage he is mainly concerned with his experiences of different kinds of dreams, and this was an example of a waking dream. Gallwey's subject was the Apostles, and Hopkins, who was very tired, closed his eyes and saw images which overlaid the images conjured up by the master's words. He saw one of the Apostles pinioned by a piece of wood shaped like a square U. The piece of wood was familiar and he had been wondering earlier that day what its function was. It was in fact used to hold a few cinders against an earthenware pipe, which projected briefly from a wall of the water-closets, to prevent it becoming frozen. It had been Hopkins's task that week to clean out the closets, so he had seen the piece of wood more frequently than usual. Such unexplained images, he decided, forced their way into the mind, demanding to be processed and understood.

A cumulative effect of developing the mental reality of so much spiritual reading and meditation occurred in the refectory when a passage from Sister Anne Catherine Emmerich's *The Dolorous Passion of Our Lord Jesus Christ* was being read aloud. Emmerich (1774–1824) was a German stigmatic and visionary who dictated an account of her visions of being an eyewitness of Christ's passion. The passage in question concerned the agony in the garden of Gethsemane. One minute Hopkins was listening quite calmly, with no forewarning of any particularly strong reaction. The next he was sobbing uncontrollably; yet, even while this was happening, part of him stood aside wondering at this unpredicted outburst. That ability to stand aside, while at the same time being genuinely overcome by the description of Christ's agony, marks that the fundamental dichotomy of Hopkins the observer/writer, guardian of his selfhood, and Hopkins the submissive religious, was set during his novitiate.

When he had been at Manresa House for fifteen months, he was made Porter, or chief novice, for ten weeks. One of the duties that this entailed was the recording in the house journal of the bare events of each day, and these may be found reproduced in full in Alfred Thomas's *Hopkins the Jesuit*. He preached his first sermon on the Feast of St Stanislaus (13 November 1869), an important day for the community, and after his death it was recalled as 'brilliant and beautiful' and 'out of the usual routine of pulpit deliveries'. These facts indicate that, as far as these things may be judged, he was considered by his superiors to be making satisfactory progress. As was customary, he spent a period working in the kitchens with the novice lay brothers (who were trained in the spirit and discipline of the Order but did not aspire to priesthood). They were Irishmen and he wrote down the stories of ghosts and fairies with which they regaled him, and the Irish expressions which he had not heard before; 'as weak as a bee's knee' was one.

He continued to make detailed visual notes, and to try to develop his own metaphysic concerning the apprehension of sense-data. That he considered his attempts unique is demonstrated by the fact that in the process he coined two new words: 'inscape' and 'instress'. (The first appearance of these is in some notes on Parmenedes which he made early in 1868.) By inscape he meant the inherent and distinctive design of an object (be it a group of trees, a frozen clod of earth, or a poem) which gives it its 'oneness' and which has to be discovered through concentrated observation. It is not found entirely by analysis, but by a counterpoise between attention and reception, and all the senses may be employed in its perception. On 12 March 1870, he used the word in the form of a verb when describing a sunset:

A fine sunset: the higher sky dead clear blue bridged by a broad slant causeway rising from right to left of wisped or grass cloud, the wisps lying across; the sundown yellow, moist with light but ending at the top in a foam of delicate white pearling and spotted with big tufts of cloud in colour russet between brown and purple but edged with brassy light. But what I note it all for is this: before I had always taken the sunset and the sun as quite out of gauge with each other, as indeed physically they are, for the eye after looking at the sun is blunted to everything else and if you look at the rest of the sunset you must cover the sun, but today I inscaped them together and made the sun the true eye and ace of the whole, as it is. It was all active and tossing out light and started as strongly forward from the field as a long stone or a boss in the knop of the chalice-stem: it is indeed by stalling it so that it falls into scape with the sky.

Instress is more difficult, more vague. It is the actual stress of energy which permeates an object and determines its inscape, and which also flows into the senses of the perceiver. Once, walking on the fells near Stonyhurst with a companion, Hopkins perceived a familiar inscape in a new way 'as if my eye were still growing', but the presence of another person prevented him from feeling the instress. As with so many potent abstract concepts, it is possible to find connections between Hopkins's inscape and instress and many other fields of awareness. It is worth remembering that he was interested in the work of Friedrich Max Müller, who pioneered studies in comparative mythology and was a leading Sanskrit scholar. Hopkins took down many quotations on Eastern religion from one of Max Müller's books.

It was in May 1870, when he was nearing the end of his novice-ship, that he wrote in his journal one of his most famous prose passages—a description of a bluebell.

> I do not think I have ever seen anything more beautiful than the bluebell . . . I know the beauty of our Lord by it. Its inscape is mixed of strength and grace, like an ashtree. The head is strongly drawn over backwards and arched down like a cutwater drawing itself back from the line of the keel. The lines of the bell strike and overlie this, rayed but not symmetrically, some lie parallel. They look steely against the paper, the shades lying between the bells and behind the cockled petal-ends and nursing up the precision of their distinctness, the petal-ends themselves being delicately lit.

It is possible, if fanciful, to project another implication on to the appeal of the bluebell besides its honey scent, azure colour and gummy white stalk reaching down into the earth. This is the link with its Linnaean appellation, *hyacinthus non-scriptus*, and the legend of Hyacinth, the slain youth whom Apollo loved, and from whose blood a deep red or purple lily is supposed to have sprung.

Hopkins took his vows on 8 September 1870, following an eight-day retreat. The ceremony was a simple and a secret one, as a precaution against the fact that a clause in one of the Catholic Relief Acts forbidding the administering or taking of such vows was still technically enforceable.

In the small chapel on the second floor of Manresa House, lit by a diamond-paned skylight, he knelt in front of the novice master and silently vowed to be perpetually poor, chaste and obedient. Gallwey answered 'Amen' and took the written formula of the vows from him. Any remaining thread of possibility that Hopkins might reject the absolute life of a religious was severed: he was not a man who would go back on his word.

He wrote to his mother that he was now bound 'to our Lord', a fact which delighted him and enabled him to speak more freely. Equipped with a new gown, biretta and Roman collar, a crucifix and other gifts from Gallwey, he set out on 9 September for Stonyhurst College, the Jesuit school and seminary in the fells near Blackburn, Lancashire. It stands on the southern slopes of Longridge Fell, looking across to the Pendle range. The rivers Ribble—with its tributary the Hodder—and Calder run through the intervening valley; to the east lie the Yorkshire wolds, and twenty miles to the west is the sea. It has been said that 'no more bracing situation could be imagined'.

At that time the school accommodated about 250 boys and the seminary thirty-five scholastics, and throughout the nineteenth century ambitious additions and improvements were being made to the buildings, gardens and playing-fields. The Stonyhurst Observatory was particularly well equipped, and between 1865–83 functioned as one of the Board of Trade's meteorological stations.

On his arrival Hopkins received a bustling welcome and he was caught up in the excitement of a strange place, a room of his own, and new companions. During most of the night he lay awake, watching the full moon over the fells. But in the morning he had pangs of homesickness, missing the familiarity of Roehampton and Father Gallwey's kindly presence. His new home, the seminary, is called St Mary's Hall and is situated three hundred yards from the main College. It is a dour building, described by a contemporary as having 'nothing specially attractive to visitors . . . all being set apart strictly for close, earnest study'.

It was still vacation time, and this gave Hopkins an opportunity to acquaint himself with his new environment. Besides portions of the original old mansion of Stonyhurst and its dull but extensive additions which made up the main school building, there were the Gothic revival church, the chapels and library, the yew-walks and greens and ponds, vineries and gardens, two Queen Anne summer-houses, cricket fields, and a covered playground. The Lancashire landscape ranged from the bleak but beautiful heather-capped fells to the 'branchy bunchy bushybowered' banks of the Hodder. Though, as Hopkins was to write to Baillie, the commonest outlook in that district of high rainfall tended to seem to be that of 'total obscuration'. One phenomenon which he had never seen before, and which elated him, was the Northern Lights.

My eye was caught by beams of light and dark very like the crown of horny rays the sun makes behind a cloud. At first I thought of silvery cloud until I saw that these were more luminous and did not dim the clearness of the stars in the Bear. They rose slightly radiating thrown out from the earth line. Then I saw soft pulses of light one after another rise and pass upwards arched in shape but waveringly and with the arch broken. They seemed to float, not following the warp of the sphere as falling stars look to do but free though concentrical with it. This busy working of nature wholly independent of the earth and seeming to go on in a strain of time not reckoned by our reckoning of days and years but simpler and as if correcting the preoccupation of the world by being preoccupied with and appealing to and dated to the day of judgement was like a new witness to God and filled me with delightful fear . . .

There was an especially spectacular display late in October, similar to one reported to have been seen in Rome earlier and taken as a sign of God's anger at the occupation of Rome by Victor Emmanuel, and the seizure of the Jesuit houses. Five Irish refugees from Rome were received at the seminary, and the students were kept informed of the situation in the refectory readings.

The timetable Hopkins had to follow was strict. They rose at 5.30; prayed and meditated until 7.30; had lectures from 10 to 12.30 and recreation or discussions after lunch; studied from 5 until 8; and prayed and meditated between 9.30 and 10.15. The subjects studied by first-year students were minor logic and epistemology, and mathematics. The philosophic emphasis prevalent at the time was a scholastic, neo-Thomist one. The method by which it was inculcated is described by Clarke:

Besides the lectures, which are given in Latin, the students are summoned three times a week to take part in an academical exercise which is one of the most valuable elements in the philosophical and theological training of the Society. It lasts an hour, during the first quarter of which one of the students has to give a synopsis of the last two lectures of the professor. After this, two other students, previously appointed for the purpose, have to bring against the doctrine laid down any possible objection that they can find in books or invent for themselves. Modern books are ransacked for these objections, and the 'objicients' do their best to hunt out difficulties which may puzzle the exponent of the truth, who is called the 'defendant'. Locke, Hegel, Descartes, Malebranche, John Stuart Mill, Mansel, Sir William Hamilton, and other modern writers, are valuable contributors for those who have to attack the Catholic doctrine. Everything has to be brought forward in syllogistic form, and to be answered in the same way. The professor, who of course presides at these contests, at once checks any one who departs from this necessary form and wanders off into mere desultory talk. This system of testing the soundness of the doctine taught, continued as it is throughout the theological studies which come at a later period of the young Jesuit's career, provides those who pass through it with a complete defence against difficulties which otherwise are likely to puzzle the Catholic controversialist. It is a splendid means of sifting out truth from falsehood. Many of those who take part in it are men of ability and experience and who have made a special study of the subjects discussed, and are well versed in the objections that can be urged against the Catholic teaching. Such men conduct their attack not as a mere matter of form, but with the vigour and ingenuity of practised disputants, and do their best to puzzle the unfortunate defendant with difficulties, the answer to which is by no means simple or obvious at first sight . . .

When the two objicients have finished their attack, there still remains a quarter of an hour before the circle is over. This time is devoted to objections and difficulties proposed by the students. Every one present has full freedom to ask of the professor any question he pleases on the matter in hand, and may require of him an explanation of any point on which he is not satisfied. It is needless to say that full advantage is taken of this privilege, and the poor professor has often to submit to a very lively and searching interrogatory. If any question is proposed that is foolish, or beside the subject, the questioner is soon silenced by the open marks of disapprobation on the part of the rest of the class, and a good objection is sometimes received with quiet applause. Any fallacy or imperfect knowledge on the part of the professor is very speedily brought to light by the raking fire he has to undergo, and while all respect is shown him in the process, he must be well armed if he is to win the confidence of the class by his answers.

The Professor to the first year, who was responsible for initiating Hopkins into this fail-safe intellectual process, was Fr. Heinrich Bochum, a thirty-year-old German who, according to one account, 'could not speak a word of English'. This obstacle, plus the nature of the course itself, made the studies very uncongenial to the less academic students—particularly Henry Kerr. And for Hopkins it must have seemed a long remove from sympathetic tutorials on Plato in Walter Pater's study at Oxford.

Besides reading modern philosophers in order to be fore-armed against doctrinal attack, the seminarians were encouraged to take an interest in the affairs of the world, from which Hopkins had been virtually shut off for two years, and subjects for discussion included the Forster Education Act, photography, and the Prussian Army. Hopkins reintroduced himself to current events by noting down incidents recorded in *Whitaker's Almanack*.

His winter at Stonyhurst was extremely cold, and gave him ample opportunity to record various effects of freezing. There were crystals in the mud, hailstones like cut-diamonds, icicles like tusks, ice-lace meshed across garden mould, and miniature pillars of ice which raised up clods and crumbs of earth 'like a little Stonehenge'. There is a traditional story of a lay brother who remembered Hopkins at Stonyhurst and said that one of his special delights was the path between the seminary and the College: he would bend down and examine it closely when the sun came out after a shower because of the way the crushed quartz glittered. 'Ay, a strange yoong man,' the brother is supposed to have said, 'crouching down that gate to stare at some wet sand. A fair natural 'e seemed to us, that Mr 'Opkins.'

The late arrival of spring in the north was not at all to his liking. In a jokey letter to his sister Kate, now fifteen, he complained at the end of April that Lancashire was still in 'a whity-greeny' January. The letter is reminiscent of those he wrote when younger, full of puns and witticisms, but ending on a serious note. The community had been vaccinated against smallpox, and he told Kate how, after laughing and chatting with friends waiting their turn in the infirmary, he had noticed one young man standing alone in the adajacent galleries looking at a picture. A glance at his already deeply pock-marked face made Hopkins realise that he could not join the others in their fun, and he felt sad for him.

Despite the cold, however, spring seemed to herald a rise in his spirits and a need to contact old friends. He wrote to Bridges, asking to hear all his news and aplogising if he had behaved 'unkindly' on the occasion that he visited him at Roehampton. And he wrote to Baillie, to whom, it seems, a reply was long overdue. He complained quite cheerfully of the wet weather and the arduous course, which left him fagged out, and expressed pleasure at receiving items of literary news; he regretted having so little time for general reading, especially as he felt that for the first time he now knew '*how* to read', how to receive the full burden of a text. His life was, he admitted, hard, but because he 'intimately' knew he was submitting to God's will it was also more to him 'than violets knee deep'. There are passages in his letters from Stonyhurst that indicate he was anxious to get back on a footing with his friends that could be fruitful and acceptable to both sides. He discussed events of general interest, indicated his approval of a thoroughly professional attitude to work, and sometimes sent off a flurry of witticisms. In one letter to Bridges, written after the 1871 Paris Commune had murdered five Jesuit Fathers among their hostages, he stated his very simple and clear views on communism. Efforts have been made to establish that he did not really mean what he said, that they are the views of a politically-naive young man; but there is nothing especially idealistic or extravagant in what he says. He just states a commonsensical view with elementary clarity. There would be, he felt, a great revolution in the not too distant future. He deplored the violent means by which it inevitably would be carried out, but considered that its causes were sadly justified. The nation's riches depended on the majority of her people living in poverty and without dignity. The majority were also deprived of education so could not be expected to respect, or wish to preserve, the monuments of civilisation. The future was, Hopkins decided, black; but it was 'deservedly black', and although he found it a horrible thing to say, he was in some respects a communist himself. Bridges apparently could not bring himself to reply, and it was two and a half years before Hopkins wrote to him again.

By mid-June there had been no really hot summer days; nevertheless since May the seminarians had been permitted to bathe daily in the Hodder in a beautiful pool between waterfalls and surrounded by trees and bushes. Hopkins wrote to his mother that when he stopped swimming and looked around he saw 'fairyland pictures'. In his journal he noted that the river was swollen after

much rain, and looked golden and like 'hills of melting candy'.
Seventeen years later in *Epithalamion* (159, RB 72), he would write
of a valley

> That leans along the loins of hills, where a candycoloured, where
>   a gluegold-brown
> Marbled river, boisterously beautiful, between
> Roots and rocks is danced and dandled . . .

Each year a holiday was arranged for the students and in August
1871 they rented a house in Innellan, overlooking the Firth of
Clyde. The journey was made by steamer from Liverpool to
Greenock—where Henry Kerr and his brother William succeeded
in temporarily losing two portmanteaux—and nearly two weeks of
visits and recreation followed. Hopkins joined a party of fifteen on a
visit to Edinburgh, arriving at noon and being given lunch at the
station by Lord Kerr, father of Henry and William. They visited
the Castle and Holyrood, and Hopkins wished he could have stayed
longer in order to appreciate fully the inscape of that most dramatic
of cities. When they were on the Castle ramparts a violent gale
sprang up, and the boat which later took them across the Firth of
Clyde back to Innellan was tossed around while hailstones as big
as pebbles cut their ears.

The day after the party returned to Stonyhurst, they went into
retreat for nine days; thus their vacation time was carefully punc-
tuated to alternate between freedom from their normal rigorous
timetable and a concentrated renewal of their dedicated compliance
with the will of God. On 8 September, when the retreat ended,
Cyril Hopkins came to spend the weekend at Stonyhurst—an
illustration of how, as Hopkins's profession as a religious became
established, the Society encouraged more freedom of relationship,
and his own family became accepting of the *status quo*. There was
no question of any of them being converted, nor did he any longer
expect it.

On Monday, 11 September, he and Cyril left Stonyhurst and
travelled to Blackburn, where they separated: Cyril to go to
Liverpool, Hopkins to go to Hampstead. It was the first time
he had been home since he entered the novitiate three years
earlier. The homecoming was quiet, only Milicent and his father
being at Oak Hill. Milicent had become an 'out-sister' of All
Saints' Home, devoting herself to nursing and other good works

while still living with her parents. The following day he visited
Aunt Annie and Grandmamma, and found the latter looking older.
When talking of her to his father in the evening, Manley told him
that she remembered her grandfather saying he had met an old man
who could recall soldiers searching the hedges for Charles I after a
battle.

On the next day he went to Bursledon, on the river Hamble in
Hampshire, to join his mother and other members of the family for
five days of their summer holiday. One evening he walked through
stubble fields with her and Grace and noticed beams in the eastern
sky, opposite the sunset. It was a phenomenon he was to remark on
other occasions, and ten years later write about in letters to *Nature*.
On the Saturday he went into Southampton for confession. Walking
back afterwards he again noticed the setting sun:

> In returning the sky . . . was in a great wide winged or shelved
> rack of rice white fine pelleted fretting. At sunset it gathered
> downwards and as the light then bathed it from below the fine
> ribbings and long brindled jetties dripping with fiery bronze had
> the look of being smeared by some blade which had a little
> flattened and richly mulled what it was drawn across. This
> bronze changed of course to crimson, and the whole upper sky
> being now plotted with pale soaked blue rosetting seized some of
> it forward in wisps or plucks of smooth beautiful carnation or of
> coral or camellia rose colour.

As far as his personal relations with his family were concerned,
we know from a remark made in a letter he wrote to Garrett six
months after the holiday that he had 'found things pleasanter' than
at any time since his conversion. This had, he added, been 'a great
comfort'. Presumably the gradual breaking of the ice—Cyril's
weekend at Stonyhurst, the short stay at Oak Hill, the final reunion
with his mother—had been fairly deliberate. The secular severance
and commitment to Christ had proved steadfast; now a carefully-
orchestrated 'normality' could be resumed.

But it is perhaps necessary to underline the fundamental
surrender of choice which Hopkins had made. This is Clarke's
description of Jesuit obedience:

> The special object of his life in the noviceship has been to train
> him up in that spirit of implicit and unquestioning obedience

which is the aim of the Society of Jesus to cultivate more than any other virtue in her sons, simply because it is the virtue that underlies all the rest, and without which no other virtue can attain its full perfection in the soul of man. The routine of monotonous and often apparently useless employment has for its object to foster the habit of what is rightly called blind obedience. The novice is taught to obey his superior without ever questioning the wisdom of the order given; the perfection of Jesuit obedience includes not only the obedience of the will, so that he does what is commanded promptly, bravely, and thoroughly, but also an obedience of the judgement, so that he regards what is commanded as the best thing possible for him. . . . In all cases where there is any sort of doubt, he must, if he is true to his rule, and loyal with Jesuit loyalty, bend his will to a favourable judgment of what has been ordered by his superior, and abstain, as far as with God's grace he is able, from all unfavourable criticism, using all the force of a loyal will, to induce his judgment to approve, and not to condemn, what his superior has enjoined. It is this obedience of the judgment which is one of the chief causes of the power exercised by the Society. It ensures a remarkable unity of action, and prevents the waste of energy, which in other corporate bodies is the result of disunion, mutual criticism, and internal disaffection and strife.

CHAPTER EIGHT

'Realty's unraveller'

A WEEK before Christmas 1871 Hopkins was disturbed around midnight by a cat mewing in the distance. He found the sad cries unbearable and went in search of their source. Stuck on a window-sill over a sink he found a kitten, which he rescued and tried to lead towards the kitchens. It followed him down the stairs, but each time they turned sharply into a new flight it would run back and try to lick him through the banisters. He made a note of the incident in his journal because he was touched by the kitten's gratitude. In fact it was probably hungry as much as grateful, but it is perhaps significant that its action so impressed Hopkins. He had little opportunity for any direct emotional or physical contacts, and this isolated midnight meeting affected him keenly.

During the Christmas holidays the boys at the College gave, as was customary, a series of concerts and plays. He saw only their *Macbeth*, having little time to spare from his studies, and went to that in order to hear the accompanying music by Matthew Locke rather than to see the play. It was, he wrote to Baillie, a production that was 'very very short of Castalia-water'—not least because all the female characters were transposed into male ones. This was the inexorable Stonyhurst rule, with the result that Lady Macbeth was metamorphosed into Uncle Donald—the text being duly altered where necessary. The effect, Hopkins remarked rather defensively, was not quite as bad as Baillie must suppose.

On 5 March 1872, he received a letter from Challis announcing that he had left the Catholic Church. Bearing in mind they had been at the Oratory School together—indeed Challis had been almost the only stimulant during that rather gloomy period—Hopkins must have felt depressed by his apostasy. He recorded a week later that he had been going through a time of trial, and again was reduced to tears on one occasion by a reading in the refectory. This was an account of a worldly French priest's decision to become a monk on hearing a choir sing the words '*Qui confidunt in Domino*, *sicut mons Sion'*. It was almost as though the words prompted a reaffirmation of Hopkins's own trust in God after a period of anxiety. Besides the news of Challis, he had been hearing conflicting stories about another ex-Oxford friend, and these perhaps served to remind him how difficult it was to communicate with non-Catholics of whom he was fond. The disparity arose in accounts of the death of Miles Fletcher, who had been at Balliol, and the accounts were given by Hopkins's two closest Balliol friends, Addis and Baillie.

Addis, who had joined the London Oratory in 1868 and was shortly to be ordained and become a parish priest, described the demise of the luckless Fletcher thus:

> Do you remember Fletcher a Scotch Catholic? He was a penitent of one of our FF. and used to spend a great deal of time in our church. He married a young lady of good family whom he had converted from the Scotch Kirk and went out with her to the Red River. There he was the great support of the Catholic Chapel. One morning he said to his wife 'I have made my meditation this morning on the best way to spend the last day of my life'. That same day he was frozen to death in the snow. He had served as a pontifical Zouave shortly before his marriage. The last time I saw him I was commiserating him about his health, which had been shattered by a fall from a horse, and he said quite simply 'No, I think it was a providential accident, for it took me away from Oxford'. When he bid his confessor here goodbye he burst into tears and said how much he felt leaving our church. His uncle told me all the particulars of his death. He had another uncle a Jesuit Fr. of the Irish province.

Whereas commonsensical Baillie wrote:

> He had a house in some very out of the way place and I fancy was not very well off. He started off a walk of some 10 or 12 miles to a town to try and get a servant and on returning was caught by a snowstorm. He was found dead only a few hundred yards from his own house. Is it not sad? He had only been married a few months.

Hopkins did not reply to Baillie's letter for nine months (not that this was unusual—there were often long gaps between his receiving and answering a letter), and then he remarked briefly that Baillie had been mistaken about the circumstances of Fletcher's death and that his end had been 'happy & providential', not 'untimely'. However, despite the fact that they differed so fundamentally, the friendship between Hopkins and Baillie never petered out. When crossing London to catch the train to join his mother in Hampshire the previous summer, Hopkins had had time to spare and on the off-chance had called at Baillie's chambers in the Temple. Disappointingly he had been out, his door, Hopkins wrote to him, closed like a prison. He very much regretted that his impulse to see 'the nicest man in London' had failed.

It was in the summer of 1872 that Hopkins began to read Duns Scotus, the thirteenth-century Franciscan philosopher who had perhaps the greatest single impact on his mature thought. In Scotus he found confirmation of the direction of some of his own ideas, plus a Catholic philosophical framework in which to try to develop them. The book he found in the library at Stonyhurst was *Scriptum Oxoniense super Sententiis*, a commentary on the work of the twelfth-century theologian Peter Lombard, printed in Venice in two volumes in 1514. Hopkins cautiously noted that his elation and enthusiasm might come to nothing—but on the other hand it could prove to be that rare occurrence 'a mercy from God'. In the end it did no good to his career as a Jesuit, though it strengthened and vitalised the philosophical element in his mature poetry. Scotus followed Plato rather than Aquinas (who was the central influence on Jesuit training), believing that each individual thing or person differed in essence. Aquinas, on the other hand, held the theory that pure matter consists of undifferentiated parts, which are distinguished only by their differences of position in space; thus the differences between objects made up of undifferentiated parts is purely physical and has no qualitative, essential difference. Scotus's emphasis on the principle of individuation (wrapped up in the customary impersonal syllogistic method) was obviously a comfort to Hopkins: it accorded with his deepest intuitions. *Duns Scotus's Oxford* (44, RB 20) which he wrote seven years later when he was living in Oxford, contains the lines:

> Yet ah! this air I gather and I release
> He lived on; these weeds and waters, these walls are what
> He haunted who of all men most sways my spirits to peace;
>
> Of realty the rarest-veined unraveller . . .

Two of Scotus's main theological teachings were also compatible with Hopkins's own developing thought. The first was that Christ's descent to earth was not an act of reparation for the Fall, but a free act of love which would have taken place with or without the Fall. It is this operation of free will, this choice of 'the great sacrifice', that Hopkins saw as the model for man to emulate. God had chosen to come to earth even though it was not ideal, not sinless, and therefore not a place where Christ could become King. But the image of that ideal still existed, and inspired by Christ's great sacrifice, man could make his own sacrifice to God's glory and could endeavour to aim at least towards the ideal.

The seminarians' August holiday was taken in the Isle of Man that year, and it was a happy one for Hopkins. He found the Manx people exceptionally good-natured, and his notes on walks and visits are enthusiastic and full of visual detail. The fell-sides were 'plotted and painted' with the square hedged fields; in *Pied Beauty* (1877) this image would reappear as 'Landscape plotted and pieced'. He went mackerel fishing, baiting the line with a piece of gleaming mackerel skin. (This fact perhaps contradicts William Empsom's view—expressed in his *Milton's Gods* (1961) when discussing *The Windhover*—that Hopkins 'was an excessively sensitive person; if he had actually seen the bird catch a rabbit he would be more likely to vomit than to write a poem'.) Because of the low tide, they could not take the fishing boat back into the bay at Douglas and had to row hard under the cliffs to the headland.

On the return journey to Stonyhurst, he called on Cyril who was working in Liverpool for their maternal uncle John Simm Smith, and walked the last ten miles from Blackburn. He felt he had never seen Lancashire look more beautiful; the breeze was warm and the grass brilliant and fresh. The Rector welcomed the homecomers by waiting on them at supper—an action which touched Hopkins and made a fitting end to the holiday. A major part of his contentment during this period was almost certainly caused by his discovery of Scotus, which sharpened and heightened his relationship with himself and with the landscape surrounding him.

Before the customary September retreat he wrote to his mother to thank her for sending the 3 August 1872 edition of the *Illustrated London News* containing a picture by his brother Arthur. The latter had studied at the Academy Schools and Heatherley's and was now endeavouring to earn his living as an artist. Hopkins had in fact already seen the magazine—and had obtained permission to cut out the illustration and keep it. It was called 'The Paddling Season' and he acknowledged that it was probably Arthur's 'best yet', but nevertheless proceeded to criticise it quite severely. It shows two little girls walking into the waves, their backs to the viewer, and a boy half-kneeling on a rock, his head turned towards them. The boy's expression was 'poor', Hopkins decided, and by giving the girls so much back hair Arthur had 'again evaded difficulties'—i.e. had not needed to draw their heads properly. After these remarks he relented and said Arthur was sure to have financial success because the drawing was so good and bold; nevertheless he hoped he would stick 'to his metatarsals' and life-drawing because his work would not be thorough without. He continued to praise and damn Arthur's work in about equal Ruskinian measures for the rest of his life.

After the retreat, Cyril and Uncle John spent a weekend at Stonyhurst. Cyril was very shortly to marry Harriet Bockett, daughter of a prominent Hampstead churchman, and Arthur was engaged to her younger sister, Rebecca—hence the pressing need for some financial success. The day after their visit, Hopkins wandered over Pendle Hill with Henry Lucas, a fellow student with whom he used to discuss Scotus, and developed a curious fantasy. There were black, bare patches on the hillside which he thought looked suitable sites for a witches' sabbath, especially one patch which stretched to the top where there was a sheer drop and a wide view. He could imagine the witches dancing round and round, moving higher and higher up the hill, until they flung over the edge on their broomsticks, one after the other, to sail away over the flat country below.

Three days before Cyril's wedding, a golden-crested wren flew into Hopkins's room at night, attracted by the gaslight on the white ceiling. He removed the bird once, but it came in again. When he captured it, he smoothed the small feathers in its crest before putting it out a second time. In the morning he found it had shed several of these brilliant little feathers, orange and yellow. He gathered them up and enclosed them as a token in the letter he sent to Cyril for his wedding day.

Towards the end of October, he became ill. He had been suffering from piles for some time, and when he developed a fever following a chill, the piles worsened and he lost a great deal of blood. So

much, indeed, that for a short time he feared he might not recover.
One evening when he had to remain in bed, Gallwey arrived at
Stonyhurst and came to see him while he was making his nightly
examination of conscience. Gallwey sat by his bed and, taking his
hand, spoke affectionately and with encouragement. He managed to
reassure Hopkins, and by the time the newly-appointed Bishop of
Salford visited the community on 17 November he was recovered
and had written some Greek iambics as a contribution to the literary
reception prepared for the bishop. He told Baillie that it had been
a welcome request because it gave him a chance to raise 'a blister' in
his desiccated Greek and also to read Euripides—an opportunity
that occurred all too rarely.

The piles, however, were only alleviated, and it had been decided
that he should go to Hampstead for Christmas in order to have an
operation. The festivities took place first, with a family dinner on
Christmas Day, and the operation was performed (by the family
doctor, Mr Prance, and a Hampstead surgeon, Mr Gay) on
30 December. When his sister Grace was allowed to see the invalid,
Hopkins told her that he had lain awake during the night after the
operation and kept thinking of the lines

> Puts the wretch that lies in pain
> *In remembrance of a shroud.*

The operation had lasted for half an hour, but Hopkins claimed it
had seemed to him more like ten minutes.

His convalescence provided an opportunity for reunions with old
friends. Baillie, Bond, Addis and Wood all came to Oak Hill, the
latter relaying a complicated story about the death in France of
Poutiatine—with whom Hopkins had visited the Paris Exhibition
in 1867. As with Miles Fletcher, the circumstances were obscure;
there were elements of melodrama and the possibility of suicide.
Hopkins recorded the story in detail, concerned no doubt for the
chances of Poutiatine's salvation. He noted that a cross had been
found on his body.

Two young novitiates from Manresa House also visited him,
Archibald Campbell and Henry Marchant. The latter had arrived
at Roehampton a year after Hopkins, and when Humphry House
was preparing the first edition of Hopkins's *Note-books and Papers*
sent him the following remarks:

Some would perhaps say that he appeared 'effeminate': he was *certainly not* that. He had a certain *natural* grace of carriage that was pleasing and attractive but he was quite unconscious of the fact and too manly to wish to be taken notice of, and would have hated being noticed. He had a strong manly will of his own. He was quite simple and did not show off his learning. He was naturally somewhat eccentric in his views and ways: but these ways were pleasing and many of them original. He spoke out pretty straight what he thought; once he said to me 'I admire you and I despise you'. I quite understood why. It gave no offence . . .

Hopkins was in bed for a fortnight. It was a mild January, with gales tearing at the trees outside his window. He noticed the buds on the elms were already rounded, and the twigs of some of the trees were the colour of smoky claret. By the end of the month he was recovered sufficiently to visit the Old Masters exhibition at Burlington House, and then he went to stay a few nights at Roehampton. While he was there, Father Gallwey took him to see the doctor who attended the novices—presumably for a confirmatory check on the results of his operation and his general health—and on 4 February he returned to Stonyhurst to finish the remainder of his final year as a student of philosophy.

Some of the notes he made during this period are very free and rich. One summer day he described as:

Very hot, though the wind which was South, dappled very sweetly on one's face and when I came out I seemed to put it on like a gown, as a man puts on the shadow he walks into and hoods or hats himself with the shelter of a roof, a penthouse or a copse of trees, I mean it rippled and fluttered like light linen, one could feel the folds and braids of it and indeed a floating flag is like wind visible; and what weeds are in a current, it gives it thew and lives it and bloods it in.

Another time he noted that the fells

were all melled and painted with colour and full of roaming scents, and winged silver slips of young brake [bracken] rising against the light, trim and symmetrical and gloried from within, reminded me of I do not remember what detail of coats of arms, perhaps the lilies of Eton College.

Everywhere there was inscape and a sense of order; from the ankle-deep footsteps in snow in February to the light beating up from the glassy heads of the May bluebells in Hodder wood. But one day: 'The ashtree growing in the corner of the garden was felled . . . a great pang and I wished to die and not to see the inscapes of the world destroyed any more.'

His oral philosophy examination was held on 23 June. This took the form of defending (in Latin) a list of theses which had been given out five weeks before. It is not known what was on the list, but the following are two examples given by Alfred Thomas as typical:

The soul is immortal both intrinsically and extrinsically.
The objective reference of ideas is an underived and non-demonstrable truth.

He took the examination earlier than the other students in order that he might be free to teach for six days in the boys' College while one of the masters was away.

It had been decided by his superiors that after the summer holidays—taken once more in the Isle of Man—he should be given a year's teaching before proceeding to the theology course at St Beuno's. He informed his mother that the reason for this was in order to give him 'a rest'. Clearly, therefore, his health was giving some concern, and since teaching could not be said to be less physically arduous than studying theology, it must have been his mental stamina as much as anything else that was taken into account. In an anonymous article written by some Jesuits and published in the *Dublin Review*, September 1920, quite a lot is made of Hopkins's 'droll extravaganza' as recalled by his contemporaries. The writers draw a comparison between him and Newman:

One was Wisdom and the other Simplicity, for if there are both Merry-Andrews and Simple-Simons among the apostolic, Gerard Hopkins was of the latter.

And they recount an anecdote, which may or may not be apocryphal, but presumably has some bearing on an aspect of Hopkins's character. It concerns Bernard Vaughan (1847–1922), who later became a rather sensational popular preacher and was an ebullient figure during Hopkins's Stonyhurst days:

[Hopkins's] freakishness became a legend with the fathers. Once at table he was seized with minor ecstasy at the conjunction of tartlets and Father Vaughan. He rose calling out: 'Tartlets! tartlets! My kingdom for a tart. Bernard, I love you,' and subsided into fantastic mirth. It was only necessary for the Father Rector to mention that no encore was necessary for the solemnity of the religious meal to proceed.

If there were elements of usually-suppressed hysteria developing in Hopkins's character, a year's teaching would no doubt be considered more fruitful—as an expressive, out-going occupation—than immediate continuation of studies.

His physical health was not entirely recovered. While mackerel fishing on holiday he was in pain and 'could not look at things much', and on the return to Stonyhurst on 16 August, the walk from Blackburn, which he had performed with ease in the fine weather the year before, knocked him up. His companions went too fast over the 'infinite stiles and sloppy fields' and when they arrived they found the seminary occupied by secular priests holding a retreat and had to stay in unprepared rooms in the College. Everything was 'darkness and despair' and it seemed to him that nature was in danger of falling apart, like a clod of earth which is held together only tenuously by the strings of a root.

The mood did not envelop him for very long, however; there was a party of German Jesuits staying at the College and the first and third days after his return the visitors entertained the seminarians with concerts. In order to return the courtesy, Hopkins—who found the Germans 'kind, amiable and edifying'—quickly organised an evening of 'music, comic and half-comic pieces' which the Beadle's journal recorded as being 'a decided success'. On 27 August the Germans gave a farewell concert during what proved to be Hopkins's final day as a student at Stonyhurst. Afterwards he walked with them down to Whalley, and then later strolled by the river with Lucas, talking of Scotus. In the evening he was told he should go to Roehampton the following day to teach rhetoric for a year. Orders were usually given in this abrupt manner; thus binding attachments to place or person were never encouraged to develop. Similarly students were not allowed to keep the same rooms for long periods, but were shifted around.

Hopkins viewed all these changes—and the continual staff

changes—with a certain wryness; but he realised that with a new intake every year, plus deaths, illness, default and foreign missions, they were inevitable. And he accepted with pride the tradition of readiness 'for instant despatch'. When he arrived at Manresa House, Gallwey, recently appointed Provincial, spoke to him 'most kindly and encouragingly'. Three days later he went into retreat.

The fact that young bracken spirals could remind him of the heraldic patterning on the arms of Eton College alerts us to the fact that Hopkins had by no means forgotten the allusions of his Oxford days. During the retreat he received, as he thought, 'a great mercy about Dolben'. It was six years since Dolben had died. Not having been received into the Roman Catholic Church his salvation would have been a matter of concern to Hopkins. There is among his papers a copy in his own handwriting of the poem found after Dolben's death (quoted on page 101). Another factor which may have steered his thoughts towards Dolben was the publication in 1873 of a book of poems by Alfred Wyatt-Edgell (later Lord Braye). He had been an intimate friend of Dolben's at Eton and Prichard's rectory, and a member of Ignatius Lyne's order, and had become a Catholic in 1868. The title poem of the book, *Amadeus*, was an elegy for Dolben, and others of the poems were concerned with his death. Hopkins was acquainted with him, and though he probably would not have seen the volume of poems, he may have heard of their publication.

Six years of torment for a soul is a long time, and Hopkins must have prayed for Dolben throughout this period. The forces of God or psyche then conspired to make him feel that Dolben's soul had been saved. He had a nightmare about ten days later. It was as though something or someone leaped on to him and fastened him down. This woke him, and he felt he had lost all ability to move his muscles. If only he could just move a finger, he felt, he would be all right.

The feeling is terrible: the body, no longer swayed as a piece by the nervous and muscular instress, seems to fall in and hang like a dead weight on the chest. I cried on the Holy Name and by degrees recovered myself as I thought to do. It made me think that this was how the souls in hell would be imprisoned in their bodies as in a prison and of what St Teresa says of 'the little press in the wall' where she felt herself to be in her vision.

During his teaching year at Roehampton, Hopkins had the title Professor of Rhetoric, which implies something rather more grand than the actuality. He was responsible for teaching the twenty-three Juniors (men who had taken their first vows but were not scholastics) and five of the novices. Rhetoric, Alfred Thomas explains, was 'an omnibus expression' which covered the teaching of Latin, Greek and English. According to Clarke the syllabus had in it 'nothing specially distinctive of the Society'; and was 'much the same as that of the higher forms of our public schools, and of those who take a classical degree at the Universities'. That Hopkins tried to impinge some of his own interests on his students may be judged from some surviving intricate notes on rhythm, metre and rhyme (published in *The Journals and Papers*), and that he was not very successful can be gathered from his description to Bridges of his teaching activities as bad and painful. From the scattered references made by and about Hopkins as a teacher, it seems the only pupils to whom he could really do justice were those who were intelligent enough to absorb all he said, but were not too argumentative or original. The dimmer ones who could not appreciate his scrupulous detail, and the challengers, fell outside his scope; he had no reserves of strength to draw on with which to try to adapt himself to accommodate their needs. That year at Roehampton, which was supposed to provide him with 'a rest', in fact left him feeling more burdened and cast down than he could remember. One can only guess at the elements that combined to cause this depression—a state which was to recur with deepening intensity for the rest of his life. His physical health was one factor: he tired easily and became 'weak', though when some activity engaged him he seems to have been energetic enough. His teaching was not sufficiently successful or engrossing to provide any replenishment to his vitality. And, one must assume, his personal spiritual contemplations and worship did not always integrate his thoughts and reinforce his devotion. He had, in those far-off Oxford days, sought Love: 'Let me be to Thee as a circling bird'—a being who could joyfully state, 'Love, O my God, to call Thee Love and Love.' As in any love affair, the ecstasy could not be perpetually sustained. But, like most romantic souls, Hopkins found this discovery painful. He was perhaps having intimations of the despair he would feel during his last years in Dublin; despair which he then expressed in images of longing such as this (fragment 151, RB 57):

Hope holds to Christ the mind's own mirror out
To take His lovely likeness more and more.
It will not well, so she would bring about
An ever brighter burnish than before
And turns to wash it from her welling eyes
And breathes the blots off all with sighs on sighs.
Her glass is blest but she as good as blind
Holds till hand aches and wonders what is there;
Her glass drinks light, she darkles down behind,
All of her glorious gainings unaware.

I told you that she turned her mirror dim
Betweenwhiles, but she sees herself not Him.

In contrast to the apparently unsatisfactory days of teaching,
Hopkins enjoyed a varied range of visits on his free days during that
year. After High Mass on Christmas Day 1873, he went home for
a week, during which time he talked about music with his sister
Grace, now sixteen. She was developing into quite a gifted pianist
and composer, and Hopkins had for some time been trying to teach
himself to play the piano. She remembered he had once had a
setting written by Bridges of William Cory's 'O earlier than the
rosebuds blow' and urged him to look for it. He went through his
belongings twice, but could not find it. Arthur accompanied him to
an exhibition of watercolours, and Hopkins picked out Frederick
Walker's *Harbour of Refuge* (of which there is also a version in oils)
for particular note. The young man scything, he thought, was 'quite
made up of dew and grace and strong fire'; and the way his body
swayed to the sweep of the scythe was so fresh and strong it was as
though the subject had been painted for the very first time.

His third brother, Lionel, was now aged nineteen, and had left
school with a report saying he was 'modest and most faultily
unambitious'. In appearance he was not unlike Gerard, being
described as 'of slight build and dapper habit', and was very fond
of his eldest brother though not sympathetic to his religious
beliefs. He himself gradually became agnostic, and at the time of
Gerard's conversion—when he was twelve—had found it difficult
to see what all the fuss and distress was about. He had once visited
Gerard when he was a novice, and was immediately asked, 'Do you
say your prayers?' When he replied 'No', Gerard remarked that at
least he was honest. Two months after the Christmas vacation he

was to set sail for Peking as a Student Interpreter in the British
Consular Service.

In the new year, Hopkins read a recent issue of *The Academy* and
came across a review of Robert Bridges's first volume of poems. He
had never received a reply to his letter about communism, and he
took the opportunity to try to re-open their correspondence. He
remarked that he could not recall exactly what he had said in his
'red letter', but that it would have been excessive of Bridges to be
much offended by it. Hopkins, it seems, had never been told of his
friend's attempts to write poetry at Eton, nor could he recall seeing
anything by him at Oxford. The review had been, therefore, an
agreeable surprise. Bridges did not, apparently, reply for more than
a year—probably because he was about to take his medical finals
and then go on a touring holiday in Italy.

Two of Hopkins's other Oxford friends visited him at
Roehampton during March. Alexander Wood came to announce
that he was about to marry 'a Miss Fulton of Bath'; and Challis—
who had left the Catholic Church—called with his fellow-barrister
friend Richard Bellasis. The latter returned after a few days to
make a retreat. He had been one of Hopkins's senior pupils at
Birmingham and would decide to return to the Oratory to become
a priest. On several occasions during the first half of the year
Hopkins visted art galleries with Jesuit colleagues, and in February
he attended one of the twenty days in which the Lord Chief Justice
summed up the long-drawn-out Tichborne Claimant case. This had
been a talking point among the Jesuits because of the defendant's
counsel's proposition that his client had been corrupted by the
authorities at Stonyhurst where he was supposed to have been a
pupil. The case whipped up a lot of anti-Roman prejudice, but
Hopkins was very satisfied by the Lord Chief Justice's manner. It
was, he wrote to Bond, both clear and casual, demonstrating that
there was no better way to conduct important matters than the
informal way in which one conducted unimportant ones. Business,
he averred, had to be businesslike. To which he then added, 'The
Day of Judgment however will be dramatic throughout'—an
indication that during secular dramas his mind seldom strayed
entirely from the expected and culminating heavenly rite.

In July he paid visits with parties of Juniors to both Houses of
Parliament in order to listen to debates. The one in the Commons
was on the Schools Endowment Bill and they watched Gladstone

F

taking notes and preparing to speak, but had to leave for Roehampton before hearing him. The member sitting next to him was an albino, and Hopkins described his head as looking rather like an apple surrounded by snow.

On Easter Monday, 12,000 men of the Volunteer Rifle Corps held field manoeuvres on Wimbledon Common, and Hopkins was among the 100,000 spectators. Despite the flaming furze, which had been set alight, and the general pandemonium, his perception was not obscured and he was able to catch the inscape of the horses. He noticed the thing that always fascinated him—the way their hair flows outwards from the groin—and he was reminded of the bas-reliefs on the pediment of the Parthenon and some lines from *Oedipus Coloneus* in which Poseidon is addressed as creator and tamer of horses, and the likeness of a horse to a curling wave is implied. Later in the day he stood by the gate of Manresa House and watched the volunteers march past, some of the cavalry unsheathing their swords. Hopkins felt this to be a 'stirring naked-steel lightning bit of business'. In a year when he spoke of weariness and depression it is interesting to see how uplifted and excited he was by this dramatic soldier-play. Always patriotic, he loved the accompanying pageantry. In *The Soldier* (63 RB 39), written in 1885, he would remark this involuntary laudation:

> Yes. Why do we all, seeing of a soldier, bless him? bless
> Our redcoats, our tars?

And on 27 December, when he was at St Beuno's College in Wales, he would move in their flourishing debating club a motion stating that 'Eminence in arms is a better object of national ambition than eminence in commerce'; then, on 18 April 1875, his lack of jingoism was illustrated by his opposition to the motion: 'There is no patriotism without some prospect of a fight or a competition, a struggle with a foreigner.' (Both motions were defeated.) One might judge that one of the causes of his low spirits at Roehampton was a simple lack of such popular excitement as the Wimbledon manoeuvres provided. When Edward Bond wrote a fortnight later to suggest they meet for a walk in the park, Hopkins's imagination took flight. They need not stop at Ham Common, he replied, but proceed via Berkshire to the Arthurian realms of Caerleon, Lyonesse, Avilon and Atlantis. He begged Bond to 'Be pregnant' and bring news and ideas of all kinds.

On 23 July he attended the celebrations for the Rector's day at Beaumont College, a Jesuit establishment at Old Windsor which was visited quite often from Roehampton. During the dinner Hopkins felt that he had talked 'too freely and unkindly', and imposed a custody-of-the-eyes penance on himself on the way home so that he could not look again at the cornfields, ripe for reaping, that had so delighted him on the outward journey.

There were examinations for his students a few days later, and then he left for the yearly summer holiday—this time in Teignmouth—feeling deeply tired and downcast. At first the town seemed dull and the wind flung the sand into his face. But gradually his senses revived, and from appearing to be simply red on the first day, the bright Devon soil of the ploughed fields became like 'rosy cocoa-dust-coloured handkerchiefs' on the second.

After the holiday was over, Hopkins was informed that he was to be sent to St Beuno's College in north Wales to study theology. Two days later, 28 August, he rose half an hour earlier than usual to make his departure; a brassy, dappled full moon hung low over the pasture outside his window.

When he arrived at St Asaph, the town near St Beuno's, one of the two people waiting to meet him was Henry Kerr, and he found a warm welcome at the college itself. Francis Bacon, whom he also already knew and in whose hand survive the only texts of some of his poems, had put some scarlet geraniums in his room and during the next few days several of the theologians showed him around the neighbouring countryside. With William Kerr he looked westwards from the top of a hill towards clouded Snowdon, and then down along the Valley of Clwyd between lower hills where a blue, mealy bloom seemed to seep up from the south. The 'instress and charm' of Wales momentarily replenished his spirits and fired his energies. He would work for her conversion. And he would learn to speak Welsh. On just the day after his arrival he had told his father of the latter intention, and had described the neo-Gothic exterior of Joseph Hansom's (inventor of the cab) building, and the corresponding interior whose staircases, galleries and bo-peeps it would take a fortnight to learn, and whose heating left much to be desired. (Hopkins suffered from chilblains.) The garden was a sort of dramatic wonderland, full of terraces, heights, tree-platforms and flights of steps.

But, just as quickly as his enthusiasm for learning Welsh developed, so was it dashed. James Jones, Rector of the College, returned from a visit to Beaumont on 9 September, accompanied by Henry Coleridge who was to give the autumn retreat. Hopkins asked Jones about learning Welsh, but was told he should only do so if his intention was purely to facilitate his work among the Welsh people. But it was not—Hopkins was fascinated by the language for its own sake. This disappointment made him bitterly weary, and he recorded that he 'shed many tears'. At the same time he lost inclination to continue with his music: no doubt due to scruples as to his intention. Then he revived, feeling that after all the conversion of Wales was his entire motivation, and at some stage he was given permission to start lessons with a Miss Susannah Jones. This particular episode is probably indicative of the problem Hopkins posed to his superiors. There is no indication that they would have forbidden him to learn Welsh for any punitive reason, but their job in carrying out the objects of the Order was to find the most useful way of employing Hopkins's talents in the furtherance of their mission. The usefulness of a fascination with Welsh rhythms and assonance was presumably not immediately apparent.

After the retreat, Hopkins and six others received from Bishop Thomas Brown of Newport the minor orders known as Doorkeepers, Readers, Exorcists and Acolytes. Their use, he explained to his mother, was almost obsolete, and the Bishop, who had to cut five little snips from his hair during the ceremony, must have found it difficult because he had recently trimmed it himself very close to the scalp.

The actual course at St Beuno's was, Clarke writes,

hard especially during the first two years. On three days in the week, the student who has passed successfully through his philosophical course has to attend two lectures in the morning and three in the afternoon. The morning lectures are on moral and dogmatic theology; and those in the afternoon on canon law or history, dogmatic theology, and Hebrew, the last for half an hour only. Besides this, on each of these afternoons there is held a circle or disputation such as I have described above. In theology these disputations are as a rule fiercer and more searching than in the philosophical courses.

Once a week a 'case of conscience' (a fictitious case study which would place a priest in a moral dilemma) would be pinned up on the notice board, and two of the theologians would be asked to prepare solutions, and the rest to study it. The case could be something quite melodramatic.

The dominant ingredient of the theological teaching was the Thomism of Francisco Suarez, whose work, Hopkins once commented approvingly, lacked brilliancy. He was approving because it was not the aim of Jesuits to be brilliant and attract attention. Suarez's weighty prose covered everything satisfactorily, even though it never fired the mind. What did fire his mind, however, was the legend surrounding St Beuno, after whom the college was named, and St Winifred, whose sacred spring gushed abundantly at Holywell six miles away. Winifred, a virgin, had repulsed the unwanted attentions of Caradoc, a chieftain's son, who promptly struck off her head with his sword, whereupon the earth opened up and swallowed him. Beuno, her uncle, restored her head to her shoulders and brought her back to life. Where it had fallen, a spring suddenly appeared. She became a nun, and the spring acquired a reputation for curing diseases.

On 7 October an item appeared in the *Montgomeryshire Mercury* about 'Roman Catholics at Holywell' and containing the original (plus translation) of a poem written in the fifteenth century by Tudur Aled in honour of a pilgrimage made to the well by Edward IV. Hopkins apparently kept a cutting of this article, though it is not known if he saw it on the day it appeared. On the next day, however, he walked to the well with a companion. The weather was bright and fine, and there were crests of snow on the mountains. When they reached the well, they bathed in the clear, aquamarine water. Hopkins revelled in its buoyancy, and listened fascinated when the priest at the church nearby related a story of a young man who had been cured of rupture after bathing in it. Hopkins wrote to the man to check the facts of the story, but although he received a reply he never got answers to his list of searching questions. His father expressed an interest in the case, and Hopkins promised to try to find out about another cure that had been reported. Whatever the facts in specific cases, Hopkins undoubtedly believed in the power of the spring, and told Bridges he was filled with devotion every time he went to see it. These verses from Tudur Aled's poem relate to the healing properties of the well:

As the Baptismal Font conveys
A fiery unction all divine,
So Sychnant's Well the virtues hath
Hidden in Water and in Wine.

Such gift was to a mortal giv'n
That holy water sprang from tears;
As from the drops on Calvary spill,
Here, too, a healing fount appears.

Come hither, hither, all that ail,
Ye deaf, ye speechless, too, and blind,
From God, and sweet Saint Winefrede,
Full speedily your cure to find.

Thou crippled wight, come, hither crawl,
The crutch cast from thee in the deep;
Thyself shalt on the edge be fain
Without its aid to run and leap.

From tongue-tied lips words glibly flow,
Ears closed to sound are open laid,
The soul and senses all have weal,
When such physician lends her aid.

Five years later Hopkins started to write his own verse drama about the legend (152, RB 58). He gave to Beuno a speech about the well:

O now while skies are blue, now while seas are salt,
While rushy rains shall fall or brooks shall fleet from fountains,
While sick men shall cast sighs, of sweet health all despairing,
While blind men's eyes shall thirst after daylight, draughts of
    daylight,
Or deaf ears shall desire that lipmusic that's lost upon them,
While cripples are, while lepers, dancers in dismal limb-dance,
Fallers in dreadful frothpits, waterfearers wild,
Stone, palsy, cancer, cough, lung wasting, womb not bearing,
Rupture, running sores, what more? in brief, in burden,
As long as men are mortal and God merciful,
So long to this sweet spot, this leafy lean-over,
This Dry Dene, now no longer dry nor dumb, but moist and
    musical
With the uproll and the downcarol of day and night delivering

Water, which keeps thy name, (for not in rock written,
But in pale water, frail water, wild rash and reeling water,
That will not wear a print, that will not stain a pen,
Thy venerable record, virgin, is recorded).
Here to this holy well shall pilgrimages be,
And not from purple Wales only nor from elmy England,
But from beyond seas, Erin, France and Flanders, everywhere,
Pilgrims, still pilgrims, more pilgrims, still more poor pilgrims.

Living in this part of Wales, with its myths and holy places, charmed Hopkins deeply; there was, he once told his mother, hardly anything in the world that could 'best the Vale of Clwyd'.

CHAPTER NINE

'A great dragon folded in the gate . . .'

EARLY IN 1875 Hopkins received a belated reply from Bridges to the letter he had sent from Roehampton. Bridges wrote of his current enthusiasms—Hegel and Heine—and invited his friend to call on him at Maddox Street provided that the suggestion presented no moral difficulty. One of the awkwardnesses in their relationship was that Bridges would, from Hopkins's point of view, over-emphasize the impediments to freedom of friendship that being a Jesuit imposed. He pointed out that there would have been no *moral* difficulty, simply one of limited free time. His reply was, however, enthusiastic. It started 'My dearest Bridges' and said how he liked to hear about his latest intellectual interests even if he was unable to share them. He had no time to read Hegel, and, regret-fully, had even had to put Aristotle back on the shelf. However he had some opportunity to read Scotus whom he cared for more even than Aristotle and certainly more 'than a dozen Hegels'. Bridges did not reply for two years. One reason was his objection that his letters could be opened and read by Hopkins's superiors—an objection Hopkins found exaggerated since, although letters were torn open, they were not often read, and would only, he later teased Bridges, have been found interesting if they contained, say, an offer of a wife, or a legacy, or a bishopric. Linking to his lack of op-portunity to read Aristotle—whom he had once claimed to find the be-all and end-all of philosophy—is the stance Hopkins took in a debate held on 17 January when he supported the motion that 'A theological student should eschew all literature not bearing on his studies'.

From this year onwards there are no surviving journals of his day-to-day activities and observations, though it is known that he wrote others and, to judge from another debating society motion, there was no objection to their being kept. This motion, discussed on 20 September 1874, had stated: 'The practice of keeping a diary is exceedingly useful and worthy the adoption of all'; it had been supported by Hopkins and was carried.

The year proceeded quietly. In July he passed examinations in moral theology and dogma, and in August the yearly holiday was taken in Barmouth, on the Merioneth coast. For some reason he and the Rector went only for a week instead of the usual fortnight. Twenty-five ordinations took place after the September retreat (including Capuchins from a neighbouring monastery), the largest number of Roman Catholic priests ordained at one time in Great Britain since the Reformation. On 3 December, the feast of St Francis Xavier, Hopkins preached an ad lib sermon at dinner, and on 12 December he moved a debating motion: 'That the state does well in compelling parents to educate their children.' It was defeated: Hopkins's stance in social debates was often more radical than that of the majority. On another occasion he supported the admittance of women to degree courses—'under proper arrangements'.

A few days before the education debate, reports had started to appear in the newspapers of a shipwreck that had taken place near Harwich in the early hours of Monday, 7 December. In the terrible weather—characteristic of that winter—the captain of the iron-vessel *Deutschland* (British-built, and working for the North German Lloyd's Company on the Bremen–New York route) lost his bearings and the ship went aground on the shifting sands of the Kentish Knock. That Hopkins should have taken an interest in any shipwreck was quite usual, but this one was particularly horrific and had the added pathos that among the drowned were five Franciscan nuns on their way to make a new life in America after being exiled from Germany. It was the particular account in *The Times*, 11 December 1875, that impressed Hopkins most deeply. The following is an extract:

At 2 a.m., Captain Brickenstein, knowing that with the rising tide the ship would be waterlogged, ordered all the passengers to come on deck . . . Most of them obeyed the summons at once; others lingered below till it was too late; some of them, ill, weak, despairing of life even on deck, resolved to stay in their cabins and meet death without any further struggle to evade it. After 3 a.m. on Tuesday morning a scene of horror was witnessed. Some passengers clustered for safety within or upon the wheel-house, and on the top of other slight structures on deck. Most of the crew and many of the emigrants went into the rigging, where they were safe enough as long as they could maintain their hold.

But the intense cold and long exposure told a tale. The purser of the ship, though a strong man, relaxed his grasp, and fell into the sea. Women and children and men were one by one swept away from their shelters on the deck. Five German nuns, whose bodies are now in the dead-house here, clasped hands and were drowned together, the chief sister, a gaunt woman 6 ft. high, calling out loudly and often 'O Christ, come quickly!' till the end came. The shrieks and sobbing of women and children are described by the survivors as agonising. One brave sailor, who was safe in the rigging, went down to try and save a child or woman who was drowning on deck. He was secured by a rope to the rigging, but a wave dashed him against the bulwarks, and when daylight dawned his headless body, detained by the rope, was seen swaying to and fro with the waves. In the dreadful excitement of these hours one man hung himself behind the wheelhouse, another hacked at his wrist with a knife, hoping to die a comparatively painless death by bleeding. It was nearly 8 o'clock before the tide and sea abated, and the survivors could venture to go on deck. At half-past 10 o'clock the tugboat from Harwich came alongside and brought all away without further accident.

Three years later Hopkins explained to R. W. Dixon:

... I was affected by the account and happening to say so to my rector he said that he wished some one would write a poem on the subject. On this hint I set to work and, though my hand was out at first, produced one. I had long had haunting my ear the echo of a new rhythm which now I realised on paper ...

Aided by newspaper cuttings sent by his mother (unfortunately she had omitted the graphic *Times* piece, a copy of which Hopkins would have liked to keep by him for reference, sending by mistake duplicates of another cutting), he tentatively embarked on the poem. He mentioned that he was working on it in a letter written to his mother on Christmas Eve, and he later told Bridges that Stanza 12 was the first to be written—'before I had fixed my principles'. It started simply enough, with a short, swinging quatrain:

> On Saturday sailed from Bremen,
> American-outward-bound,
> Take settler and seamen, tell men with women,
> Two hundred souls in the round—

Then Hopkins established the principle of using longer lines for the second half of each stanza, leading up to a complex six-stress line at the end, urgent and emotional:

> O Father, not under thy feathers nor ever as guessing
>   The goal was a shoal, of a fourth the doom to be drowned;
>   Yet did the dark side of the bay of thy blessing
> Not vault them, the million of rounds of thy mercy not reeve
>   even them in?

Whether this form was intended from the start, so that he aimed all along at a lyrical ode rather than a narrative poem, or whether intuition dictated the form as he started to write, we cannot be sure.

For ten years he had embarked on no ambitious poetry, and for seven had written only a few pious verses for specific occasions. So he began tentatively. But 'the echo of a new rhythm' soon became the reality, and took charge. How long *The Wreck of the Deutschland* took to write we do not know. Certainly it was completed by June 1876. Nor do we know the circumstances which made Hopkins feel able to include the first ten, personal, stanzas which precede the narrative of the wreck. He would have had to fit the poem's production around his normal timetable, but there would have been a break in lectures during the Christmas holidays. The weather was bitterly cold, and the gas light in his room flickered—it needed a new burner. (The man in the neighbouring room had been given a new one, but Hopkins had to wait his turn.) Among the usual more light-hearted holiday recreations the community experimented with a spelling-bee—a parlour game recently arrived from America. The Rector donated a prize, which was won by R. F. Clarke. Hopkins was, as he put it, 'disgracefully felled' by 'allegiance'. (When they held another spelling-bee on Shrove Tuesday, he won.)

Before looking at the poem itself, and guessing at what point Hopkins's total personal imagination took over, it may be worth indicating why the appearance of this major and original poem, after such a long silence, is really no surprise. Hopkins was thirty-one. When he was twenty, and writing to Baillie about his theory of Parnassian verse, he mentioned another kind of poetry—Olympian. This, he explained, was 'the language of strange masculine genius' which suddenly forced its way 'into the domain of poetry, without naturally having a right there'. One of the last references he made to his own poetry, before becoming a Jesuit, was to write to Bridges that he hoped he would be able to 'master the peculiar beat' he had used in *For a Picture of St Dorothea*.

Six years later, when he was teaching at Roehampton, he made some notes on the differences between poetry and verse; poetry, he declared, was speech which had been 'framed for contemplation of the mind'. Sometimes poetry could be heard just for its own sake, over and above the interest of its actual meaning. It was essential that it should contain some meaning and content, but only to provide a support or structure to the shape which was the poem, and which might be described as the inscape of speech. For Hopkins, who was so exact about facts and meaning, to have set a semi-abstract concept in the forefront of his approach to true poetry shows how highly he held the art of juxtaposing word-sounds, and how effective he knew that art, when perfected, to be. He was pursuing ideas which would preoccupy so-called avant garde 'sound poets' a century later, and he was, for a Victorian, most unusually sympathetic to the primitive aspects of poetry. During this period he was also exploring the relationship between music and poetry, together with the effects of stress and rhythm—particularly in Greek and Latin verse.

The descriptive notes in his journal, written since becoming a Jesuit, had frequently come close to poetry. These are random one-line fragments:

Then I saw soft pulses of light one after another rise
the sun sitting at one end of the branch in a pash of soap-sud-
      coloured gummy bimbeams
a floating flag is like wind visible; and what weeds are in a current,
      it gives it thew and lives it and bloods it in
from the same window the full moon at night in a pale coloured
      heartsease made of clouds
Balks of grey cloud searched with long crimsonings

And this entry on sighting a comet, made on 13 July 1874, at Roehampton, could almost be set as a poem (though not one that would have passed muster with Hopkins):

I have seen it at bedtime in the west, with head to the ground, white, a soft well-shaped tail, not big: I felt a certain awe and instress, a feeling of strangeness, flight (it hangs like a shuttlecock at the height, before it falls), and of threatening.

Then, with the start of his lessons in Welsh, he had an opportunity to approach, from a completely new direction, the effects of language. By the time he came to write *The Wreck of the Deutschland* he had a fair working knowledge of Welsh prose and had studied classical Welsh metrics. (With the five shillings he was to win at the Shrove Tuesday spelling-bee, he planned to buy the work of the Welsh poet Goronwy Owen.) He later told Bridges that he partly learned his 'chiming of consonants' from Welsh, and his natural tendency to condense meaning was abetted by what Dr Idris Bell describes as the tendency of the early Welsh poets to be

exclamatory rather than predicative; such minor but useful parts of speech as articles, prepositions, pronouns and the copula are freely dispensed with.

The cessation of his imaginative writing had not been paralleled by a cessation of his thoughts about forms of expression; the idea of 'the language of strange masculine genius' was no chimera. When Rector Jones spoke the words—whether casually or thoughtfully—that enabled him to undertake the creation of a poem without guilt or scruple, he unwittingly unleashed a mature artist.

It was not difficult for Hopkins to imagine conditions on the Kentish Knock. His childhood memories of Manley Hopkins's concern with shipping, the recent accounts in the papers, and his daily experience of the bitter Welsh winter, all served his narrative.

> Into the snows she sweeps,
>   Hurling the haven behind,
> The Deutschland, on Sunday; and so the sky keeps,
>   For the infinite air is unkind,
> And the sea flint-flake, black-backed in the regular blow,
> Sitting Eastnortheast, in cursed quarter, the wind;
>   Wiry and white-fiery and whirlwind-swivellèd snow
> Spins to the widow-making unchilding unfathering deeps.

There follow three stanzas describing the grounding of the ship, and the hours of being lashed by storm with no sign of rescuers. 'Hope had grown grey hairs, / Hope had mourning on . . .' Then, in Stanza 17, the leader of the Franciscan nuns, the 'gaunt woman 6 ft. high', makes her appearance in the penultimate line:

> They fought with God's cold—
> And they could not and fell to the deck
> (Crushed them) or water (and drowned them) or rolled
> With the sea-romp over the wreck.
> Night roared, with the heart-break hearing a heart-broke rabble,
> The woman's wailing, the crying of child without check—
> Till a lioness arose breasting the babble,
> A prophetess towered in the tumult, a virginal tongue told.

Suddenly the narrative stops, and Hopkins speaks to his own heart, which, it seems, has been moved to not unenjoyable tears:

> Ah, touched in your bower of bone
> Are you! turned for an exquisite smart,
> Have you! make words break from me here all alone,
> Do you!—mother of being in me, heart.
> O unteachably after evil, but uttering truth,
> Why, tears! is it? tears; such a melting, a madrigal start!
> Never-eldering revel and river of youth,
> What can it be, this glee? the good you have there of your own?

Had he already decided to include, perhaps already started to write, Part One of the poem, describing his relationship with God; or was Stanza 17 the first directly personal one which he wrote, as an immediate and involuntary response to his tears? Either way, it shows his meticulous habit of self-examination. The fact that his tears for the nun had an element of the 'madrigal' in them, of the enjoyment common to children when they submit to a 'good cry', and that his heart was about to enjoy an 'exquisite smart' from his description of the tragedy, seems a truthful enough admittance of what he considered to be unduly selfish, bordering perhaps on the sadistic, pleasure in the subject he was contemplating. (*The Times* account quoted earlier, which triggered him off in the first place, has a potency likely to quicken anyone susceptible to images of violence.) But 'this glee?', the private enjoyment of the heart emitting 'Never-eldering revel and river of youth', was surely as much to do with the sheer enjoyment of placing due words on paper once more ('make words break from me') as illicit response to the subject in hand. Combined, the dual experience must have shaken the citadel of Hopkins's carefully-nurtured selflessness. But, once shaken, it seems there was nothing for it but for him to include the drama of his own submission to God as a parallel theme to his reaction to the wreck of the ship—which he saw as the enactment of God's will; for, despite its indubitable tragedy, the wreck enabled the nuns to make an exemplar of their faith and find glory in heaven.

When he edited and finally published Hopkins's poems in 1918, Bridges described *The Wreck of the Deutschland*, which opens the main section of the book, as 'like a great dragon folded in the gate to forbid all entrance, and confident in his strength from past success'. Here he referred to his own initial avowal that he would not for any money read the poem a second time, for it offended his deepest sensibilities. His objections were twofold: technical, and on grounds of emotional and spiritual good taste.

Hopkins's technique has been examined and explained many times* (and most clearly by himself). Since he had a strong influence on some twentieth-century poets, and since technical permissiveness has long been the norm, that stumbling block no longer looms large. However Hopkins's reasons for wishing to inject new blood into prosody, and his overall method of doing so, give a good deal of insight into his character. What it really amounted to was that he, perhaps more than any other writer, was aware of, and in touch with, the effect of words on the senses, and the power that this placed in the hands of a dextrously manipulative poet.

Bridges once wrote that 'all technique in art consists in devices for the mastery of obstinate material'. Hopkins took almost the opposite course, allowing 'obstinate material' to have its head, but intuitively finding a form for it through a method of expression that engaged his mind, heart, and sense of sound, in unison. It is the difference, if one may use the simile without bathos, between an inflexible rider who trains a high-spirited colt with a restricting double-bridle and unyielding wrists, and a more instinctive man who implements a light snaffle with his voice, thighs, calves and hands. Both will end up with a trained horse, but the latter may find, through releasing the animal's individuality, that he has a champion.

---

* As I. A. Richards wrote: 'It is much easier to measure line-lengths than sprinklings of grace. Moreover, the first is an Examinable activity, the second not.'

Hopkins called his irregular metre 'sprung rhythm' and in his description of his technique (with which he prefaced, *c.* 1883, the manuscript book of his poems later kept by Bridges) he states:

Sprung Rhythm is the most natural of things. For (1) it is the rhythm of common speech and of written prose, when rhythm is perceived in them. (2) It is the rhythm of all but the most monotonously regular music, so that in the words of choruses and refrains and in songs written closely to music it arises. (3) It is found in nursery rhymes, weather saws, and so on; because, however these may have been once made in running rhythm, the terminations having dropped off by the change of language, the stresses come together and so the rhythm is sprung. (4) It arises in common verse when reversed or counterpointed, for the same reason.

Herbert Read believed that he invented the theory of sprung rhythm in order to 'justify his actual powers' for 'there can be no possible doubt—and it is important to emphasise this—that the rhythm of Hopkins's poems, considered individually, was intuitive in origin...' This is supported by Hopkins's later statement to Coventry Patmore that his 'thoughts involuntary moved' and that he did not write from preconceived theories. It was not so much that he 'invented' a theory, as that he had for a long time been fascinated by the sound impact of words, and had amassed a lot of evidence to illustrate his views. When he was actually writing a poem, however, he relied on his ear rather than his notes. Later he began to write a commentary on Greek lyric art which, among other things, was to explore the counterpointing between the 'over-thought' and 'half realised' 'underthought' of so much Greek poetry. Whether he already had this in mind as an example when melding the subjective and objective elements in *The Wreck of the Deutschland*, or whether this happened involuntarily (prompted partly by familiarity with Greek poetry) is again open to question. But that intuition was the over-riding source of his poetry is surely true, and it is one of the reasons why he has remained so popular with a particular audience.

That audience is one which does not mind having its nerve-ends played on; that enjoys the delicate stop and start, crest-of-the-wave rise and packed syntactical descent of Hopkins's unpredictable lines. His rhythms, if they are reminiscent of anything, are similar to those of imaginative sexual touch; not the regular pounding of beat that can make sex, music, poetry or field-work dull, but the inventive cross-rhythms and suspense that may be found in lovemaking, in Beethoven and ragtime, in street rhymes, and in black work-songs where the beat hangs in temporary limbo over the rest bars. (W. H. Gardner wrote that 'Sprung rhythm is, in effect, a synco-pated rhythm, and stands in the same relation to the regular syllabic metres as the prevalent syncopation of modern dance music stands to the regular musical rhythm.')

Bridges would have found such remarks as these insupportable, a dire consequence of the errors of taste that turned him against *The Wreck of the Deutschland*. He summed up these errors as 'mostly efforts to force emotion into theological or sectarian channels'. Bridges's reaction was, of course, coloured by his knowledge of Hopkins, and by his own excursions into emotional religiosity. He now rejected his adolescent Puseyism, and probably felt that Hopkins would have ridden out his Oxford doubts and passions if only he had not become a Catholic and compounded the error by joining the Jesuits. The combination of sensation and religion had become particularly distasteful to him, one of the follies of his youth, and Hopkins presented the combination, not with the allow-ably immature poetizing of a Dolben, but with the intellectual conviction of a mature man. Years of undergoing the *Spiritual Exercises* had sharpened his already keen ability to re-live and describe the sensations of sight, sound, touch, taste and smell; so that, although his natural social and emotional life had been contracted, his mental imagery had received a rare form of fertiliza-tion. Bridges probably thought it had been warped; but some at least of Hopkins's popularity is due to his Ignatian training—though the sensibility on which it was imposed was unique.

Ten years before, at Oxford, he had written *The Half-way House* and *Let me be to Thee as the circling bird* in which he strove to describe the difficulty of making a final dedication to God, and how he needed earthly evidence of His love. Now he could write of God much more directly. The terror and majesty of the divinity had increased, but the relation between earth and heaven seemed closer, and more real. His ways of describing this relation are various. There is the lyrical acceptance:

I kiss my hand
  To the stars, lovely-asunder
Starlight, wafting him out of it; and
  Glow, glory in thunder;
Kiss my hand to the dappled-with-damson west:
Since, tho' he is under the world's splendour and wonder,
  His mystery must be instressed, stressed;
For I greet him the days I meet him, and bless when I understand.

There is the description of a glimpse of heaven, which Hopkins simply fills with his favourite May-time stars and bluebells:

For how to the heart's cheering
  The down-dugged ground-hugged grey
Hovers off, the jay-blue heavens appearing
  Of pied and peeled May!
Bluebeating and hoary-glow height; or night, still higher,
With belled fire and the moth-soft Milky Way . . .

And there is the straining effort to grasp and share the glimpse that the drowning nun may have seen:

But how shall I . . . make me room there:
  Reach me a . . . Fancy, come faster—
Strike you the sight of it? look at it loom there,
  Thing that she . . . there then! the Master,
Ipse, the only one, Christ, King, Head:
He was to cure the extremity where he had cast her;
  Do, deal, lord it with living and dead;
Let him ride, her pride, in his triumph, despatch and have done with his doom there.

The years of pictorial meditation made it possible for him to see Christ on the Kentish Knock, to watch the nun as she died and, in the phrase 'lord it with living and dead', link her relation to Christ with his own, as expressed in the opening lines of the poem:

Thou mastering me
  God! giver of breath and bread;
World's strand, sway of the sea;
  Lord of living and dead . . .

Both relationships have a strong element of physical submission: 'Thou mastering me' and 'Let him ride, her pride, in his triumph'. Hopkins's Christ is not the humane but static figure of a pre-Raphaelite painting, He is the active divinity whose agonised and loving life he had frequently relived, and He is also the being to whom all his strongest emotions were now directed. What he wanted to happen above all things was that Britain, the country which he loved so deeply, should come under Christ's true Catholic rule once again. So he ended the poem with a plea to the nun to intercede in heaven on Britain's behalf, and a prayer of his own delivered in shiningly romantic chivalric phrases:

> Dame, at our door
> Drowned, and among our shoals,
> Remember us in the roads, the heaven-haven of the Reward:
> Our King back, oh, upon English souls!
> Let him easter in us, be a dayspring to the dimness of us, be
> a crimson-cresseted east,
> More brightening her, rare-dear Britain, as his reign rolls,
> Our hearts' charity's hearth's fire, our thought's chivalry's
> throng's Lord.

The Wreck of the Deutschland is not so much a dragon forbidding entry as an intricately-wrought gateway to the workings of Hopkins's imagination and psyche. I. A. Richards remarked of him that 'few writers have dealt more directly with their experience or been more candid', and it is that quality of candour, with the accompanying innovative exactness of its expression, that subsequent generations, without the awkwardness of friendship and personal memory, have valued. Bridges was repulsed by the self-revelatory aspects, and in his own work and life was habitually concerned to check the expression of impulse and to strive towards a reasoned ideal. Suspicious of religious dogma, and of any passion that overwhelmed the rational faculty, he systematically mastered the 'obstinate material' of his life, and closely guarded the secrets of his psyche. Programmed as Hopkins's life was to religious and confessional ritual, his emotions ranged freely within the strict limits set by the cordons of the regime. The result repelled Bridges and made him proclaim that he could not read the poem again for 'any money'. Hopkins sharply reminded him that, besides money, there was love. Such blanket criticism, he declared, was useless; there was no point in his friend trying to reverse his 'whole policy and proceedings'.

But this setback was in the future: Hopkins did not show *The Wreck of the Deutschland* to Bridges until 1877. For the present he prepared to send it to his friend Henry Coleridge, editor of *The Month*. Permission to do so must have been obtained from his Rector, and for a few weeks, in the summer of 1876, he had the satisfaction of having completed a major poem and of believing it would find its natural outlet in the journal of his own Society.

CHAPTER TEN

'The world was saved by virgins'

HOPKINS WAS told that *The Wreck of the Deutschland* would appear in the August issue of *The Month* as long as the accents he had put in to mark the scanning could be deleted. When it did not appear, he tried unsuccessfully to find out whether it would be printed in the September issue. Towards the end of that month he wrote to his mother bidding her to 'sigh no more' about the fate of the poem, and telling her that he was glad it had not appeared, while to his father he admitted that it had cost him much trouble.

When Humphry House enquired in 1944 why the poem had been rejected, he received the following letter from Mgr. J. M. Barton:

The facts, as told to me by my old and dear friend the late Fr. Sydney Fenn Smith, S.J. [1842-1922], were these. The editor at that time was Fr. Henry Coleridge, a convert clergyman and a scholar of the old-fashioned classical type. He read the poem and could not understand it, and he did not relish publishing any poem that he himself could not master. He then handed the poem to Sydney Smith who did his best to master the author's elaborate system of diacritical signs. But it was not of any service to him. He told me that the short line 'Thou hadst glory of this nun?' was one that he read and read again, without ever being sure that he was reading it with the exact rhythm desired by G. M. H. In the end, as he said to me, 'the only result was to give me a very bad headache, and to lead me to hand the poem back to Fr. Coleridge with the remark that it was indeed unreadable.' This conversation may well have been in 1918 or 1919, after the publication of the *Poems*.

—and therefore forty years after the poem was written, so that the substance of this evidence may not be absolutely exact. Anecdotally the idea of the poor father making himself ill over the ambiguities (rhythmical or otherwise) of 'Thou hadst glory of this nun?' now has its comic side, but this rejection—however well meant—of

Hopkins's mature work by the Society was, in the long run, a tragedy for him.

He had warned Coleridge in advance that he would dislike the poem, but Coleridge had replied that he knew there was a new sort of poetry in America that did not rhyme or scan or construe, and as long as Hopkins's poem did those three things, made sense, and contained no bad morality, it should be acceptable. Hopkins—who had read one or two poems by Walt Whitman—did not feel his own poetry was influenced by Whitman's freedom in either morality or technique. (That he privately regarded him as a kindred spirit, however, was to be revealed in a letter to Bridges a few years later, see p. 207.) Two years after the rejection, when Hopkins's correspondence with Canon Dixon was just beginning, he explained to him that, although *The Month* had at first accepted the poem, they changed their mind and 'dared not print it'. Its composition had, however, enabled him to feel he could continue to write, just so long as he did not spend any considerable time upon it.

On 12 June he was one of the two defendants in that term's theological disputation; its subject is known to have been concerned with the sacrament, and Hopkins would have spoken in Latin, stating and defending his thesis and then answering objections. A week later he wrote the fragment *Moonrise* (137, RB 65), presumably as a direct result of rising very early and watching the waning moon:

I awoke in the Midsummer not to call night, in the white and the
    walk of the morning:
The moon, dwindled and thinned to the fringe of a finger-nail
    held to the candle,
Or paring of paradisaïcal fruit . . .

And two weeks later came *The Woodlark* (138, RB 64) in which he identified with the small bird flying joyfully over ripe corn and 'crush-silk poppies', sunspurge and oxeye, until the feeling of good and celebration was exhausted and it dropped down to its nest. The poem was never completed, being disordered fragments on a single small sheet of notepaper in memory of a sudden moment of happiness at the sound of birdsong and sight of fields near harvest time.

A celebration for the Bishop of Shrewsbury's episcopal silver jubilee was to be held at St Beuno's at the end of July. By April it had been decided to present the bishop with an album of verses and prose addresses, the former in many languages. A German student with a nose like a bugle horn supplied verses in Chinese and Manchu written in a beautiful script. Hopkins was the only member of the community who could write in Welsh, and he composed *Cywydd* (172) in which he expressed the hope that the work of the bishop would help to convert the men of north-west Wales. He also supplied some Latin verses for the album, but their original opening had to be scrapped because others found them unintelligible. (This was due to the tortuousness of his imagery rather than any deficiency in his superiors' Latin.) And his skills were called upon a third time to supply a poem, *The Silver Jubilee* (29, RB 6), which was set to music and sung as a glee during dessert at the celebratory dinner. The poem was printed, together with the commemorative sermon preached by John Morris, lecturer in history at St Beuno's, by Burns & Lambert the Catholic publishers. Morris wished to use 'The Silver Jubilee' as his title, but would only do so if Hopkins allowed his poem to appear too. This small recognition probably pleased him, and shows that—apart from Francis Bacon who admired his work as a whole—there were others at St Beuno's who took an interest in his occasional poetry.

In mid-August he went to Barmouth for the traditional holiday, and one morning with some others rowed up the river Mawddach to 'The George', where they had breakfast. They remained there for a few hours until the ebb tide would facilitate their return, and Hopkins probably wrote his first draft of *Penmaen Pool* (30, RB 5), which carried the inscription 'For the Visitor's Book at the Inn'. The beer apparently pleased him; following the mildly defiant and parenthetical aside, '(who'll / Not honour it?)', he described it as 'ale like goldy foam / That frocks an oar in Penmaen Pool'.

On their return from holiday, the community were told that Jones had been appointed Provincial and was leaving for London immediately; his post of Rector was taken by Gallwey, who arrived a week later. Hopkins was no doubt pleased to be once more under the guidance of Gallwey, who, according to his biographer Michael Gavin, 'noted and encouraged signs of exceptional ability in younger men, and left nothing undone to develop them'. He was not at all lax, however, and tightened up the discipline in the college, insisting that all students should consult a professor or superior 'on the advisability of reading this or that author or book', and should remember the rules concerning silence and speaking in Latin. In

mid-September he requested that they should not walk in the
garden after dark. Perhaps he felt the unlit dells and winding paths
might provide undue opportunity for unguarded conversation or
friendship.

Hopkins apparently wrote several letters to various friends, aunts
and other relatives at Christmas without receiving replies, so he was
particularly pleased to get a spontaneous letter from Baillie. His
pleasure was compounded by the fact that Baillie had recently
returned in good health from North Africa, whither he had been
sent to die after a bad lung haemorrhage. The untroubled affection
he had always felt for Baillie shows in the last paragraph of
Hopkins's reply, where he announced that he would like to record
and acknowledge the fact that Baillie had always been so kind to
him, much more so than he deserved since his own nature and
behaviour was 'blackguardly' compared to those of his friend. The
appellation 'blackguard', when referring to himself or his verses,
was to become quite obsessive. Since the word means 'a criminal'
or 'unprincipled scoundrel', and since Hopkins did not use words
lightly, it indicates how unsatisfactory he still found his persona
and behaviour. It also indicates—there being no evidence of outward scoundrelly behaviour—that the life of his mind and imagination continued to gainsay his scruples.

In February he heard briefly from Bridges for the first time for
two years. It seems that Bridges was reluctant to write at length for
fear of his letter being opened: he suggested, however, that he could
write a long and interesting one, and could send Hopkins some
pamphlets he had published. Hopkins told him that it was unreasonable and superstitious of him to mind about the cursory letter
inspection, and that he could send the pamphlets right away without
waiting to write. He was very curious to find out their contents.
Bridges had addressed him by his surname, and in a postscript
Hopkins asked him to return to his old custom of using his
Christian name, which he liked better. In 1867, also in a postscript,
he had explained that while Bridges sometimes used his Christian
name he would continue to use his friend's surname, since it felt
more natural and was 'the prettier' name. He almost invariably
from 1877 addressed both Bridges and Baillie as 'dearest'.

During these early months of 1877 Hopkins was studying for the
examination in moral theology. It was bitterly cold inside the college,
and the battle to keep the students' rooms at a bearable temperature

appears to have been a losing one. The Minister's log records that 'at consultation all were agreed that something should be done to guard against the danger to which students' health is exposed, but what?' In some of the rooms the temperature could not be raised above 46°. One student even suffered 'a rush of blood to the head' which the doctor put down to excessive cold. During Lent Hopkins fasted only once a week, but he became excessively tired as a result of continual, and hurried, revision. However he still managed to dash off 'in a freak' *God's Grandeur* (31, RB 7) and *The Starlight Night* (32, RB 8) on consecutive days in late February, and send them to his mother on her birthday, 3 March. They were the first sonnets he had written for nearly twelve years.

Bearing in mind that Gallwey had objected to students walking in the garden after dark, one presumes that *The Starlight Night* must have been the result of Hopkins leaning out of a window, or returning late from some engagement. It contains sixteen exclamations, revealing that despite his weariness he still experienced moments of ecstasy, and could sustain the memory of the feeling long enough to assemble appropriate words. 'Look at the stars! look, look up at the skies!' It is a poem that eagerly embraces the magnificence of a clear sky filled with stars—'bright boroughs', 'circle-citadels'.

God's Grandeur, Hopkins said, might almost have been written especially to use the image of God's grandeur flaming out 'like shining from shook foil'. This memory of lightning (that always excited and disturbed him), the undertone of weaponry (echoed in the phrase 'Why do men then now not reck his rod?'), shows his absolute view of God as the great, and invigorating, master. *The Starlight Night* has the more domestic image of Christ, enclosed by the stars, 'Christ and his mother and all his hallows' (saints). In both the poems nature supplies the fruitful, sensuous imagery:

> nature is never spent;
> There lives the dearest freshness deep down things;

and

> The grey lawns cold where gold, where quickgold lies!
> Wind-beat whitebeam! airy abeles set on a flare!
> Flake-doves sent floating forth at a farmyard scare!

(Whitebeam is a tree, the white undersides of whose leaves are revealed when blown by the wind; and abeles are white poplars.)

And what about man? He is mentioned only as the destroyer of environment and rejector of God:

> all is seared with trade; bleared, smeared with toil;
> And wears man's smudge and shares man's smell . . .

Loss of man's contact with nature is symbolised by the fact that he no longer walks barefoot and touches the soil. (Hopkins had a predilection for the benefits of going barefoot.)

These sonnets contain a précis in images of his view, when happy, of the world: God as master, Christ domesticised with his virgin mother, nature fresh and fruitful, man in need of redemption. And over this version of the world the Holy Ghost 'broods with warm breast and with ah! bright wings'. Psychologically it is tidy and, for the moment, Hopkins's presence is that of an observer, acknowledging his debt to nature's munificence with 'Prayer, patience, alms, vows'. His own doubts and temptations are—just for this brief interlude in February, in cold Wales, while he anticipates the spring—absent.

On the same day that he posted these sonnets to his mother, he took his examination in moral theology 'to see whether I am fit to hear confessions'. He then had to prepare a sermon for the following Sunday, 11 March, and its reception demonstrated all too clearly the difficulties he was to get into as a preacher. Disconcertingly, he had to stop before he reached the end because people were laughing 'prodigiously': some were even rolling in their chairs. Since the sermon does not contain any jokes, and since he was speaking to a religious community and not a gathering of ribalds, this effect was a serious one.

The sermon was about the feeding of the five thousand. Hopkins tried, in the Ignatian tradition, to make his audience picture the event as clearly as possible by comparing the Sea of Galilee with the Clwyd Valley. His method of doing so no doubt engendered the first suppressed feelings of hilarity. The sea, he claimed, was shaped like a man's left ear, with the river Jordan entering at the upper rim and exiting by the lobe. Imagining the ear to be in place on a head, various towns were then positioned, as it were, in the hair, on the cheek, and in the ear, and these Palestinian towns could be related in position to those bordering the Clwyd. The combination of Hopkins's packed and urgent detail, as he developed his convoluted narrative, and the almost childish way he extended his images, was clearly too much for an audience who were anyway used to him in the occasional role of humorist. By the time he came to the paragraph which depended for its impact on the repetition of Jesus's request to Andrew to 'Make the men sit down', the congregation was out of control and half-way through it Hopkins had to stop.

Two weeks later, during the Easter holidays, he was given leave to go to stay with John Jones, a priest in Caernarvon, in order to improve his Welsh—Jones being the only Catholic priest who could preach in that language. The original plan was that he should stay a fortnight, but he had to return after three days because of 'a misfortune' which occurred to Jones's servant. Gallwey had presumably decided that it would be advisable for Hopkins to concentrate on developing his ability with Welsh to a practical end, and at the same time to have a spell away from what apparently rather too easily developed into an hysterical atmosphere within the college community. His holiday being thus curtailed, he had the small compensation of a day's outing in the college's pony trap with two others.

Some days later he developed a cold and cough, and thought he was growing even thinner than usual. Nevertheless, during April he completed various pieces of work. There was a presentation poem written in Latin (174) on St George's Day for Thomas Burke, the Dominican orator, who came to St Beuno's for a retreat. There was another sermon (subject unknown) preached during dinner on 26 April. Then two days later he read a paper at the recently established Essay Society which met on alternate Saturdays. The subject of his essay was 'The composition of place in the Spiritual Exercises' and the records of the Essay Society give this summary of its content:

> The essayist maintained that 1° the composition was always of a real, never of a fictitious place—2° it is not principally intended to keep the mind from wandering or to assist the imagination— 3° Its true object is to make the Exercitant present in spirit at the scenes, persons, etc., so that they may really act on him and he on them.

This gives direct proof of how singlemindedly Hopkins approached this mental discipline, as his 'Make the men sit down' sermon, and *The Wreck of the Deutschland*, have already indicated.

But perhaps the most important piece of writing he accomplished during that April, was a letter he wrote to Bridges on the 3rd. The 'pamphlets' which Bridges had mentioned turned out to be a Latin poem about the history of St Bartholomew's Hospital, and *The Growth of Love*, a sonnet sequence published anonymously. Anyone tempted to reproach Bridges for the outspoken way he objected to much of Hopkins's poetry should perhaps remember that the tone of their critical exchange was set by Hopkins in this letter. Although he complained of lack of time and overwhelming tiredness, he set about his friend's poems with a terrier-like agility and thoroughness. But (and we do not know if the same could be said of Bridges's letters) the criticism was interlaced with encouragement and love. He thought the sonnets were 'full of manly tenderness and a flowing and never failing music' and he was proud of Bridges for writing them. However, he added, that did not mean that Bridges should be proud for himself, being already quite enough given to conceit. The letter enclosing the pamphlets had evidently discussed the subject of rhythm and metre, and when elaborating on this in his reply Hopkins suddenly seized the opportunity to announce that he had recently composed two experimental sonnets 'which I think I will presently enclose'.

Bridges's first publications could not have come at a better time, coinciding as they did with Hopkins's rebirth as a poet and establishing a ground for their relationship that could, by and large, operate outside the strictures of Jesuit life and Bridges's objections thereto.

May was always a special month for Hopkins, even before he became a Catholic and it took on the special significance of being Mary's month. It was the time of the bluebell, of birds' nests and pear blossom; a season of sweet fecundity. And indeed it is the almost perfect month, the brief span when green leaves and white blossom permeate the English (or Welsh) landscape, and there is still no hint of summer's over-ripeness or autumn's decay. It is possible to stand in a field in May and feel that youth and freshness comprise the world. The May of 1877 was no exception. It was the culmination of what Hopkins later described to Bridges as 'my salad days ... my Welsh days', and during it he wrote *Spring* (33, RB 9), *In the Valley of the Elwy* (34, RB 16), *The Sea and the Skylark* (35, RB 11), and *The Windhover* (36, RB 12). The latter he referred to in 1879 as 'the best thing I ever wrote'.

His health was still not good, and part of the month he spent by the sea in Rhyl. The poems are a consummation of his now-familiar themes, briefly summarised here, with the quotations identified by the poem's number in the fourth OUP edition.

Spring was perfect, counterpoised exactly between innocence and fertility:

> What is all this juice and all this joy?
> A strain of the earth's sweet being in the beginning
> In Eden garden.
>
> (33)

The ecstatic rise of feeling brought about by experiencing God's lovely world, and the subsequent distancing from man's 'sordid turbid time' (35), is expressed—as so often before—by identification with the movement and song of birds.

> Through the echoing timber does so rinse and wring
> The ear, it strikes like lightnings to hear him sing;
>
> (33)

Or, unconsciously mirroring sexual gratification:

> I hear the lark ascend,
> His rash-fresh re-winded new-skeinèd score
> In crisps of curl off wild winch whirl, and pour
> And pelt music, till none's to spill nor spend.   (35)

And finally, the ease of the falcon, master of the air:

> striding
> High there, how he rung upon the rein of a wimpling wing
> In his ecstasy! then off, off forth on swing ...   (36)

In three of the poems, the dichotomy between man's graceless, sinful state and nature's rapture is not bridged:

> Have, get, before it cloy,
> Before it cloud, Christ, lord, and sour with sinning,
> Innocent mind and Mayday in girl and boy ...
>
> (33)

The inhabitants of Wales's lovely 'woods, waters, meadows, combes, vales' (34) are incomplete, unworthy of their setting. And, in Rhyl, the sea and the skylark 'shame this shallow and frail town' with their purity.

Only in *The Windhover* does a synthesis, a transformation, occur. Here the exhilaration is caused by the sight of the falcon, an exhilaration which has stirred Hopkins's suppressed affections into a transport of joy. But, as he praises the freedom and bravery of the bird, so he commands himself to crush ('buckle') the sensations aroused by the qualities of 'Brute beauty and valour', for only by so doing will he be ready to receive Christ. Just as the 'blue-bleak embers' of a fading fire topple and break open into red and gold, so will his restraint and sacrifice lead through pain to the revelation of his intrepid love for Christ—'O my chevalier!' It is a metaphor for sexual suppression. It is a great love poem. It is Hopkins combining his passion for nature and love of chivalry into an expression of ecstasy for his lord; the only ecstasy permitted during his earthly existence when he had deliberately placed his 'heart in hiding' lest it be subject to temptation.

He was now nearing the end of his third year at St Beuno's, and normally he would have stayed to do a fourth. From the references to his health, and the number of daytrips he made to Rhyl, it would seem his superiors were concerned about him, and it was decided to curtail his theology course. It may simply have been that they considered he had studied long enough (Lahey claims he left St Beuno's 'with the reputation of being one of the best moral theologians among his contemporaries'); or it may be that his enthusiasm for Scotus was developing his thought in a direction they did not approve. Whatever the reason, he took his final examination on 24 July, and the next day travelled home to Oak Hill for a holiday.

He was in London for nearly three weeks, spending one night with Bridges who was living with his lately widowed mother. It was their first extended meeting since Hopkins became a novice. Bridges continued to pass faintly sardonic remarks about the Jesuit regime, and Hopkins did not invite him back to Oak Hill because he thought he 'would not care to come', but nevertheless their friendship seems to have been strengthened by the meeting. Before returning to Wales, Hopkins sent him a copy of *The Wreck of the Deutschland*. He was back at St Beuno's when he received Bridges's reactions. These included the stricture that he would not read the poem again for any money, and a parody of sprung rhythm. Hopkins's comment on the former was Forsterian: 'Besides money, you know, there is love'. So was another of his remarks; Bridges had inquired if he might call the style 'presumptious jugglery', to which Hopkins replied 'No' but only because 'presumptious is not English'. The whole reply, jauntily—but not hysterically jauntily—countering the outright rejection of a masterpiece, is itself a colloquial masterpiece.

Bridges's comments did not throw Hopkins into a fit of despair; if anything, they seemed to put him on his mettle. Eleven days after countering the criticisms, he wrote the (even for him) incredibly erotic and joyful *Hurrahing in Harvest* (38, RB 14). Initially it was called *Heart's Hurrahing in Harvest* and he said it 'was the outcome of half an hour of extreme enthusiasm as I walked home alone one day from fishing in the Elwy'. The date was 1 September, three weeks before he was to be ordained. It is a love song to Christ and to the Welsh hills.

> . . . I walk, I lift up, I lift up heart, eyes,
>   Down all that glory in the heavens to glean our Saviour;
> And, eyes, heart, what looks, what lips yet gave you a
>   Rapturous love's greeting of realer, of rounder replies?
>
> And the azurous hung hills are his world-wielding shoulder
>   Majestic—as a stallion stalwart, very-violet-sweet!—
> These things, these things were here and but the beholder
>   Wanting; which two when they once meet,
> The heart rears wings bold and bolder
>   And hurls for him, O half hurls earth for him off under his
>   feet.

Bridges considered the stallion metaphor an error 'of what may be called taste'—which, in conventional terms, it probably is: Hopkins was very taken by the potency of horses. One of his diary confessions, in the emotional spring of 1865, had been about looking at, and thinking about, a stallion. This shows at what a childish stage his sexual curiosity had been censored. And it also shows that twelve years later he was able to transmute these juvenile stimulations unselfconsciously.

There was a six-day retreat before the ordination ceremonies which Hopkins shared with fifteen others. They took place over three days, the major orders of subdeacon, deacon and priesthood being conferred on successive days in accordance with Jesuit practice. The final day was a Sunday, 23 September. The ordinands were allowed to sleep until eight, and after the ceremony there was a festive luncheon. The tables were decorated with fruit and flowers, and the menu included soup, roast mutton, ham, fowl and tongue. Afterwards there was an impromptu concert, and more music in the late evening after dinner. Interestingly, 23 September is the feast day of St Thecla, a virgin-martyr to whom Hopkins had written part of a poem which carries no date but was probably composed in 1866. The story goes that Thecla, on hearing St Paul preach on the beauty of chastity, had left her would-be bridegroom to follow the apostle; over the years she suffered much persecution until, at the age of ninety, when local medical men came to torment her in her hermit's cave, the rock opened to receive and save her. Hopkins's fragment deals with the early part of the story, describing Thecla's beauty and the effect of Paul's words in praise of continence, particularly the slogan: 'The world was saved by virgins.' It is a legend which illustrates perfectly his obsession with beauty that is constrained just at the point when it is ripe for consummation. Certainly the significance of being ordained on St Thecla's day would not have escaped him.

The next recorded event in his life is a curious one. Six days after the ordination, Hopkins was circumcised by a Dr Turnour and a Denbigh house surgeon. The reason was apparently medical, the ritual practice of circumcision having been banned by Pope Eugenius IV in 1441.

While he was in bed for a week recovering from the operation, he heard that his grandfather had died at Croydon. He wrote to his mother saying he was glad that she and her brothers and sisters had witnessed his peaceful end, and stating his own position and actions as a Catholic with regard to the death. It gives a clear picture of his fundamental feeling of estrangement from his family, no matter how friendly the relations between them had become.

He told his mother that for years he had daily recommended his grandfather (and, presumably, the rest of the family) 'to the Blessed Virgin's protection', and this fact gave him deep consolation and some hope. He had asked some members of the community to pray for his grandfather while he was ill, and in a letter to a friend had mentioned he would take it as a 'happy token' if he died on the Feast of the Holy Rosary, the anniversary of the Holy League's victory at Lepanto, following the supposed intervention of the Virgin. This turned out to be the day he did die, and Hopkins accepted it 'without questioning' as a sign his prayers had been heard and his grandfather's soul saved. It was, he said, perhaps the seventh time he had received a sign from heaven concerning the deaths of people he knew. He probably expected no comment on this from his mother, but set out the information very deliberately, telling her to make of it 'what you like'. None of his family had been present for his ordination.

In the same letter he told her he had been ill, but not the cause, and explained that when he was better he would be sent to Mount St Mary's College in Chesterfield. The work—some academic, some clerical—would, he said, be 'nondescript': a lackadaisical adjective to describe his first posting as a priest. But the prospect, and execution, of classroom teaching seldom gladdened him, and he had become very attached to North Wales—'the true Arcadia of wild beauty' as he later described it to Coventry Patmore.

G

CHAPTER ELEVEN

Fame and feeling

HOPKINS WAS posted to Mount St Mary's College for two terms only. During that time he complained to his mother of overwork—one of the other masters was sick and he had to add his duties to his own—and to Bridges that he was weakened by persistent diarrhoea, which his friend offered to come and cure. Hopkins was touched by the offer, but added that he could not possibly accept it.

Life was not entirely without reward, however. His best pupil, Herbert Berkeley, both carried off an inter-schools prize and put in a creditable performance as Lady Macbeth (this time transformed into Macbeth's younger brother Fergus rather than his uncle Donald). Hopkins wrote a deliberately farcical prologue to the play which Berkeley performed so energetically that some of the audience decided he must have been drunk. Hopkins was fond of his pupils, but there was little time for his own work and he described his muse as 'turned utterly sullen' in the air made murky by factory smoke.

He kept a strict Lent in 1878, and told his mother that he was thinner than ever before and that his cheeks resembled 'two harp-frames'. It was during Lent that another shipwreck prompted him to write his first poem since leaving Wales—*The Loss of the Eurydice* (41,RB 17). She was a training ship which sank off the Isle of Wight in a sudden storm on 28 March, losing all but two of her crew of three hundred. The first verses Hopkins wrote down described the manly beauty of a drowned sailor. These verses were later incorporated in the middle of the poem as stanzas 19–21. He had apparently heeded Bridges's remarks that the *Deutschland* would have been more interesting 'if there were more wreck and less discourse', and this time his friend found much to praise—though he also criticised what he felt were obscurities and affectations. Hopkins insisted that if the poem was read aloud it became clear, but later did admit that when he just glanced at it with his eyes (rather than listening with his ears) he was aghast at its 'raw naked-ness and unmitigated violence'.

At the end of April he was posted to Stonyhurst for a term to coach some degree students, and it was from there, on an impulse, that he sat down on 4 June and wrote his first letter to Canon Richard Dixon, whose poems he had first read when he was a student at Oxford. The letter reveals how deeply he loved to be moved by poetry, and how much he was still attracted to the romantic aura of Victorian medievalism, despite the radical developments in his own work:

Very Rev. Sir,—I take the liberty as a stranger in addressing you, nevertheless I did once have some slight acquaintance with you. You will not remember me but you will remember taking a mastership for some months at Highgate School, the Cholmondeley School, where I then was. When you went away you gave, as I recollect, a copy of your book *Christ's Company* to one of the masters, a Mr Law if I am not mistaken. By this means coming to know its name I was curious to read it, which when I went to Oxford I did. At first I was surprised at it, then pleased, at last I became so fond of it that I made it, so far as that could be, a part of my own mind. I got your other volume and your little prize essay too. I introduced your poems to my friends, and, if they did not share my own enthusiasm, made them at all events admire. And to show you how greatly I prized them, when I entered my present state of life, in which I knew I could have no books of my own and was unlikely to meet with your works in the libraries I should have access to, I copied out *St Paul, St John, Love's Consolation*, and others from both volumes and keep them by me.

What I am saying now I might, it is true, have written any time these many years back, but partly I hesitated, partly I was not sure you were yet living; lately however I saw in the *Athenaeum* a review of your historical work newly published and since have made up my mind to write to you—which, to be sure, is an impertinence if you like to think it so, but I seemed to owe you something or a great deal, and then I knew what I should feel myself in your position, if I had written and published works, the extreme beauty of which the author himself the most keenly feels, and they had fallen out of sight at once and been (you will not mind my saying it, as it is, I suppose, plainly true) almost wholly unknown; then, I say, I should feel a certain comfort to be told they had been deeply appreciated by some one person, a stranger, at all events and had not been published quite in vain. Many beautiful works have been almost unknown and then have gained fame at last, as Mr Wells's poem of *Joseph*, which is said to be very fine, and his friend Keats' own, but many more must have been lost sight of altogether. I do not know of course whether your books are going to have a revival, it seems not likely, but not for want of deserving. It is not that I think a man really the less happy because he has missed the renown which was his due, but still when this happens it is an evil in itself and a thing which ought not to be and that I deplore for the good work's sake rather than the author's.

Your poem had a mediaeval colouring like William Morris's and the Rossettis' and others, but none seemed to me to have it so unaffectedly. I thought the tenderness of *Love's Consolation* no one living could surpass, nor the richness of colouring in the *Wolfsbane* and other passages (it is a mistake, I think, and you meant henbane) in that and *Mark and Rosalys*, nor the brightness of the apple-orchard landscape in *Mother and Daughter*. And the *Tale of Dauphiny* and 'It is the time to tell of fatal love' (I forget the title) in the other book are purer in style, as it seems to me, and quite as fine in colouring and drawing as Morris's stories in the *Paradise*, so far as I have read them, fine as those are. And if I were making up a book of English poetry I should put your *Ode to Summer* next to Keats' on *Autumn* and the *Nightingale* and *Grecian Urn*. I do not think anywhere two stanzas so crowded with the pathos of nature and landscape could be found (except perhaps there are some in Wordsworth) as the little song of the *Feathers of the Willow*: a tune to it came to me quite naturally. The extreme delight I felt when I read the line 'Her eyes like lilies shaken by the bees' was more than any single line in poetry ever gave me and now that I am older I could not be so strongly moved by it if I were to read it for the first time. I have said all this, and could if there were any use say more, as a sort of duty of charity to make up, so far as one voice can do, for the disappointment you must, at least at times, I think, have felt over your rich and exquisite work almost thrown away. You will therefore feel no offence, though you may surprise, at my writing. I am, very Rev. Sir, your obedient servant Gerard M. Hopkins, S.J.

If there is any truth in the guess made earlier that the 'extreme delight' Hopkins felt at the line 'Her eyes like lilies shaken by the bees' had a connection with Dolben, then it may be significant that this letter was written on the Fourth of June, the day of the annual Eton College celebrations. What undoubtedly did appeal to Hopkins in Dixon's poetry, besides his intensity of feeling for Christianity, chivalry and nature, was his conception of earthly love as an irresistible and irrational passion, to which man falls involuntary victim and against which he struggles towards ascetic spirituality. These lines are from *Love's Consolation*, the poem Hopkins thought 'no one living could surpass' in tenderness:

All who have loved, be sure of this from me,
That to have touched one little ripple free
Of golden hair, or held a little hand
Very long since, is better than to stand
Rolled up in vestures stiff with golden thread,
Upon a throne o'er many a bowing head
Of adulators; yea, and to have seen
Thy lady walking in a garden green,
Mid apple blossoms and green twisted boughs,
Along the golden gravel path, to house
Herself, where thou art watching far below,
Deep in thy bower impervious, even though
Thou never give her kisses after that,
Is sweeter than to never break the flat
Of thy soul's rising, like a river tide
That never foams; yea, if thy lady chide
Cruelly thy service, and indeed becomes
A wretch, whose false eyes haunt thee in all rooms,
'Tis better so, than never to have been
An hour in love; than never to have seen
Thine own heart's worthiness to shrink and shake,
Like silver quick, all for thy lady's sake,
Weighty with truth, with gentleness as bright.
  Moreover, let sad lovers take delight
In this, that time will bring at last their peace:
We watch great passions in their huge increase,
Until they fill our hearts, so that we say,
'Let go this, and I die;' yet nay and nay,

We find them leave us strangely quiet then,
When they must quit; one lion leaves the den,
Another enters; wherefore thus I cross
All lovers pale and starving with their loss.
    And yet, and yet, and yet, how long I tore
My heart, O love! how long, O love! before
I could endure to think of peace, and call
For remedy, from what time thou didst all
Shatter with one bad word, and bitter ruth
Didst mete me for my patience and my truth.
That way thou hadst: once, cutting like a knife,
Thy hand sheared off what seemed my very life,
And I felt outside coldness bite within:
The lumpish axe that scales away false skin
Of some corruption clumped upon the bark,
Leaves the tree aching with the pale round mark,
And sweating till the wound be overshot
By the gums swelling out into a blot,
Where the bees lose their wings, and dead leaves stick.
Even so, O love, my flesh was sore and quick
From that astonishment, when I seemed flayed,
Torn piecemeal up, and shred abroad, and made
A victim to some brutal lack of skill;
Yet kissing still the hand so rough to kill.
So, so; I never meant but to live on
The old, old way; now the old life is gone—
Has it?—and left me living!

Hopkins's impulse turned out to be a good one; the attraction he felt to Dixon's poems was not marred by acquaintance with the character of their author.

Richard Dixon, born in 1833, had been to school with Edward Burne-Jones and at Oxford they both became members of the Ruskin-influenced idealistic Brotherhood which included William Morris. When Rossetti joined the group, Dixon fell completely under his spell, and he was one of the people involved in the painting of the famous Union murals. His friendship with the pre-Raphaelites gave him intense happiness—nothing could ever equal those elysian days—but his involvement had to end. He had neither the talent nor the income to survive as a professional artist,

and he took Holy Orders and became an underpaid and overworked
curate in Lambeth. At the time Hopkins wrote to him he was
forty-five, a recent widower, living with two step-daughters in
Hayton Vicarage near Carlisle. His poetry was, as Hopkins had
remarked, neglected, and he suffered chronic ill-health from
bronchitis. A gentle, self-deprecating man, the arrival of such an
ardent fan letter moved him deeply. In his reply he said:

> ... I was talking to my friend Burne Jones the painter a while
> ago, about three weeks: who said among other things, 'One only
> works in reality for the one man who may rise to understand one,
> it may be ages hence'. I am happy in being understood in my life-
> time. To think that you have revolved my words, so as to make
> them part of yourself, and have actually copied out some of
> them, being denied books, is to me indescribably affecting.
>
> I think I remember you in Highgate School. At least I
> remember a pale young boy, very light and active, with a very
> meditative and intellectual face, whose name, if I am not vastly
> mistaken, was yours. If I am not deceived by memory, that boy
> got a prize for English poetry.
>
> ... I may just add that I received a letter of warm & high
> approbation & criticism from Rossetti (whom you mention in
> your letter) about three years ago, when he read my poems,
> which he had not seen before. Beside that letter I place yours.

They continued to discuss in their letters the subject of renown
raised initially by Hopkins. Dixon pointed out some of the dis-
advantages of instant fame, and Hopkins reiterated his belief that
recognition of the work itself was a separate consideration from
recognition of its author. Each moral act (which included the writing
of poetry) deserved reward or punishment, and he very much
regretted the countless acts that went unwitnessed and therefore
unjudged. He did not duck the issue of personal fame, remarking
that lack of it might be as harmful to artists as excess, slightly
misquoting Milton's 'Fame is the spur that the clear spirit doth
rise ... To scorn delights and live laborious days'. He added that it
was very hard for an artist to do without that spur or to find a
substitute, but made it quite clear that he believed that for a man
who wished to enter heaven, fame was a great danger. The judgement of the public was in any case, he felt, arbitrary—Christ being
the only just literary critic. The only worthwhile praise therefore

was that which perhaps conveyed to the author some token of the possibility of Christ's approval. Hopkins hoped that this is what his praise to Dixon had done, for he knew that neglect caused embitterment and 'an aching in the very bones'. His struggle against this embitterment must have begun with *The Month*'s rejections of the *Deutschland* and the *Eurydice*. And, despite his belief that any fruits of talent were God's gift and should be dedicated solely back to Him in a spirit of sacrifice, his earthly rejection introduced an insidious corrosion into his supply of creative energy.

After a few weeks at Stonyhurst, he was directed to the Farm Street church in Mayfair where Gallwey was now Rector. Initially his only specific duty was to prepare three sermons to be delivered during August, and with his usual hesitations and scruples he arranged some meetings with Bridges. The latter even came to hear his first sermon, which Hopkins claimed to have delivered badly, with a fluster of nervousness at the beginning. He said he would welcome any criticisms of it from his friend 'which are not controversy'. Another sermon, preached to a congregation of women, came in for severe criticism from his superior: in it he employed an image likening the Church to a cow with full udders whose seven teats were like the seven sacraments, which must have deeply shocked any prudish hearers. His disregard for conventional good taste, and obstinate endeavour to achieve a full-blooded, original style, free of either mawkishness or bluster, allied with his tendency to physical frailness and nervous depression, made him an awkward priest to guide into a path of consistent development.

At first he had expected to remain permanently in Mayfair, though admitted to Bridges that 'permanence with us is gingerbread permanence; cobweb, soapsud and frost-feather permanence'. By October he was writing to Dixon that he had a good deal of time to himself but found he could do very little with it: he did not seem able to settle to any systematic programme of study, and wrote no poetry. One friend from the past who lived nearby and came to the church regularly was Edgell, Dolben's friend and admirer. Then in December Gallwey told him that he was to be sent to the parish church of St Aloysius in Oxford. Perhaps he hoped that Oxford would prove more congenial to Hopkins, and stabilise his spirits.

In fact, he found it most unsettling. He half-wished there would be no familiar University faces from his student days, and half-wanted to be accepted by his old friends. Some were welcoming—

including Pater—but others were cold, demonstrating their conventional distrust of Catholics in general and Jesuits in particular. Hopkins expressed the dichotomy to Baillie by saying that he found Oxford uncongenial, and yet that not to love his University 'would be to undo the very buttons of my being'. One remembers those early, breathless undergraduate letters to his mother—'Except for much work and that I can never keep my hands cool, I am almost too happy'—and contrasts the thirty-four-year-old priest, saddened by the fact that the townspeople were so stiff and respectful, making it seem as though a joke made by a Jesuit would 'put them to deep and lasting pain'. He tried to make up for it by writing amusingly to his mother about aspects of Oxford life, including the lectures in the Sheldonian Theatre on organ music, given and illustrated by Sir Gore Ouseley—a name which, Hopkins suggested, would get transformed by the satirist William Mallock into Sir Bloodclot Reekswell. Sir Gore tended to weep over his own playing, and tried to bully the audience into agreeing with his opinion on certain pieces, 'but we were naughty and would not'.

Despite drawbacks, the ten months in Oxford were quite fruitful ones. Hopkins's letters to Bridges became more intimate, and by introducing him to Dixon's poems—and vice versa—he initiated a friendship which culminated in 1909 with Bridges's memoir of Dixon to accompany a selection of his poems. And despite the fact that his superior, Father Thomas Parkinson (with whom he 'did not quite hit it off'), was for a time laid up first with a broken collar bone and then eczema, thus devolving all the parish duties on to him, he wrote a fair amount of poetry. Yet at the beginning of 1879 he had made it clear to Bridges that he was unlikely to write much more. This followed an apparent suggestion by Bridges that he should ask Edmund Gosse to make a reference to Hopkins's poems in one of his articles—presumably with the intention of stimulating an interest in their future publication. Hopkins could not agree to this; the only publication he could entertain must be at the suggestion of someone in authority in the Society, and that now seemed very unlikely. The one thing he could consider doing was to keep his poems together in one place in case anyone should like to publish them after his death—though he also thought that was very unlikely too. In the end, of course, it was to be Bridges who kept the fullest collection of the manuscripts, and Bridges who organised their posthumous publication nearly forty years later.

There seems to be a paradox here: that Hopkins could accept that his authorities would not publish the poems during his lifetime, but that it might be appropriate to do so after his death. Does this mean that he felt publication was withheld because it was considered to be bad for him; or did he feel that it was entirely due to the difficulty of the poems which a future generation might find more acceptable? In any event, having spelled out his thoughts on publication to Bridges, he went on to give reasons why it was unlikely that he would in fact write much more poetry. He could not, for a start, in good conscience give enough time for it, and he did not have the 'inducements and inspirations' that motivated others. Feeling, particularly love, was 'the great moving power and spring' of poetry, and the person with whom he was in love (Christ) now seldom stirred his heart with perceivable intensity—and on the rare occasions when it did happen it might be sacrilegious to 'make capital' out of it.

A week later, Hopkins made one of his complete reversals. Stimulated by receiving a copy of Bridges's anonymous pamphlet of sonnets *The Growth of Love*, which he praised very warmly, he admitted to having two sonnets of his own in preparation, while the following month he walked to Godstow, found that the aspens that had lined the river had been felled, and wrote *Binsey Poplars* (43, RB 19). He had already noted and mourned the increasing encroachment of man on the wild countryside around Oxford, and the tree-felling provided a focus for his acute feelings. The two sonnets which he mentioned were *Duns Scotus's Oxford* (44, RB 20) and *Henry Purcell* (45, RB 21), completed in March and April respectively.

In *Duns Scotus's Oxford* he continued with the theme that modern development was ruining Oxford which, in Scotus's day, had combined all the best aspects of town and country: 'Towery city and branchy between towers.' However it was still the same place, and Hopkins in his loneliness—the loneliness of finding no real home any more in 'my park, my pleasaunce'—found comfort in the fact that Scotus had walked those same streets:

Yet ah! this air I gather and I release
He lived on; these weeds and waters, these walls are what
He haunted who of all men most sways my spirits to peace...

Unhappily it was his persistent championship of this philosopher, who came nearest to matching the contours and sentiment of his own thoughts, his own inherent belief in individuation and selfhood, that sometimes met with disfavour from his superiors.

Henry Purcell Hopkins rightly considered to be one of his 'very best pieces'. One wonders what particular performance—if any—initiated the poem, or whether it was simply the need to express the love he had felt for Purcell's music for so long. (A few months before he had written to Dixon that, like Milton's, Purcell's work seemed 'something necessary and eternal'.) Perhaps he had heard some played in the house of Baron Francis de Paravicini, who had been his contemporary at Balliol and was now a Fellow and Tutor of the College. (Paravicini's name occurs in one of the deleted passages in his undergraduate diary: he chided himself for joking with Paravicini and Baillie in a dangerous way.) Paravicini was married to a Catholic convert and their home was apparently the one place in Oxford where Hopkins felt happy and at ease. Experiencing a 'mixed marriage' of people whom he liked must have activated his ever-present concern for friends and family outside the Catholic Church, the intractable tragedy of his belief that they would be damned. The poem opens with an expression of fervent hope that Purcell's soul may be at peace with God, that his heresy (in not being a Catholic) may have been discounted because of the good intentions revealed in the genius of his music. He later explained the meaning of the first four lines to Bridges with abrupt simplicity: 'I hope Purcell is not damned for being a Protestant, because I love his genius.'

After this the sonnet praises and explores Purcell's individuality, ending with what, in some moods, can seem like six of the best lines Hopkins ever wrote:

> Let him oh! with his air of angels then lift me, lay me! only I'll
> Have an eye to the sakes of him, quaint moonmarks, to his pelted
>   plumage under
> Wings: so some great stormfowl, whenever he has walked his
>   while
>
> The thunder-purple seabeach plumèd purple-of-thunder,
> If a wuthering of his palmy snow-pinions scatter a colossal smile
> Off him, but meaning motion fans fresh our wits with wonder.

Such joy and abandonment—yet disciplined abandonment, leaving room to notice the music's private inscape—combined with such eager love and praise, is removed from the mood in which Hopkins wrote to Bridges to say he seldom now experienced the kinds of feelings that inspired poetry. *Henry Purcell* shows how intense his positive feelings still could be. But he could not be consistently happy in Oxford and admitted to frequent 'black moods'.

It is seldom easy to go back to a place after a long absence if, during the interim, one has undergone considerable changes. For Hopkins, the proximity of evocative quadrangles and meadows, the glimpses of familiar characters such as Coles and Jowett, cannot but have stirred buried dreams and dilemmas. Now he had a definite message to preach, a complete commitment to Christ to demonstrate openly, but Oxford in 1879 was not a place to be stirred by militant Catholicism. Pusey, the survivor of the Oxford Movement, was old and isolated, and Hopkins claimed his followers to be 'up to some very dirty jesuitical tricks' (he made this joke to Bridges), and there were not nearly so many undergraduates devoted to religion as there had been in his day. To the aesthetes and the rationalists alike, a Jesuit priest—however intelligent—would not have much apparent relevance. And when Bridges visited him in Oxford, and they walked together along the Cowley road, he talked in a way that made Hopkins feel he was merely waiting until Hopkins would 'throw off the mask' and share his own disgust at the Jesuits. Certainly not many Gown as opposed to Town would have attended the sermon he preached on 6 July, at St Clement's, on the Feast of the Precious Blood. In it he asked why blood should be called precious, why it should seem so to God, and why it should seem so to man. Specific detail (handkerchiefs dipped in the blood of martyrs, signatures written in blood, Christ shedding blood at his circumcision and at his crucifixion) counterpointed the supernatural aspects of the subject. Strong emphasis was given to the absolute health and purity of Christ's blood: his noble lineage gave him beauty and perfection, unimpaired by any trace of sickness, and his peerless blood 'beat and sympathised with the feelings of his heart'.

Three weeks later Hopkins wrote *The Bugler's First Communion* (48, RB 23), the poem that most overtly expresses his fusion of feeling for male beauty and Christ. By most counts it is an embarrassing poem, one that falls into Bridges's 'faults of taste' category, but it is utterly central to Hopkins, demonstrating that his 'feelings' were in no way silenced nor his expression of them anything other than explicit. He had been with the Society of Jesus for eleven years, regularly disciplined in act and meditation, which conversely gave him the freedom of a kind of innocence from which to describe the beauty of a young soldier when joined to Christ through the Eucharist.

The boy was stationed at Cowley barracks before being posted to Afghanistan. Hopkins met him during a parish visit, and he asked if Hopkins would give him his first communion and came to St Aloysius to receive it.

> How it does my heart good, visiting at that bleak hill,
> When limber liquid youth, that to all I teach
>   Yields tender as a pushed peach . . .

Hopkins asks that the communion wafer ('leaf-light') which houses Christ's 'too huge godhead' will bring the following gifts to the boy: make him dauntless, 'Christ's darling'; make him truthful and modest, 'Tongue true, vaunt- and tauntless'; and breathe the 'bloom of chastity' into his 'mansex fine'. Here is the potent young perfection that Hopkins had long adored in man and nature—can the Eucharist arrest it for ever?

> Nothing else is like it, no, not all so strains
> Us: fresh youth fretted in a bloomfall all portending
>   That sweet's sweeter ending;
> Realm both Christ is heir to and there reigns.
>
> O now well work that sealing sacred ointment!
> O for now charms, arms, what bans off bad
>   And locks love ever in a lad!

Hopkins is not sanguine. Though his prayers would 'brandle adamantine heaven' were they disregarded, he fears the temptations that the young soldier will meet. The last dreadful word we hear of him is when Hopkins sent the poem to Bridges saying, 'I am half inclined to hope the Hero of it may be killed in Afghanistan', so passionate was his wish for primordial innocence 'before it cloy, / Before it cloud, Christ, lord, and sour with sinning'.

Dixon asked to see some of Hopkins's poems, and as soon as he had done so—he was sent the *Deutschland* and *Eurydice*—again took up the question of publication. He read them with 'delight, astonishment, and admiration', finding them 'extraordinary' and 'amazingly original'. 'It seems to me that they ought to be published. Can I do something?' His first offer was to mention Hopkins's name in a footnote to that section of his Church History which dealt with the Jesuits:

> You may think it odd for me to propose to introduce you into the year 1540, but I know how to do it. My object would be to awaken public interest and expectation . . .

Hopkins explained that he felt he could not agree to publication unless the suggestion came 'from one of our people', adding that, although his life was liable to many mortifications, 'want of fame' was the least of them. Six months later Dixon suggested sending the *Eurydice* 'to one of the Carlisle Papers, giving your name, and a line or two of introduction from myself'. This upset Hopkins very much and he wrote two letters entreating Dixon not to send the poem. The matter blew over, and it was agreed that Dixon might show his poems to friends as long as they were never printed.

In October Hopkins was posted temporarily to St Joseph's, Bedford Leigh near Manchester, before taking up an appointment in Liverpool. His two years in Lancashire were to provide opportunities for the kind of vigorous mission work that he had yearned for in Oxford, but according to Bridges 'the vice and horrors' which he encountered there 'nearly killed him'. At first, at Bedford Leigh, he was hopeful. It was 'a darksome place', blackened by the smoke of mills and foundries, but the congregation was fervent and warmhearted. He started to write his verse drama about St Winifred and contemplated another on Margaret Clitheroe, also a martyr. The more stirring parts of the action he found comparatively easy to write, but the 'filling in and minor parts' eluded him. As he told Bridges, he had neither the technical knowledge of the theatre nor a wide enough experience of life to flesh out a narrative convincingly. Also he had his sermons to prepare. Those he preached at Bedford Leigh were probably the most successful of his whole career, and he was popular with his parishioners. They include his famous one, preached on 23 November on Christ as the world's hero, 'the desire of nations'. Christ is praised for his beauty of body, mind and character. The physical praise has the clarity of a pre-Raphaelite painting and much more passion. Hopkins envisages his Lord as fairly tall, 'well built and tender in frame'; his features are beautiful;

his auburn hair is parted in the middle and curls around his ears and neck like the leaves of a filbert cluster around the nut; he has a forked beard which, like his hair, has never been cut. He is majestic in bearing, strong, yet also 'lovely and lissome in his limbs'. 'For myself,' he said, 'I make no secret I look forward with eager desire to seeing the matchless beauty of Christ's body in the heavenly light.' A month earlier he had attended a wedding, and when the march was played began to weep as—after contemplating the bride and groom and hoping their marriage bed be graced 'With lissome scions, sweet scions' (52, RB 28)—he turned to Christ, his bridegroom:

> Then let the March tread our ears:
> I to him turn with tears
> Who to wedlock, his wonder wedlock,
> Deals triumph and immortal years.

The most rhetorical of his Bedford Leigh sermons contained a rousing attack on drunkenness. It was one of the worst social problems he encountered in his parish work, and his offensive has the passion of experience rather than just the bombast of hell-fire preaching. 'Drunkenness is shameful,' he said, 'it makes man a beast; it drowns noble reason, their eyes swim, they hiccup in their talk, they gabble and blur their words, they stagger and fall and deal themselves dishonourable wounds, their faces grow blotched and bloated, scorpions are in their mind, they see devils and frightful sights.' Another habit which offended him was the way the men openly spat in the streets: on a frosty morning, it used to revolt him the way the pavements were starred with spit. He was, presumably, glad to be allowed to go away and spend the Christmas holiday at St Beuno's, where he bathed in St Winifred's Well and gazed over the frosty vale of Clwyd, while some of the Jesuits skated on a nearby lake. His mother sent him a gift of gloves and mittens, and also a comforter which he saved to give away to a needy parishioner. He took up his appointment in Liverpool in January, and it marked the beginning of a downward curve as far as his reputation as a preacher was concerned.

The Church to which he was assigned, St Francis Xavier's, had a flourishing reputation. Christopher Devlin, editor of Hopkins's sermons and devotional writings, quotes this extract from a history of the parish:

Sundays saw a succession of such great preachers as Fr Clare and Fr Harris ascending the pulpit to address immense crowds on the subjects of the day. People were flocking from all over Liverpool so that parishioners had to come early if they would wish for a seat. So great were the crowds, when Fr Tom Burke, O.P., preached the school sermon in October 1880, none of the congregation that heard the 10 o'clock Mass could get out of the church by the ordinary way. They had to leave by the sacristy, the outer tribune and by the back of the High Altar. Even before the congregation was half out, the crowd had forced open the doors, and it was with difficulty that tickets could be collected, and many not having tickets insisted on coming in to pay. Similar events were not infrequent, and soon the locked doors of the church, the queuing crowds and unloading trams on a Sunday were a well known sight until some years after the First World War.

Hopkins was told to prepare a series of four Sunday evening sermons during January, a task which Devlin describes as 'an honour as well as an ordeal'. He took the opportunity to develop the Scotian theme of God's original design for the sinless earth with Christ as its head, and ran into trouble with the Rector, James Clare. On the printed bills advertising the final sermon, Hopkins's title had been:

> ... on the Fall of God's First Kingdom—'Every kingdom divided against itself shall be made desolate and every city (commonwealth) or house divided against itself shall not stand' (Matt. xii. 25).

but Clare ordered blank slips to be pasted over it, and made Hopkins leave out or re-word all passages in his text referring to God's kingdom as falling.

The sermon contains a rather beautiful, if florid, account of Adam and Eve in Paradise. The congregation were asked to picture the forbidden tree 'laden with its shining fragrant fruit' and the Old Serpent 'swaying like a long spray of vine or the bine of a great creeper, not terrible but beauteous, lissome, marked with quaint streaks and eyes or flushed with rainbow colours'. His account of the Fall is full of psychological detail. Devlin remarks:

> In a different century or in a different place—say, in a hypothetically Catholic Jacobean Court—one could imagine solemn and sensitive faces, propped on long delicate fingers, watching

him with grave intensity. But under the circumstances one can only wonder at the perverse courage which tried to bridge the three-century-widened gap between theology and poetry.

He was not asked to preach again for three months. Then towards the end of April he began to prepare a sermon, at first making notes only 'for it seems that written sermons do no good', but then writing it out fully at the Rector's request. Another prepared for the end of May was never delivered because the time was re-allotted to a visiting preacher.

He did continue to preach during his time in Liverpool, but at very irregular intervals. Once during the hot July of 1880 he thought he had moved his congregation to tears, but the following week he looked more closely and perceived they were merely wiping the sweat off their faces. In October he was again in trouble, this time for using the word 'sweetheart' in a poetic sermon on 'Divine Providence and the Guardian Angels'. It was a word he had used without censure at Bedford Leigh, but Clare apparently took it as reason more-or-less to suspend him from preaching, or at least always to have to submit his sermons to him for revision. However, when Hopkins later complied with this latter order, he said Clare 'poohpoohed the matter and would not look at it'. One gets the feeling that Clare, an energetic man with a fine dramatic preaching manner, could not—like other senior Jesuits—find a way of coping without embarrassment with Hopkins's combination of originality, intractability and nervous sensitivity. Devlin points out that the type of robust outspokenness favoured by Tom Burke was welcomed at St Xavier's: he once prefaced a sermon with the phrase 'To hell with the Jesuits' repeated in crescendo three times, before adding: 'Such is the cry of today.' However, the tender phrase 'lover's sweetheart' was condemned.

Lacking success within the portals of the Church, the burden of parish work must have seemed correspondingly more depressing. The drunkards went on drinking, he reported to Bridges, the filthy remained filthy, and he himself was far too fagged, harried and 'gallied up and down' to achieve any writing. (During 1880 he did in fact manage three poems: *Felix Randal* (53, RB 29), *Brothers* (54, RB 30) and *Spring and Fall* (55, RB 31). To Dixon he wrote that Liverpool was the 'most museless' of places, an unhappy and miserable spot, and an account of the poverty and misery he prepared for Baillie he felt he had to tear up after reading it over many times because 'it would do no good'. He told Baillie he did not think he could remain there long, adding rather pathetically, 'I have been long nowhere yet.'

One task he had outside duties among the poor was to serve the private chapel of Randall Lightbound at Rose Hill, Lydiate, where he sometimes spent the night. It was walking there that he composed *Spring and Fall* (55, RB 31)—apart from *Pied Beauty* probably the most anthologised of his poems; he told Bridges that he was not very satisfied with it, and that it was not founded on a real incident. Goldengrove ('Margaret, are you grieving / Over Goldengrove unleaving) is the name of an estate near Lydiate, and the verbal connection with Jeremy Taylor's *The Golden Grove, or a manual of daily prayers and litanies (some especially for younger persons)* may have implanted the idea of addressing the poem 'to a young child'. *Felix Randal*, written after hearing of the death of a farrier, one of his Bedford Leigh parishioners, shows how Hopkins might have wrested more poetry from his daily work had the load been lighter and the social problems less overwhelming. He describes the mutual comfort experienced by him and the big-boned workman when he administered the sacrament:

> This seeing the sick endears them to us, us too it endears.
> My tongue had taught thee comfort, touch had quenched thy tears,
> Thy tears that touched my heart, child, Felix, poor Felix Randal...

It is certain that Felix Randal was not the man's real name, and it is thought 'Randal' probably came into Hopkins's mind because of Randall Lightbound. Perhaps the child-like qualities of the farrier, which became more apparent as he became more ill, reminded him of his brother Felix who had died as a baby, when he himself was nine.

He had one experience of administering the sacrament which seemed like a small miracle. The recipient was a boy, sick with typhus, whose doctor had given up all hope, and who then proceeded to make a rapid and remarkable recovery. The doctor was so impressed he brought a colleague to witness the case.

During 1881 Hopkins became increasingly interested in musical composition. He jokingly remarked to Baillie that he embarked on this task with less qualifications than ever before encountered 'in the whole history of the art', since he could neither read music nor play an instrument properly, but it seemed that the rhythms of music now haunted his mind in the way that, previously, the rhythms of words had done. He was keen to set poems—his own, Dixon's, and particularly Bridges's—and it was an interest that helped to cement the friendship between Bridges and the family at Oak Hill, since Grace from time to time supplied the accompaniments to Gerard's tunes. He wrote at length to Bridges about the connections between musical and poetic metre, and it was as though the more abstract qualities of music were able to feed his creative impulse at times when the exigencies of words, and particularly perhaps the subject matter of his experience which they would have to represent, were too daunting. He even tried to tackle harmony himself, though became rather cross when Bridges said he could not judge a melody to one of his lyrics without hearing the bass; Hopkins wrote: 'I do not understand it: a tune is a tune.'

In March, Dixon made yet another attempt to involve Hopkins in publication. Hall Caine, who had recently become Rossetti's companion, was preparing a large collection of sonnets, and Dixon sent him *The Starlight Night* and *The Sea and the Skylark*. He told Hopkins:

> . . . not of course for publication without your consent: but for inspection . . . I now write to ask if you will consent that some sonnet of yours should be published with your name by him. If so, will you send him one—I think it had better be one in ordinary rhythm: or at most a counterpointed one . . .

This time Hopkins reacted most positively, replying nine days later that he had sent off three sonnets. Caine acknowledged them with 'a somewhat effusive' postcard, promising to write more fully soon. When he did write, it was to reject the poems, the purpose of his book being, he said, to 'demonstrate the impossibility of improving upon the acknowledged structure whether as to rhyme-scheme or measure'. Hopkins thought he sounded like a she-bear whose cubs had been taken away, and was rather fed up at being treated like 'a "young aspirant" '. (Caine was nine years his junior.) What is not explained is why he suddenly felt able to contemplate publication.

He had a holiday at Oak Hill during the summer, which coincided with Bridges being dangerously ill with pneumonia. The first time he visited, Bridges was not strong enough to talk for long, and the second time Hopkins was not allowed up to see him. His recovery was very slow; in November he went abroad to convalesce, and resigned his medical appointments. (He had in any case intended to give up medicine when he reached the age of forty.)

As was customary after the summer holiday, Hopkins went into retreat when he returned to Liverpool, and it was then he wrote his famous meditation on the First Principle and Foundation of Loyola. The Principle reads:

> Man was created to praise, reverence and serve God Our Lord, and by so doing to save his soul. And the other things on the face of the earth were created for man's sake and to help him in the carrying out of the end for which he was created. Hence it follows that man should make use of creatures so far as they help him to attain his end and withdraw from them so far as they hinder him from so doing. For that, it is necessary to make ourselves indifferent in regard to all created things in so far as it is left to the choice of our free will and there is no prohibition; in such sort that we do not on our part seek for health rather than sickness, for riches rather than poverty, for honour rather than dishonour, for a long life rather than a short one; and so in all other things, desiring and choosing only those which may better lead us to the end for which we were created.

Hopkins's meditation contains the reference to the fact that when he was a child he used to ask himself: 'What must it be to be some-one else?'—and failed to find an answer. For each person was so individual, so self-determining, so highly pitched and unlike all others, that one's sense of oneself was more distinctive than the taste of ale or the smell of camphor. And since the universal being had chosen to create our world out of an infinite number of possible worlds, then the universal being was also self-determining. Nor were human beings individuated by the presence of the universal being in each. They had their own autonomy, their own shame, guilt, fate and self-taste, while at the same time being a fraction of the universal being's great selfhood. Thus did Hopkins cling passionately to the uniqueness of himself, however much that self displeased him ('my deserts and guilt, my shame and sense of beauty, my dangers, hopes, fears, and all my fate, more important to myself than anything I see'), affirming the possibility of working at self-conscious redemption through knowledge of Christ and the 'great sacrifice' rather than submission to anything that smacked of universal determinism. On the 'great sacrifice' he wrote:

> The world, man, should after its own manner give God being in return for the being he has given it or should give him back that being he has given. This is done by the great sacrifice. To contribute then to that sacrifice is the end for which man was made . . .

This may be compared with the Ishal Upanishad:

> The whole world is the garment of the Lord. Renounce it, then, and receive it back as the gift of God.

After the retreat, his Liverpool appointment ended and he was sent on supply to Glasgow for a month. Although he found it a wretched place, he preferred it to Liverpool and felt he got on better there; though, as he remarked to Bridges, 'bad is the best of my getting on'. A two-day visit into the Highlands enabled him to write *Inversnaid* (56, RB 53), in which he reiterated the theme which had haunted him at Oxford—a yearning for wildness, free from the marks of man.

> What would the world be, once bereft
> Of wet and of wildness? Let them be left,
> O let them be left, wildness and wet;
> Long live the weeds and the wilderness yet.

He had spurts of creative energy that prompted ideas such as writing a 'great ode' on Edmund Campion; but apparently they came to nothing, and he found these brief imaginings soon dried up. Living in a great town, he said, put both his mind and his heart into slavery.

He was particularly anxious to complete any compositions he had on hand while he was in Scotland, since after that he was due to go to Manresa House for his tertianship. This is the third year of noviceship, intended to 'help the young priest to renew his spirit of piety and to learn how to utilise to the best of his ability all the learning and experience he has acquired', or, as Hopkins expressed it, 'to enable us to recover that fervour which may have cooled' through living in the outside world. He intended to write no poetry during the year, and Dixon found his dedication and rigour full of pathos. Hopkins wrote to him that although, if he chose to look at things from one side rather than the other he might possibly have bitter regrets, he knew that to be unknown was holier, and brought more peace, than to be famous.

He had never wavered in his vocation, he told his friend, it was simply that he had not lived up to it.

CHAPTER TWELVE

'My go is gone'

IT WAS not so much fervour that Hopkins recovered during his tertianship, as a temporarily contented frame of mind. He confessed to Dixon that his experiences in Liverpool and Glasgow had left him with the 'truly crushing conviction' of the misery of the urban poor, and of the degradation and hollowness of nineteenth-century civilisation; but at Manresa House, with its gardens and fine trees, he could find comfort within the restricted regime of a novice. Dixon saw the rules preventing outside visits and the reading of anything other than spiritual books as sacrificially severe, but to Hopkins the enclosing timetable (which included cleaning and kitchen work) no doubt came as a relief.

Until interrupted by the November Long Retreat, given by Father Robert Whitty, he wrote long letters to Dixon setting out detailed criticism of his poems in the same punctilious yet loving way that he reacted to Bridges's work. It was this generous attention to the aspirations of others, combined with his own acceptance of obscurity, that moved Dixon to write:

> ... I will say nothing, but cling to the hope that you will find it consistent with all that you have undertaken to pursue poetry still, as occasion may serve: & that in so doing you may be sanctioned & encouraged by the great Society to which you belong, which has given so many ornaments to literature. Surely one vocation cannot destroy another: and such a Society as yours will not remain ignorant that you have such gifts as have seldom been given by God to man.

When the retreat was over, Hopkins sent a very long reply which demonstrates his mood of renewal and acceptance, and mentions that St Ignatius looked on individual fame 'as the most dangerous and dazzling of all attentions'. Some of the notes he made during the retreat referred to Whitty's references to 'the hidden life' which Christ led in Nazareth, which provided a 'great help to faith for us who must live more or less an obscure, constrained, and unsuccessful life'. He could even make a link to his own repulsion for places like Liverpool, because a traveller had told Whitty that Nazareth was still renowned for its 'rudeness and worthlessness'. Whitty impressed upon Hopkins that a great part of the lives of the holiest of men consisted in the 'well performance' of ordinary duties.

Whereas (after benevolent protestations which mingled sadness with admiration) Dixon accepted Hopkins's continuing vocation, Bridges did not relinquish the right of an old friend to dissent. The deepening intimacy of their relationship may be illustrated from a letter Hopkins sent from Bedford Leigh when Bridges had asked whether there was any point in him continuing to write poetry. Hopkins suspected the doubt arose from his own copious comments on poems sent to him, and pointed out that when he was shown work for the purposes of criticism he usually saw it to the least advantage, whereas later, in print, it fell into more favourable focus. He accused Bridges of wanting to be told over and over again that he was a genius, a poet, and wrote beautiful verses. But then he relented and said that since 'being biassed by love' he was not perhaps the most appropriate critic, nevertheless if he were not his friend he would 'wish to be the friend of the man that wrote your poems'. 'They shew the eye for pure beauty and they shew, my dearest, besides, the character which is much more rare and precious.' Bridges, he added, might not have the volume of imagery of Tennyson, Swinburne or Morris, but he had a pure and exquisite feeling for beauty, and the character of the poems combined sincerity, earnestness, manliness, tenderness, humour, melancholy, and human feeling in a way which far excelled the other poets.

While Hopkins was at Manresa House, Bridges again made some disparaging reference to the fact his letters might be opened, and seems to have assumed that Hopkins would not read his manuscript of *Prometheus the Firegiver* because he did not like it, instead of realising he was not permitted to do so for the time being. (Admittedly Hopkins, half prickly, half resigned over these continuing minor conflicts, did not spell out the reason for the delay.) During Lent, as part of the tertianship, he was sent to take part in a mission in Maryport on the Cumberland coast, and to do some parish work in Preston. From Preston he wrote to Bridges, now recovered from the after-effects of his pneumonia, saying, 'I hope, my dear heart, you are now really better; not better, well; strong, vigorous, lusty, beefish . . .' He had, he said, enjoyed the mission, for it had enabled him to speak out and call 'a spade a spade'.

When he returned to Roehampton, they arranged for Bridges to visit Manresa House as Hopkins could not go up to London. He brought his nephew with him, which Hopkins felt to be 'a restraint upon confidential talk', and the incident of the peach took place which many years later Bridges included in *The Testament of Beauty*:

> And so,
> when the young poet my companion in study
> and friend of my heart refused a peach at my hands,
> he being then a housecarl in Loyola's menie,
> 'twas that he fear'd the savor of it, and when he waived
> his scruple to my banter, 'twas to avoid offence.

It seems the gardener then offered to sell some peaches to Bridges, but Hopkins would not let him buy them. Afterwards the gardener complained that he would have charged a reasonable price. The whole scene has elements of embarrassment, mild fuss and slight bluster that could not be eradicated from a relationship founded in the adolescent days of high church Oxford, from which one partner had developed in worldliness and the other in denial; yet Bridges grew to discipline his poetry with utmost rigour in taste and form, while Hopkins unleashed his lines to capture pure feeling in whatever way seemed immediate and fresh. He might try to refuse to eat a peach, but he provided the experience of eating a sloe for posterity:

> How a lush-kept plush-capped sloe
>   Will, mouthed to flesh-burst,
> Gush!—flush the man, the being with it, sour or sweet,
> Brim, in a flash, full!

Bridges's next visit to Roehampton accidentally coincided with the procession for Corpus Christi, and Hopkins was grieved that it was a dull affair and that Bridges was not given a book from which to follow the hymns. Again he had the feeling that, because such a ritual had no significance now for Bridges, the latter was waiting—not without distate—for the time when it would no longer have significance for Hopkins either. Such cynicism, Hopkins felt, was not a characteristic vein in Bridges, and he was hurt that it should 'bulk out' in a 'diseased and varicose way' over this one matter. Bridges was placed in an impossible position. He cared for Hopkins and hated the Jesuit regime. Also, probably better than anyone, he understood why Hopkins had sought such discipline. But it ill-matched his own development. He was about to move to the old Manor House in Yattendon, Berkshire, where he would devote himself to culture and friendship, and, after his marriage in 1884, to family life. Having served a long and varied apprenticeship, he was able to use his financial inheritance to create the environment of his choice. More secure now—not least through Hopkins's encouragement—in his estimation of his literary worth, he could wholeheartedly develop his work, leaving time for other pursuits such as his interest in sixteenth-century music. Both men were thirty-eight years old.

Bridges wrote to Hopkins describing the beauty and advantages of Yattendon. Hopkins, having completed his tertianship, was beginning a two-year teaching appointment at Stonyhurst and tried to match his friend's enthusiasm for his new home by listing in great detail all the virtues of the college and its surroundings—right down to a jackdaw, a rookery and a goldfish. And if, he added, he could show it to Bridges—a tour which could take up to three hours—'you could not make me wretched now by either stealing or buying fruit'. His job entailed coaching students in classics for the London University examinations. At first he had energy for his own work too, and by mid-October had completed *The Leaden Echo and the Golden Echo* (59, RB 36), which he had begun two years earlier. It is the maidens' song for his never-completed St Winifred drama, and he told Dixon, 'I never did anything more musical.' Bridges wondered if he had been influenced by Whitman when writing it, and this brought forth a long reply which Hopkins referred to as a 'de-Whitmaniser'. In it he admitted that 'I always knew in my heart Walt Whitman's mind to be more like my own than any other man's living', but denied—rightly—that their styles of poetry were similar. He had read only half-a-dozen pieces by Whitman, including extracts from *Leaves of Grass* in a review by George Saintsbury in the *Academy* of 10 October 1874, a year before he wrote the *Deutschland*. Despite the passage of eight years, he could still half-remember one of the lines quoted in the review. And since it is likely that it was this review which made him feel 'Walt Whitman's mind to be . . . like my own', extracts from it may be of interest:

It is not difficult to point out the central thesis of Walt Whitman's
poetical gospel. It is briefly this: the necessity of the establishment of a universal republic, or rather brotherhood of men. The
ideal man... is to be a rather magnificent animal, almost
entirely uncultured... possessing a perfect *physique*, well
nourished and clothed, affectionate towards his kind, and above
all things firmly resolved to admit no superior. As is the ideal
man, so is the ideal woman to be... The key-word of all his
ideas and of all his writings is universality. His Utopia is one
which shall be open to everybody; his ideal of man and woman
one which shall be attainable by everybody; his favourite scenes,
ideas, subjects, those which everybody, at least to some extent,
can enjoy and appreciate.... The exclusion of culture, philosophy, manners, is owing to this desire to admit nothing but
what is open to every human being of ordinary faculty and
opportunities. Moreover it is to this that we may fairly trace the
prominence in Whitman's writings of the sexual passion, a
prominence which has given rise, and probably will yet give rise,
to much unphilosophical hubbub... Yet it would be a great
mistake to suppose that sexual passion occupies the chief place
in Whitman's estimation. There is according to him something
above it, something which in any ecstasies he fails not to realise,
something which seems more intimately connected in his mind
with the welfare of mankind, and the promotion of his ideal
republic. This is what he calls 'robust American love'. He is
never tired of repeating 'I am the poet of comrades'...

Hopkins told Bridges that it was not pleasant for him to have to
confess an affinity to Whitman since he regarded him as 'a very
great scoundrel'—a fact which made him long to read more of his
work and also to be quite determined that he would do no such
thing. As far as style went, he pointed out that Whitman's lines
were in essence rhythmic prose, whereas his own maidens' song
was 'very highly wrought'; the long lines were not 'rhythm run
to seed' but with every syllable 'weighed and timed'. And, above
all, the poem was supposed to sound like the thoughts of a 'good
but lively girl' and not at all like those of Walt Whitman. They
sound, in fact, like Hopkins elaborating in a most complex and
compelling chant his attitude to mortal beauty and its inevitable
decay:

... Come then, your ways and airs and looks, locks, maiden gear,
    gallantry and gaiety and grace,
Winning ways, airs innocent, maiden manners, sweet looks,
    loose locks, long locks, lovelocks, gaygear, going gallant,
    girlgrace—
Resign them, sign them, seal them, send them, motion them
    with breath,
And with sighs soaring, soaring sighs, deliver
Them; beauty-in-the-ghost, deliver it, early now, long before
    death
Give beauty back, beauty, beauty, beauty, back to God,
    beauty's self and beauty's giver.

Inevitably, for the pattern was quite set now, the shot of vitality
which came from a change of scene soon ebbed. By the new year
1883 he complained to Baillie of the heavy and weary state of both
his body and mind 'in which my go is gone'. He had been told by
his superiors to use his spare time for writing a book, and had
several vague plans—including one for a study of Greek Lyric
Art. But he could scarcely rouse the energy even for sustained
serious reading, and seemed to himself to be 'but half a man'. As
usual, he wrote to Newman in February to send good wishes for
his birthday, and this time asked if he might be allowed to prepare
a comment to accompany some new edition of his *Grammar of
Assent*. Newman thanked him for his complimentary proposal,

But I cannot accept it, because I do not feel the need of it, and I
could not, as a matter of conscience, allow you to undertake a
work which I could not but consider at once onerous and
unnecessary. The book has succeeded in twelve years far more
than I expected. It has reached five full editions. It is being
translated in India into some of the native tongues—broken into
portions and commented on. It is frequently referred to in
periodical home publications—only last Saturday week with
considerable praise in the *Spectator*—Of course those who only
read so much of it as they can while cutting open the leaves, will
make great mistakes about it, as Dr Stanley has—but, if it is
worth anything, it will survive the paper cutters, and if it be
worthless, a comment, however brilliant, will not do more
than gain for it a short galvanic life, which has no charms
for me.

Hopkins hastily denied that his proposal had been 'complimentary', which drew this reply from Newman:

> In spite of your kind denial, I still do and must think that a comment is a compliment, and to say that a comment may be appended to my small book because one may be made on Aristotle ought to make me blush purple! As to India, I suppose all English books, even Goody Two Shoes, are so unlike its literary atmosphere, that a comment is but one aspect of translation.
>
> I must still say that you paid me a very kind compliment. You seem to think compliments must be insincere: is it so?

As before, when he felt jaded, Hopkins turned to music, and this time he tried to work out an exercise in counterpoint. When he played it himself he thought it sounded rather good, but when someone else tried it, it seemed to maunder and wander 'in a wilderness'. The month of May did not at first appear to bring its usual inspiration, but when he was asked to write something to hang up in honour of the Blessed Virgin he produced *The Blessed Virgin compared to the Air we Breathe* (60, RB 37), the best of his devotional poems, in which he knew he must 'compromise with popular taste'. In an essay on Plato which he had once written for Pater, he had remarked on the aim of recognizing the underlying law and order in the world so that such unity could be experienced 'like breathing wholesome air'. A similar image of all-enveloping unity—rather like living in an open womb—is developed in detail in the poem:

> Wild air, world-mothering air,
> Nestling me everywhere,
> That each eyelash or hair
> Girdles; goes home betwixt
> The fleeciest, frailest-flixed
> Snowflake; that's fairly mixed
> With, riddles, and is rife
> In every least thing's life;
> This needful, never spent,
> And nursing element . . .

And he goes on to compare the sea of air which prevents us from being burned by the sun to the Incarnation which made the God of the Hebrews more approachable without dimming His glory.

He would have sent the poem to Dixon, but said he had no leisure to copy it out. Yet in the same letter he remarked that someone else in his job would probably have time to do a good deal of his own personal work. He did, however, send it to Bridges, despite its subject, and Bridges found it 'admirable'.

Towards the end of July, he waited gloomily for the autumn appointments. He did not particularly want to leave Stonyhurst, yet felt he had achieved nothing during his year there. He told Bridges he was like 'Fortune's football' awaiting 'another kick of her foot'. The only immediate instruction he received was to take leave of absence once term was over.

On 30 July, however, something interesting did occur. Coventry Patmore, then aged sixty, came to stay as a guest at Stonyhurst for their speech day on 1 August, and Hopkins was given the task of looking after him. As an undergraduate he had noted in his journal 'Fair with clouds. Walking down towards Sandford with Coventry Patmore in hand' and he had continued to admire his work—defending it against attacks by Bridges: 'For insight he beats all our living poets, his insight is really profound . . .'

The central theme of Patmore's work is spousal love (he had recently married happily for the third time, his previous wives having died). Claude Colleer Abbott refers to the difficulty in accepting 'his Sultan-like conception of woman and her sphere' plus his blurring of the boundaries between spousal and divine love. But it was territory that suited Hopkins, and the two men got along very well in a formal kind of way. Richard Garnett described Patmore as 'haughty, imperious, combative, sardonic,' though 'at the same time sensitive, susceptible, and capable of deep tenderness'. He did not normally like priests (indeed was on occasion extremely rude to them), but Hopkins's informed admiration for his work was exactly what he needed after being out of favour with the critics for a long time. Three days after his visit, Hopkins was able to report to Bridges that, before bringing out the next edition of his poems in the autumn, Patmore was going to send them to him for suggestions. He suspected he was bragging by mentioning it, but there it was 'all blubbering in wet ink'.

The conclusion must finally be drawn, from Hopkins's reactions to meeting Patmore, from the enthusiastic and meticulous hard work he put into criticising his poems, and for all the time he devoted to commenting on Bridges's and Dixon's poems over the years, that in order to be fully vitalised, he needed to belong—as an integral part of his life—to a recognized and accepted literary society. Piecemeal correspondence, and arbitrary chance meetings, were not sufficient to keep his 'vein flowing'. It may be argued that there is no proof he would have sustained his creative energies had a way been found officially to recognise his life as a poet as well as a member of the Society of Jesus. But the fact he continued to write, however intermittently, and to improve his powers, does indicate that with some kind of established acceptance he might have written a great deal more. It is not suggested, however, that there was ever any question of Hopkins wanting to leave the Society, or that he would have survived better outside it. And it is mainly hindsight—with access to his literary correspondences, and a perspective on his achievement—that makes one see how desperately he needed to put down roots within the professional literary world in which he was so well equipped to flourish. His poetry might have met with brickbats, but he had ample critical resources with which to defend himself.

He had been given leave of absence in order to spend time with his family at Oak Hill and then to accompany them to Holland for a few days. From there, his parents were to make a sad journey to East Prussia to collect Grace, staying with the parents of her late fiancé in Sensburg. She had met and fallen in love with Henry Weber in Switzerland the previous year and an engagement had been allowed despite his frail health. But he had died in June, and she had gone to Sensburg to visit his grave. Hopkins assured Bridges that she was 'too simple-minded and too sweetnatured to let herself be soured or enfeebled by a grief'.

After his holiday he went into retreat at Beaumont. In the notes which he made, he remarked that it was fifteen years since he came to the Society, and he prayed to be lifted into a higher state of grace (which also meant being lifted on a higher cross), with more zeal to do God's will. He regretted he was able to perform so few hard penances, but remembered Father Whitty's teaching about the 'well performance' of ordinary duties. And he prayed that the Lord would watch over his compositions: not necessarily preserve them (he was willing for them to be lost) but to see they did him no harm through other men's enmity or imprudence. They belonged to God, and he should 'employ or not employ them as He should see fit'.

Then, contrary to his earlier expectation, he was sent to Stonyhurst for a further six months, where he immediately settled down to go through Patmore's poems with a fine critical toothcomb. Patmore responded with gratitude, and uncharacteristic humility. He said that in his 'present state of poetical incapacity' he could not embark on any changes demanding creative imagination—such as the emphases in moral tone or taste which Hopkins had questioned—but he accepted many minor verbal and metrical suggestions. (Of the lines 'Yes, she had read the "Legend of the Ages", / And George Sand too, skipping the wicked pages' in *Girl of All Periods*, Hopkins remarked that they may have been observed from life, but were unpleasant. And while praising *The Kiss* as a 'gem of execution' he found something in it offensive and could not help wishing that its characters, Victor and Amanda, 'might both once be well whipped'.)

Hopkins's own compostion was still confined to music, and he attempted a Gregorian setting for Collins's *Ode to Evening*. He told Bridges that he groped in his 'soul's very viscera' for the tune and 'thrummed the sweetest and most secret catgut of the mind': a description which might also be applied to the making of some of his poems.

When the time came to write Newman's 1884 birthday letter, Hopkins was in Dublin. The management of University College, which was then associated to the Royal University of Ireland, had been handed over to the Jesuits the previous October, and the College's president, Dr Delaney, was organising new staff appointments. The Jesuit authorities in England presumably told him about Hopkins, and it seems that a recommendation from Jowett influenced the Senate to elect Hopkins Fellow of the University and to appoint him to the Chair of Greek at University College. Unfortunately the dignity of the appointments' titles were not reflected in the reality of the work. Hopkins approached Ireland in a state of weakness and fear; his condition was not suited to exile in a strife-torn country, most of whose inhabitants hated the English.

It had been the removal of Protestant bishops in Ireland which had ignited the Oxford Movement. And it had been Newman who, thirty years earlier, had set out to create a Roman Catholic 'Oxford' in Dublin in the guise of the University of Ireland. After a series of squabbles and intractable difficulties, he withdrew, and the University virtually died; but now politics made the establishment of a

Royal University expedient. University College was mainly an examining body (though it had some students), and Hopkins's task for the remainder of his life was to conduct six examinations a year, whose candidates ran into hundreds, and to take classes in Latin and Greek. When he told Bridges the news, he said that if Stephen's Green, the biggest square in Europe and site of University College, were paved with gold, it could not compensate for such work. To Newman he remarked that the college buildings had fallen into 'deep dilapidation' by the time the Jesuits took over. Personally, however, he had been warmly welcomed and kindly treated.

He had introduced Patmore to the work of Bridges and Dixon, and through contact with the former Patmore discovered that Hopkins also wrote poetry and asked to see some of it. A month after he arrived in Ireland, Hopkins learned his reaction:

... System and learned theory are manifest in all these experiments; but they seem to me to be *too* manifest. To me they often darken the thought and feeling which all arts and artifices of language should only illustrate; and I often find it as hard to follow you as I have found it to follow the darkest parts of Browning—who, however, has not an equal excuse of philosophic system.

Hopkins once said of Browning's verse: 'The general effect, the whole, offends me, I think it repulsive.' Patmore told Bridges: 'To me [Hopkins's] poetry has the effect of veins of pure gold imbedded in masses of unpracticable quartz . . . I wish I had not to tell him of my objections. But I had either to be silent or to say the truth . . .' Hopkins laconically told Bridges that Patmore 'did not on the whole like my poems' and in the same letter broke into despairing capitals: 'AND WHAT DOES ANYTHING AT ALL MATTER?' He said a fortnight later that he thought he was recovering from a deep fit of nervous prostration in which he had felt he might be dying.

It was at this time that Bridges wrote to him saying he had become engaged to Monica Waterhouse (the daughter of Alfred Waterhouse who lived in the house he had designed above Yattendon), and asking Hopkins to be his best man. Since Bridges had many friends, this shows how closely he now esteemed their friendship. Hopkins had to refuse, but he was genuinely delighted at the news. Some time after the marriage had taken place on 3 September, he told Bridges he loved to hear about his new life

H

because he had 'a kind of spooniness and delight over married people', especially if they used the words 'my wife', 'my husband', or displayed their marriage ring. Bridges had apparently expressed some doubt that Hopkins might approve of his friends marrying, but was told that he liked men to marry because a single life was difficult and not altogether natural. For a celibate life to be manageable, 'special provision' such as the Jesuits had was needed, but most people could not have that. The nature of the 'special provision' is not elaborated.

A July holiday in Galway, which he enjoyed, did not repair the state of his nerves, and by the end of September, when examinations and lecturing were pressing heavily upon him, he felt that he was in danger of permanently injuring his eyes. Although he completed no poems this year, he was preparing draft fragments of two in his notebook. One was the soliloquy (152, RB 58) by Caradoc (see p. 153) who remained unrepentant after striking off Winifred's head:

> Down this darksome world ' comfort where can I find
> When 'ts light I quenched; its rose, ' time's one rich rose, my
>   hand,
> By her bloom, fast by ' her fresh, her fleecèd bloom,
> Hideous dashed down, leaving ' earth a winter withering
> With no now, no Gwenvrewi. ' I must miss her most
> That might have spared her were it ' but for passion-sake. Yes,
> To hunger and not have, yet ' hope on for, to storm and strive and
> Be at every assault fresh foiled, ' worse flung, deeper disappointed,
> The turmoil and the torment, ' it has, I swear, a sweetness,
> Keeps a kind of joy in it, ' a zest, an edge, an ecstasy . . .

And the other was *Spelt from Sibyl's leaves* (61, RB 32), his desolate contemplation on the nature of judgement and hell, which he said should be 'almost sung', in 'loud, leisurely, poetical' recitation. It ends with an image of life as

> a rack
> Where, selfwrung, selfstrung, sheathe- and shelterless, thoughts
>   against thoughts in groans grind.

His contact with his family during that first year in Ireland was minimal. Grace complained that writing to him was like throwing letters into a well. At the end of December he wrote to tell his mother he would not be home for Christmas, since it was a short holiday, the travel would tire him, and he had an examination immediately afterwards. He told her that Dr Delaney was one of the most generous and openhearted men he had ever lived with, and that Robert Curtis, who had been elected Fellow at the same time as himself, was more of a comfort to him than he could describe—'a kind of godsend I never expected to have'. Curtis's father was a Q.C. and lived in Dublin, and Hopkins was made very welcome at his home. However, the ill-equipment of the College itself meant it was like living in a 'temporary Junction'. To his sister Kate he wrote a Christmas letter, partly in cod Irish, in which he said one of the fathers, an elderly Frenchman called Jacques Mallac, was trying to encourage him to take up drawing again.

One has the feeling that the inquietude of Hopkins's being, expressed most forcibly to Bridges, was an entrenched plant, feeding on the psychological patterns of forty years, and that no amount of good fellowship or friendship could now change the nature of the plant. Certainly his colleagues could not alter the incredible scrupulosity with which he approached his examination duties, which meant that he agonized for hours over a complex system he developed in which half and quarter marks were allotted, and the resulting totals repeatedly checked and balanced one against the other. He failed to make much impression on his classes, and his pupils were frequently inattentive, and sometimes rude. 'I do not object to their being rude to me personally,' he told an acquaintance, 'but I do object to their being rude to their professor and a priest.'

When he heard that Bridges and his wife had visited Oak Hill during the Christmas holiday and they had all played music together, Hopkins regretted not going home. As usual he felt jaded, in need of a change, and the thought of that shared music made him wistful. 'Change' seemed to be the only relief he could ever find for the 'fits of sadness' which, he told Bridges, 'resembled madness', although they did not affect his judgement.

CHAPTER THIRTEEN

'Time's eunuch'

DUE TO Mallac's influence, a young count from the Austrian Empire came to board at University College, and Hopkins wrote an amusing letter to his mother describing the preparations for this royal visitation. His advice had been sought about good English story books suitable for the count's younger sister to read, and he appealed to his mother and sister for help. The characters must be born before the stories started as birth was too strong a subject to be presented to the young countess; and there must not be the slightest hint of lovemaking. This, Hopkins declared, posed a difficulty, as even the 'most highly proper' English stories tended to have love in them, and he did not particularly care for the kind of all over 'slobbery niceness and good humour' that characterised pure-minded stories such as *Christmas-Tree-Land* by Mrs Molesworth. When the count arrived, Hopkins was able to report to his mother that he was a 'splendid sample of young nobleman', particularly on horseback.

Mallac seems to have done his best to befriend Hopkins, pronouncing on his health, persuading him to draw, and—on 1 March 1885—taking him to Phoenix Park to see a political protest meeting. The crowds were well-behaved, and Hopkins did not find the event disturbing, but he told his mother that the grief of mind he endured because of Irish politics in general was so strong that he could not bring himself to express it. This grief was caused partly by living among people who were in perpetual 'peaceful rebellion' against his own people, and partly because he understood very well that the Irish problem brooked no solution. He wanted Home Rule (although he disliked Gladstone deeply and regarded him as a traitor) since he was sure the alternative was war, but he feared the Irish people's lack of allegiance to any existing law or government, along with their fierce passion for national recognition, aggrandisement and glory. He expressed his loneliness and exile, his separation from family, country and heaven, in this sonnet (66, RB 44):

To seem the stranger lies my lot, my life
Among strangers. Father and mother dear,
Brothers and sisters are in Christ not near
And he my peace my parting, sword and strife.
England, whose honour O all my heart woos, wife
To my creating thought, would neither hear
Me, were I pleading, plead nor do I: I wear-
y of idle a being but by where wars are rife.
I am in Ireland now; now I am at a third
Remove. Not but in all removed I can
Kind love both give and get. Only what word
Wisest my heart breeds dark heaven's baffling ban
Bars or hell's spell thwarts. This to hoard unheard,
Heard unheeded, leaves me a lonely began.

It is one of the six sonnets of desolation he wrote (virtually
certainly) during 1885 and never sent to anyone. Once he told
Bridges he would send him all of them, describing how four had
come 'unbidden and against my will'; but he never did, and they
were found among his papers after his death. They include
(*Carrion Comfort*) (64, RB 40), *No worst, there is none* (65, RB 41),
I wake and feel the fell of dark (67, RB 45), *Patience, hard thing!*
(68, RB 46), and *My own heart let me have more pity on* (69, RB 47).
One, he said to Bridges, 'was written in blood' if ever anything was.
Bridges thought it was probably (*Carrion Comfort*):

Not, I'll not, carrion comfort, Despair, not feast on thee;
Not untwist—slack they may be—these last strands of man
In me or, most weary, cry *I can no more*. I can;
Can something, hope, wish day come, not choose not to be.
But ah, but O thou terrible, why wouldst thou rude on me
Thy wring-world right foot rock? lay a lionlimb against me? scan
With darksome devouring eyes my bruisèd bones? and fan,
O in turns of tempest, me heaped there; me frantic to avoid thee
    and flee?
Why? That my chaff might fly; my grain lie, sheer and clear.
Nay in all that toil, that coil, since (seems) I kissed the rod,
Hand rather, my heart lo! lapped strength, stole joy, would
    laugh, cheer.
Cheer for whom though? The hero whose heaven-handling flung
    me, foot trod

Me? or me that fought him? O which one? is it each one? That
    night, that year
Of now done darkness I wretch lay wrestling with (my God!) my
    God.

They are not poems that need any exposition. Their narrative of the
stage of Hopkins's mind and feelings is painfully clear. Their
expression is sometimes as near to perfection as words might
achieve, as in the last six lines of *No worst, there is none*:

O the mind, mind has mountains; cliffs of fall
Frightful, sheer, no-man-fathomed. Hold them cheap
May who ne'er hung there. Nor does long our small
Durance deal with that steep or deep. Here! creep,
Wretch, under a comfort serves in a whirlwind: all
Life death does end and each day dies with sleep.

After this period of painful but consummate fecundity, he still felt
the need to write to Bridges: '. . . if I could but produce work I
should not mind its being buried, silenced, and going no further;
but it kills me to be time's eunuch and never to beget.'
    His spirits briefly revived in the summer when he spent time at
Oak Hill and Midhurst with his parents, and a few days in Hastings
with the Patmores. The edition of *Angel in the House* incorporating
some of his revisions had appeared, and Patmore told him, 'A very
good critic assures me that your suggested corrections have had a
very decided effect on the impression made by the whole poem. It
is wonderful how two or three awkward and unfinished lines
deteriorate from a whole volume.' When he returned to Clongowes
Wood College in County Kildare to make his retreat, he wrote a
patriotic hymn, *What shall I do for the land that bred me* (156, RB 59),
his eulogy in praise of the armed forces (*The Soldier*) (63, RB 39)
and *To what serves Mortal Beauty?* (62, RB38). If any poem could
be said to represent the earthly Hopkins, the passion and the
problem, it is the last. What, it asks, should one do when encounter-
ing dangerous beauty, the kind that 'does set dancing blood' by the
perfection of 'the O-seal-that-so feature'? The answer is 'merely
meet it' with a glance; not 'gaze out of countenance'. He instances
Pope Gregory glancing at 'those lovely lads' 'wet-fresh windfalls of
war's storm', of whom Gregory remarked, 'Non Angli sed angeli.'
Had they not been golden-haired and blue-eyed, Hopkins suggests,

Gregory might not have noticed them and therefore not concerned himself with converting Britain. Ergo—beauty has a function. But it is evident that when 'Self flashes off frame and face' Hopkins was still vulnerably susceptible and had to remind himself to 'Merely meet it', 'then leave, let that alone'.

In the early spring of 1886, he embarked on another scheme for a book. This time it was to be on Homer's Art, which quickly altered to a study of Greek-Egyptian derivations in an endeavour to prove 'that Egyptian civilisation may well have rocked the cradle of the Greek'. He enlisted Baillie's help, badgering him for comments and facts, and Baillie good-naturedly responded promptly to a spate of letters and postcards. But, as Hopkins himself had surmised at the start, it came 'to nothing in the end'.

In May he seems to have been sent briefly to St Aloysius's in Oxford, and from there spent a day at Yattendon and a holiday at Oak Hill. It was his last visit to his childhood home, for his parents were about to move to Haslemere in Surrey. When he had first heard this news, the previous November, he told his mother, 'It seemed like death at first to leave Hampstead.' His health was temporarily improved by the holiday, and he took great pleasure in visiting the Royal Academy's Summer Exhibition. His favourite work was Hamo Thornycroft's sculpture, *The Sower*, which he thought was like one of Frederick Walker's pictures 'put into stone'. Walker had, he decided when writing to Dixon about the exhibition, the essential gift of 'masterly execution'. It was 'a kind of male gift', which marked off men from women or—on reflection—perhaps not so much 'the male quality in the mind' as 'a puberty in the life of that quality'.

Delaney unexpectedly permitted him another holiday in September, this time a walking tour in Wales with Robert Curtis. That he had energy for this kind of activity there was no doubt, and he wrote ecstatically of the beauties and inspiration of 'Wild Wales'—also of 'the heartiest of breakfasts'. He even did a little more work on his St Winifred play, telling Bridges that Wales was 'always to me a mother of Muses'. But by early October he was back in Dublin, swamped by 331 examination accounts of the First Punic War, and his improved health and spirits were quickly reduced to 'nearer my lees and usual alluvial low water mudflats'.

Nevertheless, his letters to Bridges during the rest of the year were very lively, and contained long discussions on music and

novelists. He recommended *King Solomon's Mines* as a good read
for boys, said Hyde in *Jekyll and Hyde* was certainly not over-
drawn—'my Hyde is worse', and remarked that the 'gift and genius'
that went into contemporary English novels did not fall far short of
'what made the Elizabethan drama'. He particularly admired
Hardy's great scenes, even though he did not write 'continuously
well', regretting he and Richard Blackmore were eclipsed by 'the
over-done reputation of the Evans-Eliot-Lewes-Cross woman'. (He
did then reprove himself for speaking slightingly of the 'poor
creature!') He was meeting more of Dublin's artistic society,
including the poet Katharine Tynan (whom he described as 'a
simple brightlooking Biddy') and also W. B. Yeats, then aged
twenty-one. When he visited the latter's father, J. B. Yeats, he was
presented with *Mosada: a Dramatic Poem* by his son, illustrated
with a portrait of the author by his father. It was, Hopkins felt, a
bit too much 'for a young man's pamphlet'. Another poem of
Yeats's he described as an 'unworkable allegory' about a man and a
sphinx on a rock in the sea. But, he wanted to know, how had they
got there? and what did they eat? Such criticisms might sound
prosaic, he said, but commonsense was no more out of place on
Parnassus than anywhere else.

For their part, Katharine Tynan remembered Hopkins as 'small
and childish-looking, yet like a child-sage, nervous too and very
sensitive, with a small ivory-pale face', and W. B. Yeats described
him as a 'querulous, sensitive scholar'. According to a friend
quoted in Lahey's biography of Hopkins, 'he was of a very retiring
disposition and made few acquaintances in Dublin, even these he
seldom visited, and very rarely could he be induced to ask permission to lunch or dine out. Without permission he could scarcely
be prevailed on to take a cup of tea.' Yet from his letters there is
evidence that he had a reasonably wide circle of acquaintances, and
was not averse to visiting.

He busily promoted Bridges's work among these acquaintances, including leaving copies of *Prometheus the Firegiver* and *Nero* (*Part
I*) at the house of Edward Dowden, Professor of English Literature. In an article on Bridges, published in 1894, Dowden wrote:

Father Gerard Hopkins, an English priest of the Society of
Jesus, died young, and one of his good deeds remains to the
present time unrecorded. We were strangers to each other, and

might have been friends. I took for granted that he belonged to the other camp in Irish politics . . . Father Hopkins was a lover of literature, and himself a poet. Perhaps he did in many quarters missionary work on behalf of the poetry of his favourite, Robert Bridges. He certainly left, a good many years since, at my door two volumes by Mr Bridges, and with them a note begging that I would make no acknowledgment of the gift. I did not acknowledge it then; but, with sorrow for a fine spirit lost, I acknowledge it now.

Despite his note, Hopkins told Bridges not long before he died that he would never forgive Dowden for not acknowledging the gift.

He spent Christmas 1886 and the New Year as the guest of an elderly Miss Cassidy in Monasterevan, Co. Kildare. She was a member of a prosperous family of brewers and distillers, and Hopkins came to rely on her hospitable friendship—the breaks at Monasterevan becoming 'one of the props and struts of my existence'. Indeed, Delaney seems to have been sympathetic to Hopkins's need for change, as his visits and holidays increased in their frequency.

But, as he wrote to Bridges in February, after three years in Ireland, during which he had in the main done God's will 'and many many examination papers', he had no working will, no strength or energy to complete self-imposed creative tasks. He did not even finish scholarly papers which he might have contributed to journals, although he continued sporadically to add to his diffuse thoughts on Greek metre. He realised that Ireland was not to blame, and he told Bridges that elsewhere he might have felt worse: which is probably true for, though he found the examinations a burden, he appears to have had freedom in friendship and social activity, and to have been well-treated by his colleagues. Two amicable ex-pupils of his lived in Dublin, and one of them, Bernard O'Flaherty, regularly called to take him for walks, which he enjoyed. One somewhat bizarre entertainment which he attended was a dramatic recital by Miss Romola Tynte, whom he described to Bridges as 'a beautiful Sappho' dressed in a costume designed by Oscar Wilde. A review in the *Irish Times* said that pieces by G. R. Sims (such as 'Out of work' and 'Late for dinner') were 'deepened greatly by the interpretation given them by one with the emotional capacity of Miss Tynte'.

In August he stayed with his family for the first time at Court's Hill Lodge, Haslemere, and was able to exchange visits with Bridges. Afterwards he decided he 'had never in my life met a sweeter lady than Mrs Bridges'. When their daughter Elizabeth was born on 6 December he was 'truly delighted'. At the end of September he wrote to Bridges from a hotel in Rostrevor, Co. Down, saying his 'broken holidays' were ending, and that alternating between holidays and work, 'like sleep and waking', meant he lost the effects of both, and did not feel well. But he did admit to being 'in pretty good spirits', had been touching up the sonnets Bridges had never seen, and in a few days had written two new ones which he would send. These were *Harry Ploughman* (71, RB 43) and *Tom's Garland: (upon the Unemployed)* (70, RB 42). He hoped Bridges would find nothing of Walt Whitman in the former, which begins:

> Hard as hurdle arms, with a broth of goldish flue
> Breathed round; the rack of ribs; the scooped flank; lank
> Rope-over thigh; knee-nave; and barrelled shank—

Bridges was not over-keen, and neither he nor Dixon could construe *Tom's Garland* at all. On 10 February 1888, Hopkins wrote to him:

> I laughed outright and often, but very sardonically, to think you and the Canon could not construe my last sonnet; that he had to write to you for a crib. It is plain I must go no farther on this road: if you and he cannot understand me who will? Yet, declaimed, the strange constructions would be dramatic and effective. Must I interpret it? It means then that, as St Paul and Plato and Hobbes and everybody says, the commonwealth or well ordered human society is like one man; a body with many members and each its function; some higher, some lower, but all honourable, from the honour which belongs to the whole. The head is the sovereign, who has no superior but God and from heaven receives his or her authority: we must then imagine this head as bare (see St Paul much on this) and covered, so to say, only with the sun and stars, of which the crown is a symbol, which is an ornament but not a covering; it has an enormous hat or skull cap, the vault of heaven. The foot is the daylabourer, and this is armed with hobnail boots, because it has to wear and to be worn by the ground; which again is symbolical; for it is navvies or

daylabourers who, on the great scale or in gangs and millions, mainly trench, tunnel, blast, and in other ways disfigure, 'mammock' the earth and, on a small scale, singly, and superficially stamp it with the footprints. And the 'garlands' of nails they wear are therefore the visible badge of the place they fill, the lowest in the commonwealth. But this place still shares the common honour, and if it wants one advantage, glory or public fame, makes up for it by another, ease of mind, absence of care; and these things are symbolized by the gold and the iron garlands. (O, once explained, how clear it all is!) Therefore the scene of the poem is laid at evening, when they are giving over work and one after another pile their picks, with which they earn their living, and swing off home, knocking sparks out of mother earth not now by labour and of choice but by the mere footing, being strongshod and making no hardship of hardness, taking all easy. And so to supper and bed. Here comes a violent but effective hyperbaton or suspension, in which the action of the mind mimics that of the labourer—surveys his lot, low but free from care; then by a sudden strong act throws it over the shoulder or tosses it away as light matter. The witnessing of which lightheartedness makes me indignant with the fools of Radical Levellers. But presently I remember that this is all very well for those who are in, however low in, the Commonwealth and share in any way the Common weal; but that the curse of our times is that many do not share it, that they are outcasts from it and have neither security nor splendour; that they share care with the high and obscurity with the low, but wealth or comfort with neither. And this state of things, I say, is the origin of Loafers, Tramps, Cornerboys, Roughs, Socialists and other pests of society. And I think that it is a very pregnant sonnet and in point of execution very highly wrought. Too much so, I am afraid.

In the previous month he had regretted to Bridges that he had 'no inspiration of longer jet' than to make a sonnet; and remarked that his 'quasi-philosophical' paper on Greek Negatives—if ever finished—might not pass the censors, and even if it did, what magazine would take it? 'All impulse fails me: I can give myself no sufficient reason for going on. Nothing comes: I am a eunuch—but it is for the kingdom of heaven's sake.' In September 1865 he had written: 'My sap is sealed, / My root is dry.' He had wanted his

life-force, which led to sin, to be totally replaced by God's imma-
nence which would surely supply him with energy of a less questionable kind. However, it was not a transfusion that could be easily
attained, if indeed it could be attained at all.

CHAPTER FOURTEEN

'I that die these deaths'

DURING 1888 Hopkins made little attempt to be cheerful, even to his mother. The drudgery and burden of examinations crushed him, he told her, and it was so cold he was still wearing winter clothing in July. He tried to read the long reports of Parnell's case in *The Times* which she sent him (the College no longer took the paper) but his eyesight was not really up to it. He ticked Baillie off for saying that life in London was 'intolerable'; he could picture the West End, 'cheerful and quietly handsome', with its fine trees, balmy air, and so many things to see and hear and do, and he thought there was a very great deal to be said for life in London. But his own private dream, he went on, was for 'a farm in the Western counties, glow worms, new milk . . .' Then remembrance of the fact he lived in Ireland brought him back to earth with a jolt.

In February he received a letter from Patmore saying that on Christmas Day he had burned a manuscript called *Sposa Dei* which Hopkins had read when he visited the Patmores in 1885. The book had been a series of meditations on—according to Gosse who also read it—'the love between the soul and God by an analogy of the love between a woman and a man; it was, indeed, a transcendental of human desire.' After Hopkins's death, Patmore wrote to Bridges:

> . . . there was something in all his words and manners which were at once a rebuke and an attraction to all who could only aspire to be like him. The *authority* of his goodness was so great with me that I threw the manuscript of a little work—a sort of 'Religio Poetae'—into the fire, simply because, when he had read it, he said with a grave look, 'That's telling secrets'.

He had waited two and a half years before burning the book, and had consulted one other person as well as his own conscience, but it was markedly the moral tenor of Hopkins's reaction that decided him. On 6 May Hopkins replied that he wished he had been more guarded in his comments since he was sure slight changes might have overcome any of his objections. A few weeks earlier, probably while supervising an examination, he had written the fragmentary *Epithalamion* (159, RB 72), intended as an ode for Everard's forthcoming marriage, and it had foundered on imagery possibly more questionable than that encountered in *Sposa Dei.*

It describes a 'listless stranger' who hears the noise of boys shouting, and so turns towards a river where he

               unseen
Sees the bevy of them, how the boys
With dare and with downdolphinry and bellbright bodies
 huddling out,
Are earthworld, airworld, waterworld thorough hurled, all by
 turn and turn about.
This garland of their gambols flashes in his breast
Into such a sudden zest
Of summertime joys
That he hies to a pool neighbouring; sees it is the best
There; sweetest, freshest, shadowiest;
Fairyland; silk-beech, scrolled ash, packed sycamore, wild
 wychelm hornbeam fretty overstood
By. Rafts and rafts of flake-leaves light, dealt so, painted on the air,
Hang as still as hawk or hawkmoth, as the stars or as the angels
 there,
Like the thing that never knew the earth, never off roots
Rose. Here he feasts: lovely all is! No more: off with—down he
 dings
His bleachèd both and woolwoven wear:
Careless these in coloured wisp
All lie tumbled-to; then with loop-locks
Forward falling, forehead frowning, lips crisp
Over finger-teasing task, his twiny boots
Fast he opens, last he offwrings
Till walk the world he can with bare his feet
And come where lies a coffer, burly all of blocks
Built of chancequarrièd, selfquainèd, rocks
And the water warbles over into, filleted with glassy grassy
 quicksilvery shivès and shoots
And with heavenfallen freshness down from moorland still brims,

Dark or daylight on and on. Here he will then, here he will the fleet

Flinty kindcold element let break across his limbs

Long. Where we leave him, froliclavish, while he looks about him, laughs, swims.

And then, in a few disjointed lines, the reader is suddenly informed that the scene which the stranger glimpsed was an image for marriage, and the water, in which he chose to swim, an image for spousal love. Since Hopkins felt 'spooniness and delight over married people', it is significant that his own image for marriage should be a group of naked boys swimming in a romantic natural setting.

His August holiday, another walking tour with Curtis, this time in Scotland, was not very successful. It seems that neither man was in good spirits, and though they could have prolonged their fortnight, they chose not to. They climed Ben Nevis, and walked in Glen Coe, but did not manage to get any bathing or boating. When they separated, Hopkins went to Whitby, on the Yorkshire coast, to spend a week with his brothers. After his death, Arthur wrote to their mother recalling

the marvellously beautiful expression that was in his face as he bid us Goodbye when he left us. It brought tears into our eyes then, and in some distant way I felt that I should see his face no more.

Hopkins wrote to Bridges from Scotland saying he felt very old and looked very wrinkled.

I will now go to bed, the more so as I am going to preach tomorrow and put plainly to a Highland congregation of MacDonalds, Mackintoshes, Mackillops, and the rest what I am putting not at all so plainly to the rest of the world, or rather to you and Canon Dixon, in a sonnet in sprung rhythm with two codas.

This sonnet was *That Nature is a Heraclitean Fire and of the comfort of the Resurrection* (72, RB 48) which he had written just before leaving Dublin. Their recent correspondence had revealed to Bridges how differing their reading tastes had become, and this, he seems to have suggested, affected Hopkins's writing and caused some of the difficulties he encountered therein. Hopkins's comment on this inference was:

> The effect of studying masterpieces is to make me admire and do otherwise. So it must be on every original artist to some degree. Perhaps then more reading would only *refine my singularity*, which is not what you want.

This exchange did not prevent him writing a week later to ask for Bridges's comments on *St Alphonsus Rodriguez* (73, RB 49) which he had written to order for the first anniversary of the canonisation of St Alphonsus, a laybrother who for forty years was hall porter at the Jesuit college in Majorca. 'The sonnet (I say it snorting) aims at being intelligible.' Bridges replied promptly, and on 19 October Hopkins wrote: 'I am obliged for your criticisms, "contents of which noted" . . .' and some of which he acted on. The poem was sent to Majorca.

He had to cut short his Christmas holiday at Monasterevan in order to make his yearly retreat. He had been unable to do this during the summer, he told his mother, because the University kept him 'in attendance correcting proofs' and doing other 'trifling things'. It was not that he disliked retreats, he said, but he did dislike having to curtail his holiday. During the retreat, spent at the novitiate near Tullamore in Offaly, he made quite copious notes which have survived. Again he went over the old ground concerning his incapacity, his work among people whom he felt were unlawful, his mournful life, and this led him 'on that course of loathing and hopelessness which I have so often felt before' and which had made him give up the practice of meditation—except during retreat—for fear of madness. He had no grounds on which to excuse himself, 'but what is life without aim, without spur, without help? All my undertakings miscarry: I am like a straining eunuch. I wish then for death . . .' He tried to concentrate on the Spiritual Exercises, on compositions of place, and had some success.

Paravicini visited Dublin around this time, and his wife later reported that he

> saw Father Gerard once or twice; and they spent an evening together. He thought him looking very ill then, and said that he was much depressed. That day or two seemed to bring back all the old friendship, and give it, as it were, new life . . .

His repetitive despair was translated into a sonnet (74, RB 50) on 17 March, St Patrick's day:

> Thou art indeed just, Lord, if I contend
> With thee; but, sir, so what I plead is just.
> Why do sinners' ways prosper? and why must
> Disappointment all I endeavour end?
> Wert thou my enemy, O thou my friend,
> How wouldst thou worse, I wonder, than thou dost
> Defeat, thwart me? Oh, the sots and thralls of lust
> Do in spare hours more thrive than I that spend,
> Sir, life upon thy cause. See, banks and brakes
> Now, leavèd how thick! lacèd they are again
> With fretty chervil, look, and fresh wind shakes
> Them; birds build—but not I build; no, but strain,
> Time's eunuch, and not breed one work that wakes.
> Mine, O thou lord of life, send my roots rain.

He sent the sonnet to Bridges on 24 March from Monasterevan, with the injunction: 'Observe, it must be read *adagio molto* and with great stress.' It is interesting that, whereas he had suppressed the desolate sonnets of 1885, he despatched this one quickly. He may still have been at Monasterevan when he wrote *The shepherd's brow* (75, RB 69), a sonnet which Bridges placed among the unfinished poems when he edited Hopkins because he felt it 'must have been thrown off in a day in a cynical mood, which he could not have wished permanently to intrude among his last serious poems'. But the sonnet had been through at least five drafts, and it has since been reinstated with the finished work.

On 22 April he wrote a sonnet (76, RB 51) especially for Bridges, explaining, in the procreative imagery that came so naturally to him, why his poetry often did not come up to expectations. It was to be his last poem.

> The fine delight that fathers thought; the strong
> Spur, live and lancing like the blowpipe flame,
> Breathes once and, quenchèd faster than it came,
> Leaves yet the mind a mother of immortal song.
> Nine months she then, nay years she long
> Within her wears, bears, cares and moulds the same:
> The window of an insight lost she lives, with aim

Now known and hand at work now never wrong.
Sweet fire the sire of muse, my soul needs this;
I want the one rapture of an inspiration.
O then if in my lagging lines you miss
The roll, the rise, the carol, the creation,
My winter world, that scarcely breathes that bliss
Now, yields you, with some sighs, our explanation.

This was presumably written in reference to Bridges's reaction to his *Thou art indeed just* sonnet. But for some reason Bridges destroyed two letters Hopkins wrote after 24 March which might have thrown some light on the matter.

He sent the sonnet to Bridges on 29 April, with a letter in which he announced he was ill but in good spirits. It is a long, chatty letter and the last which he wrote to the man who had become, despite all their differences, perhaps his closest friend of all, and certainly his closest literary friend.

Two days later he informed his mother that he seemed to have some kind of rheumatic fever and might have to see the doctor. On 3 May he told his father he was in bed, feeling sleepy by day but sleepless by night. By 5 May his illness had still not been diagnosed, but he was content enough to be relieved of his examination work at the busiest time of the year. His mother posted him some spring flowers from Haslemere which revived when they were put in water.

By 8 May he was too sick to write, and dictated a letter home via Father Thomas Wheeler. Typhoid had been diagnosed, but he was very well cared for and his only complaint was 'that food and medicine keep coming in like cricket balls'. Wheeler wrote to Mrs Hopkins himself on 14 May, saying, 'I think he is now well round the corner and on the high road to mending.'

But, during the night of 5 June, his condition deteriorated rapidly. Kate and Manley were sent for and attended his bedside for two days with Thomas Wheeler.

On Saturday morning, 8 June, Wheeler administered extreme unction. It is reported that Hopkins whispered, 'I am so happy. I am so happy. I am so happy.' Just before noon, prayers for the dying were begun. He could no longer speak. It appeared he followed the words and the responses of his parents.

He died at half-past one.

Postscript

WHEN HOPKINS received from Coventry Patmore Cassell's National Library edition of *The Angel in the House*, he remarked that such cheap issues were a 'great boon':

> It would seem that there is some kind of smouldering fame a writer may have, which on being fuelled with a cheap supply breaks into flame.

He never liked over-elegant, limited editions and I think the Penguin selected *Poems and Prose* which has been reprinted many times, and the OUP paperback *Poems*, would both have pleased him.

Robert Bridges has been praised by some for his careful guardianship of the manuscripts of Hopkins's poems, and criticised by others for not publishing them before 1918. In fact he arranged for poems by Hopkins to appear in four anthologies between 1893 and 1915, and edited the first volume as soon as there was an established publisher who was interested: he knew of Hopkins's dislike of private, limited editions. His criticisms of the poems do not usually strike Hopkins's admirers as just, but they probably seem so to admirers of Bridges. It would be difficult to imagine two friendly poets whose poetical chemistry was ultimately so different.

The question people most often ask about Hopkins is: would he have been a greater (or at least a more prolific poet) if he had not been a Jesuit? To which I can only reply that he *was* a Jesuit, and his decision to become one was no more arbitrary than most people's choices of career. I think he had a fundamental need to share in some kind of literary or artistic life and this was denied him; but he also had a need for protection from so-called moral danger. It is useless to blame the Society of Jesus for not providing him with literary opportunities compatible with twentieth-century lay taste.

After his death, various people described him as saintly. They do not appear to be simply indulging in pious hyperbole. He was a man who was considered 'good' by those who knew him. He once wrote to Bridges of the 'chastity of mind which seems to lie at the very heart and be the parent of all other good'. He wanted to achieve that chastity of mind, and many of his contemporaries felt that he had done so. He did not feel he had, though he continually strived.

He also told Bridges 'deliberately and before God' that 'fame, the being known, though in itself one of the most dangerous things to man, is nevertheless the true and appointed air, element, and setting of genius and its works'. His fame smouldered for a long time, but a steady supply of paperbacks now feeds the flame.

It has to be said, however, that from Hopkins's point of view some of the attraction people find in the poems is exactly the kind of attraction he was trying to avoid. Suppression developed his rhythmic and verbal ability to express physical excitement and wonder. He could make sounds that play on the senses.

Above all, he could recreate the moment of arousing wonder at physical attraction and he could describe the experience of barren despair. These two are, perhaps, the most consuming private experiences known to the majority of people. Which is the reason why, despite his having spent his adult life in a manner with which few can identify, Hopkins still affects the modern heart.

Selected bibliography

Texts

Poems of Gerard Manley Hopkins, ed. by W. H. Gardner and N. H. Mackenzie, 4th edn., Oxford 1970.
The Correspondence of Gerard Manley Hopkins and Richard Watson Dixon, ed. by C. C. Abbott, Oxford 1935.
The Correspondence of Gerard Manley Hopkins to Robert Bridges, ed. by C. C. Abbott, Oxford 1935.
Further Letters of Gerard Manley Hopkins, ed. by C. C. Abbott, 2nd edn., Oxford 1956.
The Journals and Papers of Gerard Manley Hopkins, ed. by Humphry House and Graham Storey, Oxford 1959.
The Sermons and Devotional Writings of Gerard Manley Hopkins, ed. by Christopher Devlin, Oxford 1959.

Books on Hopkins

Todd K. Bender: *Gerard Manley Hopkins, the Classical Background and Critical Reception of his Work*, John Hopkins 1966.
Margaret Bottral (ed.): *Gerard Manley Hopkins, Poems, A selection of critical essays*, Macmillan 1975.
W. H. Gardner: *Gerard Manley Hopkins*, 2 vols., Oxford 1944-9.
Jim Hunter: *Gerard Manley Hopkins*, Evans 1966.
Gerald F. Lahey: *Gerard Manley Hopkins*, Oxford 1928.
Paul L. Mariani: *A Commentary on the complete Poems of Gerard Manley Hopkins*, Cornell 1970.
John Pick: *Gerard Manley Hopkins: Priest and Poet*, Oxford 1942.
Eleanor Ruggles: *Gerard Manley Hopkins*, Bodley Head 1947.
Alfred Thomas: *Hopkins the Jesuit, the years of training*, Oxford 1969.
R. K. R. Thornton (ed.): *All My Eyes See—the Visual World of Gerard Manley Hopkins*, Ceolfrith 1975.

General

Piers Brendon: *Hurrell Froude and the Oxford Movement*, Elek 1974.
R. F. Clarke: The Training of a Jesuit, *The Nineteenth Century*, August 1896.
J. R. Briscoe (ed.): *V. S. S. Coles*, Mowbray 1930.
Richard Watson Dixon: *Poems*, with a memoir by Robert Bridges, Smith Elder 1909.

Digby Mackworth Dolben: *Poems*, with a memoir by Robert Bridges, Oxford 1915.

The Dublin Review, no. 334, July–December 1920: *Father Gerard Hopkins*, contributions by Frederick Page and 'Plures'.

Brian Elliott: *Marcus Clarke*, Oxford 1958.

Geoffrey Faber: *Oxford Apostles*, Faber 1936.

Geoffrey Faber: *Jowett*, Faber 1958.

Richard Hurrell Froude: *Remains*, Vol. 1, Part 1, Rivington 1838.

G. Gruggen and J. Keating: *History of Stonyhurst College*, Kegan Paul 1901.

Albert Guerard Jr.: *Robert Bridges*, Harvard 1942.

James Hastings (ed.): *Encyclopedia of Religion and Ethics*, Edinburgh 1917.

L. C. Hopkins: a translation of Tai T'Ung's *The Six Scripts or the Principles of Chinese Writing*, with a memoir of the translator by W. Perceval Yetts, Oxford 1954.

Manley Hopkins: *Hawaii : The Past, Present and Future of Its Island-Kingdom*, Longmans 1862.

Ralph S. Kuykendall: *The Hawaiian Kingdom, Vol. II, 1854–1874*, University of Hawaii 1953.

Mrs M. M. Maxwell-Scott: *Henry Schomberg Kerr : Sailor and Jesuit*, Longmans 1901.

Alfred H. Miles (ed.): *The Poets and the Poetry of the Century*, Vol. 8, Robert Bridges and Contemporary Poets, 1893.

John Henry Newman: *Apologia Pro Vita Sua*, Oxford 1964.

—— *Verses on Various Occasions*, Longmans 1888.

—— *Prose and Poetry*, sel. G. Tillotson, Hart-Davis 1957.

Ronald Pearsall: *The Worm and the Bud*, Penguin 1969.

Brian Reade (ed.): *Sexual Heretics*, Routledge 1970.

James Sambrook: *A Poet Hidden, the Life of Richard Watson Dixon*, Athlone 1962.

Hans Schaer (trans. R. F. C. Hull): *Religion and the Cure of Souls in Jung's psychology*, Routledge 1951.

Isaac Taylor: *Loyola : and Jesuitism in its Rudiments*, Longman 1849.

Edward Thompson: *Robert Bridges*, Oxford 1944.

Robert H. Thouless: *The Psychology of Religion*, Cambridge 1923.

Nitram Tradleg (Martin Geldart): *A Son of Belial*, 1882.

Meriol Trevor: *Newman*, Vols. I and II, Macmillan 1962.

Index